the BOWERY

the
BOWERY

The Strange History of New York's Oldest Street

Stephen Paul DeVillo

Skyhorse Publishing

Skyhorse Publishing books may be purchased in bulk at special discounts for sales promotion, corporate gifts, fund-raising, or educational purposes. Special editions can also be created to specifications. For details, contact the Special Sales Department, Skyhorse Publishing, 307 West 36th Street, 11th Floor, New York, NY 10018 or info@skyhorsepublishing.com.

Skyhorse® and Skyhorse Publishing® are registered trademarks of Skyhorse Publishing, Inc.®, a Delaware corporation.

Visit our website at www.skyhorsepublishing.com.

10 9 8 7 6 5 4 3 2 1

Library of Congress Cataloging-in-Publication Data is available on file.

Cover design by Rain Saukas
Cover photo credits: Library of Congress

Print ISBN: 978-1-5107-2686-4
Ebook ISBN: 978-1-5107-2687-1

Printed in the United States of America

Contents

Preface

The Bowery isn't what it used to be. And in fact, it never was. New York City's oldest thoroughfare, the Bowery has both reflected and shaped the ever-changing city it helped give birth to. Throughout its long, lively, and sometimes tragic history, the Bowery has hosted an endless parade of farmers, drovers, soldiers, coppers, gangsters, statesmen, showmen, magicians, poets, writers, artists, and unfortunates. Fur traders gave way to farmers, whose farms in turn gave way to taverns, tanneries, saloons, circuses, dime museums, tattoo parlors, speakeasies, flophouses, brothels, and religious missions. The Bowery's cavalcade continues today as this long-avoided boulevard experiences a dramatic rebirth. Well-dressed visitors now head to the Bowery, not as a place to go slumming, but as a world-class destination for contemporary art and music.

It's been an astonishing four-hundred-year-long story that I would like to share with you. A lifelong New Yorker, I've long been fascinated with the city's lesser-known nooks and byways, the small places that often contain a larger history. Venturing down the Bowery just as it was reemerging into the daylight in the 1990s, I wondered what tales its old buildings could tell me, and found there are many such tales to tell. Come with me as we take a walk through time as we stroll down the once infamous Bowery.

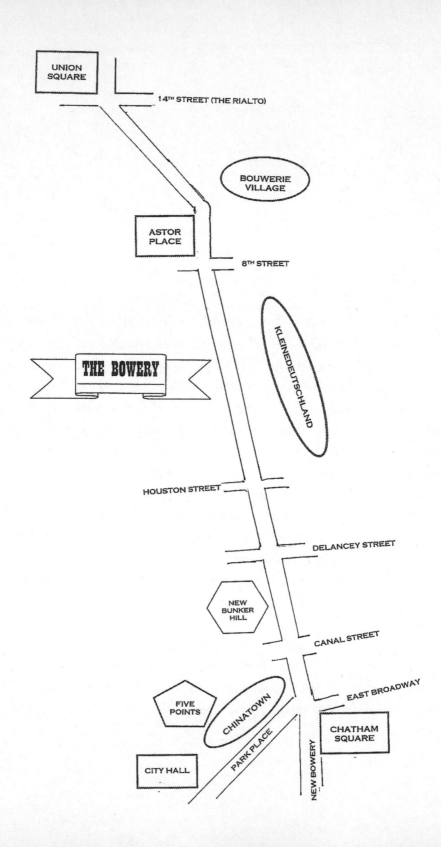

1 The Great Bouwerie

LIKE MANY LATER VISITORS TO New York, the first European settlers made their way to the Bowery. Coming from the Netherlands, they sought not thrills, but furs and farms. It wasn't yet called the Bowery back then, but it was already an old thoroughfare. From the Harlem River crossing at the far northern end of the island, a Native American trail ran down the east side of Manhattan to an area just south of a large pond. From there a short trail led to a village on Werpoe Hill on the west side of the pond. Another trail branched east to the small village of Nechtanc where Corlear's Hook jutted into the bend of the East River, while the main trail continued on to the canoe landing at the far southern tip of the island, where Castle Clinton stands today.

Running the length of the island, the trail connected different groups of the Lenni Lenape, or Delaware nation. The Canarsee (or Werpoes) occupied the southern part of the island, while the Rechgawawank occupied the north end, and the trail that was to become the Bowery served then, as it would later, as a connection and meeting ground among different groups. Apart from linking the bands living on the island, the trail served trading parties from the mainland to the north and east, and a branch led to Sapokanikan on the island's western shore, where Indians from west of the river would paddle over to trade deer and elk meat for tobacco at a place that would become the Meatpacking District.

The Bowery's reputation as a place of sharp dealings may well have begun with Peter Minuit's legendary twenty-four-dollar land deal. Minuit, the director of the New Netherland colony, is credited with swapping sixty Dutch guilders' worth of European goods for the whole of Manhattan island. However, the precise location and circumstances of this transaction are uncertain. Whether it happened at Shorakapkok near present-day Spuyten Duyvil, or if, as was more likely, it took place at Werpoe Hill by the Collect Pond, the fact was that no single group possessed the entire island. The Canarsee people at Werpoe Hill had rights only to the southern end of the island; the rest was occupied by other Lenape groups, not least of which were the Rechgawawank on the northern end, who would sell their territory only in pieces. The last of the Rechgawawank wouldn't leave Manhattan until 1715, over ninety years after Peter Minuit's legendary "purchase" of the island.

Like the thousands of commuters who today follow old Indian routes to the island, the Dutch came to Manhattan for business. The southern tip of the island faced one of the finest harbors in North America, from which ships could sail across the Atlantic to markets in Europe or outfit privateers for a bash at the Spanish Main. Manhattan moreover lay alongside the great waterway that the Dutch knew as the North (later Hudson) River, which, like the trail, pointed north toward the sources of beaver furs. Dutch fur traders had been on Manhattan for over ten years before the West India Company planted a permanent settlement there in 1624. New Amsterdam served as a trading post and overseas shipping point for furs sent down from Fort Orange, site of present-day Albany. With the Eurasian beaver long hunted out, American beaver furs were a valuable commodity, prized for making felt for the big wide-brimmed hats that in those days defined gentlemen of fashion.

The Dutch West India Company was sure that New Amsterdam would prove to be a gold mine, but it needed a stable foundation, and that meant settlers who could create an agricultural base to provide a reliable food supply. The Dutch accordingly laid out six farms, or *bouweries* in Dutch, along the trail north of New Amsterdam—five small farms plus the "Great Bouwerie," which will figure in the story later. These six bouweries were named after their owners: Blyevelt, Schout, Wolfert, Van Corlear, Leendert, and Pannepacker.

The Indian trail linked the farms together so it became known as the Bouwerie Lane. Almost immediately, however, the process began of chopping the Bowery down from its original thirteen-mile length to its current stretch of only two miles. The Dutch gave the southern end of the trail the grandiose name of Heere Straat (Broadway), which ran up to present-day Ann Street. There the trail became the Heere Wegh (Highway) following the line of today's Park Row, becoming Bouwerie Lane only once it was past today's Chatham Square.

Foreshadowing its history, the trail became the scene of New York's first mugging shortly after the establishment of New Amsterdam. A Lenape came down the trail with his young nephew, bearing a load of furs for trade to the Dutch. As the pair approached the pond, they were jumped by three men who murdered the Lenape and made off with the furs. Not wanting to deal further with the Europeans, the boy didn't try to report the murder but simply made his way back home, determined to someday settle accounts.

New Amsterdam grew into a small town and soon began to take on many of the characteristics of its mega-city successor. The Netherlands did not have a large surplus population to export to its colony, so the West India Company offered generous terms to recruit potential settlers from other parts of Europe. Those who accepted the offer, many of them French-speaking Walloons from today's Belgium, received free transportation to New Amsterdam, plus a house, barn, and tools. The company also loaned each settler a starter kit of livestock including four each of horses, cows, sheep, and pigs. As time went on, more generous land grants would be made to individuals who would recruit and outfit their own settlers to live on the land as rent-paying tenants. Among them was Jonas Bronck, who would establish in 1639 his estate in what became his namesake borough, the Bronx.

Recruiting settlers from among various refugee groups in Holland made New Amsterdam the cosmopolitan city New York remains today. In 1643, the Jesuit Father Isaac Jogues, escaping from captivity and torture among the Mohawks, passed through New Amsterdam. The Catholic priest was warmly received by the Dutch Calvinist Director Kieft, who, like many a later New Yorker, insisted on giving the out-of-towner a grand tour. Jogues found New Amsterdam to be a place where no less than eighteen languages were spoken and where several Protestant denominations practiced, even though Dutch Calvinism was the official religion of the colony.

But amid its cultural diversity, New Amsterdam experienced ethnic conflict. Dutch and English interests clashed in Connecticut, where rival settlers from New Netherlands and New England staked out conflicting claims. By 1640, English settlers from Connecticut were moving into Long Island, changing the ethnic composition of such towns as Flushing and establishing their own settlements in Hempstead and Gravesend. The old cliché "there goes the neighborhood" may well have first been muttered in Dutch regarding incoming Anglo-Saxons.

Still, New Amsterdam continued on its easygoing way, sometimes to the consternation of its ministers, called *dominies*. People taking Sunday off for secular pleasures especially annoyed them; the Reverend Johannes Backerus complained in his reports back home that the colonists were "very ignorant in true religion, and very much given to drink." Backerus's own predecessor Everadus Bogardus was himself known to imbibe a bit of "Dutch courage" before mounting the pulpit to deliver boozy diatribes attacking the sixth director of the colony, Willem Kieft. For his part, Kieft would post a drummer outside the church door to drown out the *dominie*. The congregation learned little true religion, but it was great entertainment.

With its diverse, rowdy, and hard-drinking population, New Amsterdam saw a lot of conflict, some of which was settled in court. Suits often involved the depredations of unfenced animals and verbal abuse between neighbors, while merchants and storekeepers complained against street peddlers, a contention that remains as heated at the beginning of the twenty-first century as it was in the seventeenth.

Other pleasures were avidly pursued. Nocturnal liaisons took place at a watercourse nicknamed "Hoerenkill" (Whore Creek) outside the town limits. The precise location of this colonial landmark is uncertain, but it might have been the brook called the Versch Water Killetje (Little Fresh

Water; later Old Wreck Brook) that flowed out of the Collect Pond, crossing the Bowery where the Kissing Bridge was later located. If so, it was a
portent of the Bowery's future.

Amid the good times, though, resentments festered among the Native
Americans. By the 1640s, tensions between Europeans and Native Americans were growing in New Netherlands, partly because of the sharp dealings the Indians received from the *Swannekins* (Salty People), as they
called the Dutch. Resentments were brought to a head by Director Kieft's
arrogant demand that the Native Americans still resident on Manhattan
pay taxes to the Dutch.

Meanwhile, the Native American boy who saw his uncle killed in
1626 for furs had grown to manhood bearing an obligation to avenge the
death. In 1641 he decided the time had come for retribution, and the warrior came down the old trail and went to the isolated cabin of Claes Smits
by Turtle Bay. He killed Smits and went home again, satisfied that the
blood debt occasioned by the European murder of his uncle was satisfied
in the time-honored way by the murder of another European.

To Director Kieft it was a wanton homicide, with an alleged twenty-
year-old crime serving as a flimsy excuse, and he demanded that the
natives surrender the murderer. The natives explained that this was
merely the traditional expiation of a crime and felt no obligation to coop-
erate with Dutch justice.

Unable to obtain satisfaction from the native Lenape, the Smits
murder became a pretext for Kieft's War, which began with massacres
of Native Americans on Corlear's Hook and Pavonia (present-day Jersey
City) in 1643. The conflict lasted until 1645 and did not go well for the
Dutch, rolling back the frontier of New Netherlands down the Bowery
right up to the streets of New Amsterdam. As the isolated farmhouses on
Manhattan were one by one set ablaze, Kieft tried to pass the buck and
place the blame on his officers, one of whom tried to assassinate him. The
Bouwerie Lane reverted to being a route for Native American war parties, and it was simply too dangerous for farmers to bed down beyond
New Amsterdam's wooden palisades. The war eventually sputtered out
in mutual exhaustion, but the West India Company had nearly lost New

Netherlands. It was decided that Kieft would have to go and a more effective administrator put in his place.

Into this war-ravaged colony Peter Stuyvesant came on May 11, 1647, like an avenging high school principal. Still in his late thirties, Stuyvesant had forged an interesting career with the West India Company, working his way up from clerk after his premature departure from university. His trademark wooden leg that stumped down the gangplank that May day was a souvenir of his brief term as director of the Dutch colony on Curacao, where he led an expedition to capture the island of St. Martin back from the Spanish, who had themselves captured it from the Dutch a few years before. A cannonball shot from the Spanish fort mangled his leg, and he was forced to abandon the expedition, characteristically blaming the debacle on the "unwilling dogs" that it was his misfortune to command. As Kieft's War sputtered to a close, Peter recuperated from his amputation in Holland, where he married Judith Bayard and sought reassignment with the company.

Stuyvesant found New Amsterdam run-down and demoralized, and he set about restoring discipline with an energy that made him the first of Manhattan's "reform mayors." He proclaimed the town's first Sunday "blue law," ordering the taverns closed on the Sabbath and at 9:00 p.m. on weeknights, an issue that would still reverberate on the Bowery 250 years later. He enacted stiff penalties for anyone drawing a knife in an argument and stiffer penalties for anyone using one. He laid down laws on building standards, the fencing in of animals, and fire control, and slapped an excise tax on imported wine and liquor. He topped all this off with the town's first traffic ordinance, which forced wagon drivers to lead their horses by hand through the streets of New Amsterdam, except along Broadway.

The strong-willed Stuyvesant was unapologetic about his autocratic rule; anyone who had survived having a leg sawed off without anesthesia was unlikely to be frightened by protesting burghers. He once told objecting New Amsterdamers that he intended to go on issuing whatever orders he saw fit, "especially those which tend to the glory of God, the best interest of the inhabitants, or will prevent more sins, scandals, debaucheries, and crimes."

New Amsterdam's residents continued to produce scandals and debaucheries, but Stuyvesant's rule did make New Amsterdam look like a civilized place again. Four years after his arrival the director-general decided to settle down there for good. He built "White Hall" (at the foot of today's Whitehall Street) as his official residence, but he desired a quiet place where he could reside well away from the contentions of New Amsterdam. He therefore called in his connections in the West India Company and arranged to purchase the Great Bouwerie. Previously leased by Director General Wooter van Twiller, the Great Bouwerie was the largest of the bouweries laid out by the company along the old trail, running from about the present-day 5th Street to about 17th Street, lying between the Bowery and the East River. Much of the Great Bouwerie was salt marsh, but this didn't bother Stuyvesant, who was now the landlord of several tenant families and could set about building a manor house suitable to his dignity and status.

It took another Indian war to fix Peter Stuyvesant's stamp on the Bowery. The still adventurous and aggressive Stuyvesant had just launched an expedition to take over the Swedish colony on Delaware Bay when trouble erupted over some stolen peaches.

A war party from up the Hudson was passing through Manhattan en route to attacking some Long Island tribes when one of their women helped herself to a few of the ripe peaches in an orchard belonging to Hendrick van Dyck. Van Dyck shot and killed the woman before he realized that he was facing an angry war party, and he quickly fled for his life. To the Native Americans, European notions of property ownership were bizarre enough, but to shoot someone over a handful of peaches was just too much. The war party quickly changed its objective and swept down on the Dutch in Manhattan instead of the Indians of Long Island. They stormed their way into New Amsterdam demanding the surrender of van Dyck only to become inebriated with a timely gift of gin and then hustled out by the Dutch garrison. That did not end the affair, however, and destructive raids on isolated farms began to blaze throughout New Netherlands, once again threatening to turn the Bouwerie Lane back into an Indian trail. A number of settlers along the Bouwerie were taken captive, among them the daughter of Wolfert Webber, the Bowery's first tavern keeper.

Stuyvesant's wife Judith was as strong willed as her husband. She remained at her Bouwerie mansion, fortifying the place as best she could and hiring ten Frenchmen to defend it. Peter returned in haste from his triumph at New Sweden and managed to negotiate a peace with the belligerents. Not willing to take further chances with New Netherlands' security, he ordered that henceforth groups of at least ten families would be assembled to form a village before any new farms would be authorized. The first of these villages would be formed on Stuyvesant's own Great Bouwerie.

Stuyvesant Village joined a village of free Africans down the Bowery in the vicinity of Werpoe Hill. Among them was Emanuel de Groot, who had earned his notoriety in an interesting way. Known as "the Giant," de Groot arrived in New Amsterdam as an enslaved African. In 1641, he was one of seven slaves involved in a brawl in which Jan Primero, another slave, was stabbed to death. Exactly who stabbed Primero could not be established, so the seven slaves were all equally convicted of the crime. But as the magistrates were unwilling to waste company property, lots were drawn for just one of the seven to be hanged for the crime, and the lot fell to de Groot.

Seeing the size of the man, the hangman didn't want to take any chances with "the Giant," so he took the unusual step of tying two ropes, with two separate nooses, around de Groot's neck. In spite of all these precautions, de Groot survived the hanging when both ropes broke and dropped him, still alive, to the ground. The assembled crowd, seeing God's providence in this strange event, clamored for de Groot's pardon, and he was spared further attempts at execution.

This miraculous escape from death enhanced de Groot's standing as a community leader, and in 1644 he found himself in charge of a small band of middle-aged and elderly slaves freed by order of Director Kieft and left to settle where they could beyond the town boundary. They were free, but their children were to remain enslaved, an arrangement that benefitted the bottom line of the Dutch West India Company, which thereby rid itself of responsibility for taking care of the aging slaves while retaining the services of their offspring.

With their children still enslaved, and the Indian war still raging, the little band decided to stay close to town. They moved onto the lands of the old Native American village along Werpoe Hill, thus creating Manhattan's first African neighborhood just across the pond from the Bowery. Although de Groot's little village would eventually disperse, a significant African presence along the lower Bowery would persist into the early 1800s.

Eleven years later, at the close of the 1655 war, Stuyvesant's Bouwerie Village began to take shape northeast of Werpoe Hill. Stuyvesant's authoritarian nature liked his tenants neatly assembled into a compact settlement, and as things quieted down after the end of the Peach War he set about turning the place into a functioning village. Apart from providing security, the village would be a pleasing complement to his country seat, where at last he could rule in peace, a good hour's walk away from the rowdy natives of New Amsterdam.

Religion ranked high on the list of Stuyvesant's priorities, and he built a stone chapel to join his manor house as the centerpiece of his Bouwerie Village, bringing in a dominie every Sunday to conduct Dutch Reformed services. Keeping his distance from New Amsterdam and its ever-contentious burghers, Stuyvesant paid the expenses for a minister to commute from Breuckelen (Brooklyn) instead, and provided an escort of soldiers to conduct him safely from his landing on the East River. All this cost Stuyvesant the pretty sum of 250 guilders a year, but it saved him the trouble of attending services in New Amsterdam, whose own church building never seemed to get finished.

Stuyvesant's chapel, later rebuilt into the church of Old St. Mark's in-the-Bouwerie, was the beginning of what today is the oldest currently used site of worship in New York. This distinction is both a memorial to Stuyvesant's rule and to his hard-line religious policy. Despite the Dutch traditions of granting tolerant refuge to various refugee groups, the Calvinist Dutch Reformed Church was from the beginning planned to be the only established denomination in the colony. In the early years of

New Amsterdam this did not pose a problem, for apart from the ever-uncompleted edifice of the Dutch Reformed Church, none of the other denominations had succeeded in erecting a church building of their own. And that was the way Stuyvesant intended to keep it. He would have liked to have banned all competing denominations outright, but that was impractical even for him. So instead he issued a decree in 1656 stating that other Protestant denominations were free to worship as they pleased, but only within private homes. Dutch Reformed churches would be the only religious buildings permitted in New Amsterdam, and Stuyvesant's chapel would stand as an enduring sign of his devotion.

Along with the chapel, Stuyvesant provided other amenities of village life, namely a blacksmith shop and an inn. He set the streets of Stuyvesant Village to follow an orderly gridiron pattern, in contrast to the anarchic sprawl of New Amsterdam, with the streets named for himself and members of his family. His intentions would be honored as Stuyvesant Village grew. Running due north-south, Judith, Elias, and Margaret Streets would eventually be crossed at right angles by Gerard, Governor, Peter, Stuyvesant, and Nicholas William Streets. His chapel and mansion lay on Stuyvesant Street. As all these streets lay at a 45-degree angle to the streets that would be decreed in 1811, all but one would be eventually obliterated. Today Stuyvesant Street, angling off from Third Avenue, remains as only trace of Stuyvesant's Bouwerie Village.

Peter Stuyvesant's unflinching commitment to his church would spark further controversies in his later years as director-general. The graveyard of Shearith Israel on today's St. James Place (formerly the New Bowery) is a monument to one of these controversies. The colony's first Jewish congregation arrived in September 1654, in the persons of twenty-three refugees. Descendants of Sephardic Jews who had fled Iberia generations before, they had been living as colonists in Pernambuco, the capital of Dutch Brazil. In 1654, the Portuguese captured Pernambuco, and the Sephardim had to flee again. They sailed for Holland only to fall prey to a Spanish pirate ship, which then set sail for Spain, Portugal's fellow land of the Inquisition. The Spanish ship, though, was overtaken by a French privateer, whose captain offered to convey the refugees to New

Amsterdam—at a stiff price. To raise the money, they had to sell off all their goods when they arrived in New Amsterdam, and the group found themselves in the new colony with little more than the clothes on their backs.

Stuyvesant was not pleased with their arrival. Though unable to dislodge dissident Protestants, he was determined to at least prevent the Jews from settling in his colony. To this end he wrote the Amsterdam Chamber (the governing body of the West India Company) seeking permission to expel the refugees, in order that they "be not allowed further to infect and trouble the new colony." The West India Company flatly rejected Stuyvesant's request in view of "the considerable loss sustained by this nation [the Sephardim], with others, in the taking of Brazil, as also because of the large amount of capital which they have invested in the shares of this company."

Thwarted, Stuyvesant nevertheless continued to throw obstacles in the path of this community, even refusing their request to establish a cemetery on the ground that nobody of their community had yet died. But when someone did die a year later, Stuyvesant reluctantly granted them permission to set up a cemetery. The precise location of this first cemetery is not known, but in 1683 the burials were removed to a new site east of the Collect Pond. In the mid–nineteenth century, the Bowery was extended south from Chatham Square, cutting through a corner of the burial ground. The burial ground, minus the sliced-off corner, remains, maintained by the congregation known today as Shearith Israel.

Frustrated in his attempts to expel the Jews, Stuyvesant turned his fury on the Society of Friends, the so-called Quakers, whose wandering preachers began to drift in from the English colonies. Unlike the Sephardim, the Quakers had no influential community back in old Amsterdam who could speak up for them to the Dutch West India Company, but they did have a community in nearby Flushing. Harsh punishments, such as public floggings, inflicted on the Friends who arrived in New Amsterdam provoked the disgust of many in New Amsterdam, including Stuyvesant's own sister, Annake. Eventually Stuyvesant's order forbidding all residents of New Amsterdam to even allow Quakers into their homes prompted the

Flushing Remonstrance in December 1657, wherein the director-general was reminded that the original 1645 patent for the town of Flushing guaranteed "liberty of conscience" to all residents. A century after Stuyvesant's death, the Friends quietly established their own cemetery on the Bowery, at the corner of Houston Street, and built a meeting house a stone's throw west of the Bowery at Elizabeth and Hester Streets.

Peter Stuyvesant's last rage came in 1664 when an English fleet sailed into the harbor and demanded the surrender of New Netherlands. The wooden-legged warlord was naturally inclined to fight it out, and he stumped up to the ramparts of a decayed Fort Amsterdam. Staring in defiance at the English fleet, he laid his hand on a linstock to fire the first shot before he was persuaded to back down. In a stormy meeting later that day he learned that his belligerence had no support among the residents of New Amsterdam, who were only too aware of how quickly the English warships could blow the town into splinters. The final straw came with the presentation of a petition signed by ninety-three leading citizens, among them Stuyvesant's own son Balthazar. On September 8, 1664, he met with the English officers in his Bouwerie mansion to accept the terms of surrender.

By now Stuyvesant was too attached to his bouwerie to abandon it, and after returning to Amsterdam to defend his role in the affair, he petitioned the English King Charles II for permission to return to the place now named New-York. Charles obliged, and Stuyvesant spent several years in quiet retirement on his bouwerie. Some years before, he had planted there a pear tree from Holland, saying that he wanted to leave something behind to be remembered by. Stuyvesant of all people needn't have worried about being remembered, but the tree flourished and became a landmark, living to 1867 at the corner of Third Avenue and 13th Street. Its memory may still be found today on the apartment building at the northwest corner of 13th and Third, where a brass plaque labels the building PEAR TREE PLACE. Peter Stuyvesant died on his bouwerie in February 1672, and was buried in the family vault by the side of his chapel. His widow Judith remained, as did the rest of the family, which would form an important part of old New York society. But New York had not heard the last from Peter Stuyvesant.

2   Taverns and Tea Water

THE TEA WATER SPRING HAD everything to do with how the Bowery would later develop. Though eventually some 250 wells would be dug, sweet water was a rarity in lower Manhattan, and one of its two good springs was located by the Bowery on Chatham Square. This was the famous Tea Water Spring that flowed into the Collect Pond. (The other spring was just west of the Bowery where it inspired the name of Spring Street.) While bottled "designer water" became fashionable in the 1980s, in early New York it was more a necessity than a luxury. Wells often yielded water so brackish it was said that even the horses refused to drink it, and water for cooking was bought from traveling peddlers who filled barrel wagons at the Tea Water Spring and made their way around town selling the water. Water good enough for tea was good for making other beverages as well, and the first known tavern by the Tea Water Spring was Wolfert Webber's, beginning sometime before 1664.

If the location of the Tea Water Spring was a bit inconvenient— it was still about three-quarters of a mile beyond the town limits in the 1660s—it was a copiously flowing spring, yielding nearly fifteen thousand gallons a day, providing enough water for everyone. The spring fed into the sizeable pond that the Dutch had several names for, most common being *Der Kolck* (Rippling Water) or the *Kalch-hook*, or Lime Shell Point, because of the large clam and oyster shell middens the Indians had banked up along the shores of the pond. Later, these names would be corrupted into Collect Pond. Its outline shifted over the course of time, but the Collect Pond generally lay in the low area between today's Canal Street and Worth Streets. Excess water flowed out of the pond through two streams. One, the Old Wreck Brook, made its way to the East River through the marshy areas of Beekman's Swamp, an area still called the Swamp in the 1890s, long after it had been built up and paved over. The other, the Old Kill, ran down the line of Canal Street past Lispenard's Meadow into the Hudson. Tidal surges sometimes came up the Old Wreck Brook and brought salt water into the Collect Pond, making the Tea Water Spring early New York's best source of fresh water.

The crossing of the trails and the presence of the Tea Water Spring made the lower end of the Bowery a natural place both for Native American clambakes and European revelry. Beer brewing demands clear water as much as tea does, and the spring gave Wolfert Webber all he needed. The location of his tavern on the Bouwerie Lane meant that all traffic into and out of New Amsterdam by land would have to pass his way, and travelers were invariably in need of a drink and a rest after a hard journey, or else they wanted "one for the road" as they set out on one. For those not traveling, Webber's place was located safely outside the town palisades and the patrols of the town's watchmen.

It was inevitable that as the town grew there would be competition for Webber. Shortly after the English takeover in 1664, one Richard Sackett established a tavern a bit east of Webber's near the future line of Cherry Street (the cherry orchards that Sackett planted gave the name to the street). Beginning New York's enduring tradition of ethnic bars, Sackett catered to the growing English population, who preferred mulled cider and dark ale to Webber's Dutch gin and beer. Another Englishman, Thomas Hall, was already in the area, having bought a tract of land around Bowery and Doyers Street in 1652. Finding himself pestered by thirsty travelers seeking ale and confusing his place with Webber's, Hall did the logical thing and turned his house into a tavern in 1660. It wasn't long after the English takeover that he was doing the next logical thing, at least for a New York publican: he went on record complaining about the high excise taxes on beer.

The Bowery's development accelerated in 1669, when the new English governor Francis Lovelace convened a meeting up in Harlem to consider turning the old trail into a regular wagon road. A wagon road connecting the fledgling village of Harlem with the city of New York would be "very necessary to the mutual commerce with one another."

This was good news for Peter Stuyvesant's Bouwerie Village, for the mutual commerce would naturally run past it. When the road opened, Bouwerie Village found itself at the spot where the Bouwerie Lane jogged west a bit to join the northward Bloomingdale Road. The Bouwerie and the Bloomingdale Road ran together for about a quarter of a mile before the wagon road swung east again following the line of the old Indian trail, soon to become part of the Post Road to Boston.

By the 1670s, Bouwerie Village had grown into a small but substantial community. Formed at first of Dutch settlers, after 1664 the village hosted a settlement of French-speaking Huguenots. Leaving their Dutch neighbors to worship at Stuyvesant's chapel, each Sunday the Huguenots would make their way down the Bowery to the "French Church" Du Saint Espirt down on Pine Street. Often they would be joined by other Huguenots visiting from the New Rochelle area. After the services the visitors would stop off at Bouwerie Village for lunch before heading homeward, adding to its reputation as a point of convivial departure.

Bouwerie Village was also the home of the one individual who, apart from Peter Stuyvesant and Emanuel de Groot, could be claimed as a founding spirit of the Bowery. A local legend in the late 1800s told of a pleasant though unfocused young Dutchman, Rip Schallyon, who idled about Bouwerie Village. Just about dinner time, he would manage to show up on someone's doorstep on one pretext or another. Not wishing to be thought of as ungenerous, and perhaps taking some pride in the popularity of their cooking, the Dutch housewives would usually invite him to the table to join the family for dinner. Toleration, however, didn't mean approval of Rip's freeloading career, and the women would admonish their own children not to turn into another Rip Schallyon. In time, it was said, Rip would lend his name to the English language as the original "rapscallion."

The establishment of the Royal Post Road between Boston and New York was the next step in the Bowery's development. The idea came from King Charles II, who was interested in seeing that the inhabitants of Boston and those of his newly acquired colony in New York could keep in frequent communication with each other. (King George III a century later might have wished they hadn't.) Fittingly, the mail was late on the inaugural trip to Boston. The post rider was to have left New York on New Year's Day 1673, but was held up until January 22 awaiting delayed dispatches to come down from Albany. When he finally left, it took him until February 5 to get to Boston.

As the Bowery grew in importance, more taverns sprang up alongside. By 1680, the tavern of Cornelison van Schaick sat at "the Crossroads"—present-day Astor Place, where the Sandy Hill Road (now Astor Place) ran westward south of the Bouwerie's intersection with the Bloomingdale Road at today's 17th Street and Union Square West. Broadway was not yet part of the picture; it still abruptly ended at the city limits around today's Chambers Street.

A few years later, John Clapp took over the old Bowery Village Tavern at the Crossroads and made it into an important institution. Clapp's place was popular for people making a Sunday drive or a summer evening's jaunt into the country. Building on his success and popularity, in 1697 Clapp published New York's first almanac. Clapp also founded New York's taxi industry by introducing the first hackney coach for hire in New York. Today's yellow cab drivers ought to give their horns a honk in honor of their founding father whenever they turn down the Bowery from Astor Place.

John Clapp knew how to play the role of the good host. On every twenty-fourth of June, the feast day of St. John the Baptist, he had a special celebration at his tavern for every man by the name of John. Like St. Patrick's Day when every New Yorker is Irish, there were suddenly a lot of men named John in town, all heading for John Clapp's packed tavern.

Other businesses soon joined the first taverns. A "House of Entertainment" on the Bowery, perhaps an early version of the concert saloon, was mentioned by the intrepid Boston schoolmistress Sarah Kemble Knight in 1704, when she arrived on the Bowery after her seven-day stagecoach journey from Boston, a daring journey for an unaccompanied woman to make, then and for a long time thereafter.

Stagecoach journeys weren't cheap: the standard rate was three pence per mile. It was partly to prevent arguments and price gougings and partly to regulate the rates of the Royal Mail that milestones were set up along the Bowery in 1769, shortly after Benjamin Franklin became the post-master for the Colonies. Franklin himself was no stranger to stagecoach journeys, and he invented an odometer to regulate the settings of the milestones. Along the Bouwerie Lane, the milestones marked the distance from City Hall, then at the corner of Wall and Broad Streets. The original One Mile Stone sat just below the Tea Water Spring and the Two Mile Stone at Bouwerie Village. In 1813, when the new City Hall was opened, the milestones were shifted northward to reflect the new distances, placing the One Mile Stone at about Rivington Street and the Two Mile Stone up at the future 19th Street.

The milestones became defining points on the Bowery. The Two Mile Stone at Bouwerie Village became the traditional place where people accompanying departing friends saw them off, and the Bowery Village Tavern was a convenient spot for a farewell toast. Before long there was a tavern at the One Mile Stone for those who couldn't make it that far. Curiously, long after the One Mile Stone was hit by a truck and removed in 1926, an echo of the One Mile House tavern was recalled by a liquor store called the One Mile House at the corner of Bowery and Riving-ton that continued in business until the mid-1970s. And with a nod to the place's history, a restaurant named One Mile House recently opened around the corner one block down on Delancey Street.

As New York grew in the 1700s, the importance of the Bowery grew as well, and it soon was serving several purposes for New Yorkers. The Dutch had established its role as a place of entertainment and revelry, and the English population happily expanded upon this tradition. Brew-eries and distilleries took advantage of the Tea Water Spring's never-end-ing source of fine water to service the growing number of taverns in New York. With sources of disease and infection still imperfectly known,

Europeans of the day were reluctant to trust potable water sources, even such a source as the Tea Water pump. Drinking plain water only when forced to by extreme poverty or desperate circumstances, they found it healthier to replenish their bodily fluids with beverages using boiled water such as tea, or, making the best of life as they found it, beer.

Stout's Tavern at East Broadway and Catherine Street joined Webber's and Sackett's around 1728; by the time of the Revolution, there were thirteen licensed liquor vendors lining the Bowery between the Collect Pond and Bowery Village. The licensed places were joined by any number of unlicensed places, often the homes of farmwives who would occasionally brew up a batch of ale and perhaps announce its availability by affixing the traditional "ale stake" over their doors. An ale stake jutting out over the door, usually a broom handle, was an English tradition dating from the Middle Ages; when a signboard was eventually hung from the stake, it became the origin of the familiar pub sign.

The Bull's Head Tavern opened in the mid-1700s and became one of the Bowery's longest-lived establishments, marking the combination of what was then the two main industries on the Bowery: beer and cattle.

By 1735, the plot that would become Chinatown on the lower end of the Bowery was known as the Plough and Harrow Tract, named for the tavern that stood there. Originally Thomas Hall's tavern, the place later became known simply as the Farmer's Tavern. As always, a good location ensured the continuity of business, and the Farmer's Tavern became a favorite place for cattle drovers and people who did business with them, situated as it was on the route by which cattle were brought to the city.

The salt meadows and empty lands the Dutch found on either side of the old Indian trail were first put to use as areas where cattle and swine were let loose to graze freely. As more bouweries were established the cattle needed to be contained, and eventually cattle pens were set up on the west side of the Bouwerie Lane. The Collect Pond and the brooks flowing out of it were convenient places to water the ever-thirsty cattle, and by following the path running south and east from the Collect Pond, the cattle could be brought to the main meat market for the town, the old Vly Market at the foot of Maiden Lane.

Vly was simply Dutch for ravine, and eventually the ravine was named Smith's Vly for the local English landowner. By the 1700s, the name of the Vly Market had been corrupted, appropriately enough for an open-air meat market, to Fly Market. It sat next to another important amenity for the meat trade: a brook of fresh water, handy not so much for cleanliness as for increasing the market weight of the steaks and chops. Maiden Lane was the path running down the Vly, named for the girls left to do the laundry in the brook within easy eyesight of their mothers who did their daily shopping at the Fly Market. (Despite the similarity of names, New York's Fly Market had nothing to do with the term "Flea Market," which originated centuries later in a Paris open-air used-mattress market.)

As New York grew, it became necessary to move the actual butchering of the cattle above the town, and as the Bowery was still the only road connecting Manhattan with the mainland, it was natural to place both cattle dealing and the slaughterhouses along the Bowery down which all the cattle would have to be driven.

As the eighteenth century wore on, the Bull's Head Tavern, on the Bowery just below Canal Street, took over from Bowery Village as the unofficial capital of the Bowery. The terminus both of the cattle routes into New York as well as the stage lines serving Manhattan, the Bull's Head—along with its next-door neighbor, the Black Horse Inn—became a popular place to do business, as well as a place to waste time while pretending to do business. The Bull's Head became a popular political meeting house and drew many visitors for its bustle and conversation, such as the young Washington Irving, who often dropped in even though he had nothing to do with the cattle business. There he soaked up ale and tales of Peter Stuyvesant, whom he would later lampoon as "Peter Hardhead" in his *Knickerbocker's History of New York*.

Cattle, though, remained the main reason for the Bull's Head. It was surrounded by cattle pens with an abattoir adjacent. Other slaughterhouses grew up around the Bull's Head and eventually formed a cluster lining both sides of the Bowery north of the tavern.

The area logically became a magnet for other "cattle-driven" industries such as tanneries and leather goods businesses, notably shoe and harness making. Tanneries were an exceptionally odoriferous industry, and however necessary to the economic life of a place such as New York, people naturally wanted them to be located as far outside town as possible, preferably where they would be downwind most of the time. The area around the Collect Pond suited everybody's needs perfectly, being below the end of the cattle trail where fresh hides could be collected from the slaughterhouses, and with a pond both to supply the large amounts of water the tanneries needed as well as to dump the polluted water they produced. The tanneries in Beekman's Swamp, as it was known, would evolve into a traditional locale for New York's leather goods industry that would persist until the beginning of the 1900s. A cluster of retail shoe stores around West Broadway and Chambers Streets remained until recently as a ghost of "the Swamp."

With cattle sales being done at the Bull's Head, the butchers at the Fly Market, nearly two miles down, were dependent on whatever deals were being cut over mugs of ale at the Bull's Head. One enterprising chap decided to deal with the problem head on. Henry Astor would leave his stall at the Fly Market and ride a horse up the Bowery past the Bull's Head and meet the drovers as they came down the road. The tired drovers were often happy to cut a deal with Astor right then and there and avoid both the haggling and the pen charges at the Bull's Head. This meant considerable savings to Astor, who beat out the middlemen, and enabled him to make good money by vending meat at the Fly Market at competitive prices. Canny housewives soon learned to put up with Astor's absences from his stall and wait till he returned in hopes of getting better prices.

Astor's busting of the Bull's Head monopoly made him unpopular with both the middlemen and his fellow merchants at the Fly Market. They insisted on medieval norms of proper business conduct and launched several petitions to the New York Common Council, hoping to have Astor enjoined from his "pernicious practice" of "forestalling." Astor won out in the end, and after the Revolutionary War he became the owner of the Bull's Head. The money he made became the foundation of one of New York's great fortunes, and in proper style he built a country mansion in 1796 on the Bowery just north of the Bull's Head where his wife Dolly reigned supreme as the "pink of the Bowery." His kid brother, John Jacob, would have an even greater impact on the area.

The Bull's Head would continue on, moving north as the city grew, and leaving its stamp on the landscape in a variety of ways. In the 1820s, the Upper Bull's Head was built on the corner of the Bowery and Broome Streets, and remains of its walls were eventually incorporated into what became the Occidental Hotel. The New Bull's Head was opened in 1826 at the corner of 4th Street and the Bowery. By then, the cattle market had moved further up the Bowery to what would become Cooper Square, and the New Bull's Head developed its own market for dealing in sheep, eventually creating the Tompkins Market. When the horse and cattle market shifted to the area of 23rd Street and Third Avenue later in the 1800s, the Bull's Head followed it, establishing yet another Bull's Head Tavern with a Bull's Head Village growing up around it. The name remained up to the 1940s in the form of a Bull's Head Stables and a Bull's Head Harness Company serving the dray horse industry, which persisted in New York until after World War II.

The Bowery in the 1700s served more than the leather and animal industries. The same prevailing westerly winds that blew the odors of the tanneries away from New York (and toward Brooklyn) also drove a number of windmills along the Bowery, conveniently located to transform grain from outlying farms into flour for the city. One in particular, located just beyond the Kissing Bridge that crossed the stream where Canal Street is today, became a long-lived landmark known simply as the Old Windmill, signaling to carriage drivers that they were approaching the bridge where, if they were driving with their sweethearts, they could stop and exact a kiss from their dates. (Back then, this could really make a fellow's day.) Another windmill near 10th Street ground imported "Peruvian Bark" to make quinine. Quinine was a big business in early New York, what with the extensive salt marshes lying within sight of the windmill and whose mosquitoes (or as people at the time believed, swamp vapors) made malaria a serious health hazard in the city.

In the early 1700s, the Bowery also grew to become New York's main pleasure ground. The taverns drew weekend pleasure jaunters, and the crowds soon created a market for additional entertainments. The Bowery was wide and reasonably straight, making it a good place to hold races. Footraces soon became horse races. Horse-trading flourished alongside the cattle trading, and buyers naturally wanted to take their prospective purchases out for a "road test" before deciding. Before long, the Bowery was the traditional place to hold horse races, especially on Sundays when the cattle were not moving, and the Maidenhead Race Course would be set up in 1790 on the grounds behind the old Delancey Mansion just east of the Bowery.

Amid the revelry and horse races, there were some strange things to be found along the Bowery. In May 1769, a macabre burial took place where the Bowery joined with Bloomingdale Road. Stephen Porter, in the city jail accused of piracy and murder, cheated the hangman by taking his own life. The authorities, invoking old English law, directed that he be buried "in the public highway with a stake through his heart." Following tradition, the crossroads where the Bloomingdale Road met the Bowery was selected in order that his ghost, or vampiric corpse, wouldn't know which way to go, or, if it did make up its mind, there was at least an even chance that it would head for Harlem or Westchester.

Other burials were quietly forgotten until time and chance brought them to light again. The old African Burial Ground was located in the waste ground called Cat Hollow west of the Bowery and just north of the wooden palisade marking the colonial city limits on the line of today's Chambers Street. Medical students at the nearby hospital at Broadway and Pearl Street felt free to raid what was then termed the "Negro Burial Ground" for dissection cadavers. It was only when rumors spread of them digging up bodies of white people from other graveyards that the "Doctors Riots" erupted against them in 1788.

When new office construction unearthed some of the graves in the African Burial Ground in the early 1990s, surprise mingled with controversy, and today a museum at 295 Broadway, along with a memorial, commemorates the site. Yet for all the attention that was focused on the burial ground in Cat Hollow, another nearby site remained forgotten. When the original African Burial Ground filled up, New York's African community petitioned the Common Council in April 1795 for permission to set up a second burial ground. This was located further uptown a few yards east of the Bowery at the corner of Chrystie and Rivington Streets. The graves were eventually relocated to Long Island, and tenements at 195–197 Chrystie Street were built over the plot, but the curiously named Freeman Alley still runs along what was the rear of this cemetery, serving as the entrance to a marble monument company as late as the 1930s.

The earth along the foot of the Bowery also hid evidence of horrors the city preferred to purge from its memory, and which when uncovered were quickly forgotten again. As the Bowery met Chatham Street along the line of today's Park Row, it brushed by the Common where City Hall and the Tweed Courthouse stand today. In eighteenth-century New York, the Common served many purposes, among them the site of the city's jail as well as the public execution grounds where people were hanged, tortured, and even burned at the stake.

In the eighteenth century, New York was a leading slave city, with a per capita slave population that rivaled many of the cities and towns further south. On March 25, 1712, a brief slave revolt fueled by drinks celebrating the old-style English New Year left eight whites dead and twelve wounded. A large band of slaves fled up the Bowery to seek refuge in the hills and woods north of the city. The militia, converging from New York and Westchester, rounded up nineteen slaves the next day. Bowery resident May Bickley, then the attorney general for New York, saw to it that the worst penalties were inflicted on the rebels. In all, fourteen men were hanged, two were burned at the stake, one roasted to death over a slow fire, one broken on the wheel, and one whipped and left to starve to death in his chains.

Bickley eventually lost his job as attorney general in the reaction following these executions, and New Yorkers determinedly forgot the horrors. With the civic memory thus purged, the way was left open for an even worse hysteria that erupted in reaction to the supposed "Great Negro Plot" of 1741, which was believed to be a widespread conspiracy involving wholesale murder and arson. Through the spring and early summer of 1741, interrogations alternated with executions, as confessions were extracted and the implicated were condemned. By mid-July, thirteen African men had been burned at the stake before crowds gathered on the Common, seventeen more were hanged, their corpses left hanging to rot in the summer sun, and an additional two white men and two white women were hanged. It is said that when the foundations were being dug for the Municipal Building in 1905 the burnt remains of human beings were found still with their iron chains. It is uncertain what was done with the remains, and the discovery was quickly forgotten.

But there were also lighthearted subterranean mysteries to be found along the Bowery. About this time, a legend grew up that there lurked some kind of a monster in the Collect Pond. The pond was commonly thought to be bottomless, and nobody knew what might be living in its increasingly polluted depths. Prefiguring the classic alligators-in-the-sewers story, local folklore had it that some kind of a sea monster was living down there and had grabbed a Hessian soldier during the Revolutionary War. The issue was never settled, as the pond was never drained; it instead would be filled in with earth from the nearby Bayard's Mount, burying forever what might have become a contender for the title of city mascot.

The demolition of Bayard's Mount that filled in the Collect Pond also failed to settle another legend from Colonial days. The hill was located just west of the Bowery below Grand Street, and sometime in the 1760s the idea caught on that buried treasure was to be found there, supposedly that of New York's enigmatic resident Captain William Kidd, hanged for piracy in 1701. Kidd would have needed several ships to supply all the places he was supposed to have planted treasure in. Corlear's Hook, jutting out into the bend of the East River, was one such reputed treasure site. This in itself was curious, since Corlear's Hook had been the customary place where pirates were hanged in New York, even though Kidd himself was executed in England. Still, it became a popular place for treasure seekers who often used, in those days before metal detectors were invented, various spells and incantations, to find the hidden fortune.

Eventually, those spells and incantations must have pointed toward Bayard's Mount, and the nocturnal gold bugs became a major nuisance for the Mount's resident owner, Nicholas Bayard. In 1762, he went to the length of advertising in the newspaper his complaint about the "money diggers" who had dug on his Mount the night before and had been scared away, leaving behind two spades and a pickax. Whether it was Nicholas Bayard or a more spectral apparition that frightened them away will never be known, for the money diggers never had the nerve to return and claim their tools. But if Bayard sought to keep the soil of his Mount inviolate, he was to be disappointed yet again a few years later when the Revolutionary War came to New York.

3 Bowery Bunker Hill

PAUL REVERE'S FIRST GREAT RIDE came down the Bowery in December 1773. Anxious to explain the reasons behind the recent Boston Tea Party, but fearing interception at sea, the Boston Committee of Correspondence entrusted Revere to carry their communiqués by horseback to Philadelphia via the more arduous but more secure route down the Boston Post Road. The following May, Revere rode down the Bowery again, this time bearing news of the "Intolerable Acts" the British Parliament had clapped down on Boston in response to the Tea Party and of Boston's determination to resist. His reimbursement request for this trip shows that he entered Manhattan by way of the wooden Kingsbridge at the north end of the island, then rode south along the old Post Road, which turned into the Bowery at its junction with Bloomingdale Road just above the Two Mile Stone.

The Bowery that Revere followed had grown considerably from its early days as an Indian trail. It was the still main landward entrance to a New York City clustered below present-day Chambers Street. The Bowery's status as part of the Post Road ensured that it was given a broad width and was better maintained than most roads in that day. Along with stagecoaches and post riders, the road carried much of the growing city's foodstuffs from the farms of Manhattan and Westchester—grain for the city's bakeries and breweries, firewood and hemlock bark for the tanneries, and herds of cattle driven to butchers' shambles and the aptly-named "Fly Market" at the foot of Maiden Lane.

Revere passed through New York twice again in September and October 1774, carrying messages between Boston and the Continental Congress in Philadelphia. By the time he finally set out on his midnight ride to Concord in April 1775, he had plenty of riding experience.

Events moved quickly after the battles of at Lexington and Concord a few hours after Revere's celebrated alarm-sounding ride. In June 1775, the newly appointed General George Washington passed through New York amid cheering crowds and rode up the Bowery to take command of the "Army of Observation" besieging the British forces in Boston.

Despite the cheering crowds that greeted Washington, the political mood in New York was at best ambivalent. To Royal Governor William Tryon, fleeing to the safety of his official mansion on Governor's Island, the town was rotten with rebels. To the local Sons of Liberty, notably merchant and shipmaster Isaac Sears, New York was thick with Tories.

The most prominent leader of the Sons of Liberty, "King Sears" rode up the Bowery toward Connecticut shortly after Washington passed through. With militia recruitment lagging, and two British warships already in the harbor, Sears headed to Connecticut to borrow the 1,500 men serving under General David Wooster to keep the lid on things back in New York. He convinced the Connecticut authorities to help the cause, and Wooster's Regiment duly marched down the Bowery on June 28, 1775, and set up camp just south of Bouwerie Village, in a place convenient to the Bull's Head Tavern. No cheering crowds greeted them; instead, word on the street had it that Sears had brought them in to arrest what he called "inimicals," persons of suspected Tory sympathies based on their voting records in recent colonial elections.

Though the rumored mass arrests never happened, the presence of the Connecticut militia did spur New York's recruiting drive, though many would be disappointed in the quality of volunteers that came forward. With British guns still frowning down upon the city from warships in the harbor, many people sat tight to see which way the wind would blow, and many of the men that would form the 1st New York Regiment under Colonel Alexander McDougall came from the shanties clustered about the "out ward" around the low end of the Bowery.

The Connecticut militia marched back home a few weeks later, leaving behind an uneasy Isaac Sears. He slipped out of town and returned a few weeks later at the head of a band of eighty horsemen. They had spent a couple of weeks suppressing "inimicals" in Westchester before Sears led them thundering over the Kissing Bridge to smash up the office and press of James Rivington's pro-government newspaper, the *New York Gazette*. They galloped back to Connecticut bearing sacks of hard-to-replace lead type that Sears figured could be better used to make bullets to shoot Tories. Little did Sears, or anyone else, know that the apparently pro-Tory Rivington was really a patriot all along, and would become one of Washington's secret agents, funneling information to Washington's spy "Culper Junior" that he gathered from the gossip heard in his coffeehouse. A street crossing the Bowery would be later named in Rivington's honor.

Back in Connecticut, Isaac Sears was still worried about New York's apparent apathy about the revolution, and he communicated these worries to General Charles Lee, head of the patriot forces in Connecticut. Lee, who perhaps had his own doubts about the commitment of New Yorkers to the cause, readily passed Sears's concerns on to Congress, which authorized Lee to mount a fact-finding mission to the city. Lee interpreted this as orders for a military occupation of New York, and so marched his troops down from Stamford, Connecticut, at the end of January 1776.

The New York Committee of Safety found Lee's attitude puzzling and a bit annoying, but decided it would be best to arrange a "politic" welcome for him. Accordingly, they organized crowds to line the lower Bowery and loudly cheer his arrival at the head of his troops. The crowds on the Bowery that day were a bit thin, but they were much thicker a few days later, when news of arriving British warships came in from the lookout posts on Staten Island. Nearly everyone who had a place in the country, or could borrow one, decided that it was a good time to visit it, and wagons loaded with families and household goods mobbed the Bowery, all trying to head north.

The midwinter panic was premature, as it would be months before the British could marshal their forces to mount a full invasion. But it was clear that the invasion was coming, and at the end of March, as soon as he had forced the British to evacuate Boston, George Washington began moving his troops down from Massachusetts to undertake the defense of New York.

Washington and Lee worked as best they could to make New York defensible against the coming British onslaught. The American troops were camped outside the city, close to the Collect Pond and the Tea Water Spring. A "Grand Camp," soon rose along the west side of the Bowery, from the Collect Pond all the way to Bayard's Mount, where the entry to the city was guarded by a redoubt named "Bunker Hill II." Captain Kidd's treasure remained unfound, as far as known, and New Bunker Hill was linked with other nearby redoubts, including the low mound of the Shearith Israel cemetery that was fortified to serve as a secondary line of defense.

By July 1776, the Grand Camp was completely organized and laid out. Three brigades were based in the middle, amid the cattle pens around the Bull's Head Tavern with two more on the Common or quartered in the town. Nathaniel Greene's forces held Brooklyn Heights, and other regiments guarded Governor's Island and Kingsbridge at the north of Manhattan Island. The Farmer's Inn and its two barns were converted into a military hospital.

Now a military road, the Bowery was the scene of all the activities common to eighteenth-century armies, including a notable hanging. On June 28, 1776, Thomas Hickey was hanged in a field just off the Bowery and north of the Commons. A member of George Washington's own bodyguard, Hickey was convicted of counterfeiting, conspiracy to burn New York, and of plotting the assassination of Washington, reputedly through a poisoned bowl of the boiled peas that was a favorite dish of the snaggletoothed general.

Two weeks after witnessing the Hickey hanging, the troops along the Bowery were drawn up again to hear the public reading of the Declaration of Independence. There being no one place where the entire army could be assembled, the Declaration was first read on the Common, then read aloud to the formations in their separate camps.

In the end, the fortified Bowery never fired a shot. In August, the disastrous Battle of Long Island forced Washington to abandon Brooklyn and escape with most of his troops to Manhattan. Then in September, the British crossed the East River and landed in the middle of Manhattan. Washington was forced to evacuate his troops from the New York City defenses before the British thrust across the waist of the island and sealed all routes of escape. The Boston Post Road was cut off within an hour of their landing, so the American troops heading up the Bowery out of New York had to turn onto the Bloomingdale Road and head for Harlem as fast as they could.

Amid the chaos some units fell through the cracks. General Henry Knox found himself in temporary command, but without any orders or any clear idea of what was going on, until Washington's aide Major Aaron Burr (not yet one of New York's more controversial figures) slipped past the advancing British troops and rode to New Bunker Hill to extricate Knox. Thinking himself completely cut off, Knox was planning to hold the fort and fight to the last cartridge, and rejected Burr's advice to retreat to Harlem. Burr instead rallied the troops himself and led them north along the Bowery and the Bloomingdale Road, with a very annoyed Knox following along. By using a few farm lanes that he had scouted out, Burr eluded the British and brought the men to the American lines on Harlem Heights. Thanks to Burr, the Battle of New Bunker Hill was one Bowery bloodbath that never happened.

A triumphant British Army marched down the Bowery and moved into what remained of the American defenses, which they soon set about improving. The Bunker Hill redoubt on Bayard's Mount became a key point of the new line of British defenses of the landward side of New York. Anxious to secure the freshwater sources, they drew the main line of defense well north of the city, crossing the Bowery along the approximate line of today's Grand Street, leaving the Collect Pond and the Tea Water Spring safely within British lines. The point where the defense line crossed the Bowery was fortified and became known as the Bowery Gate. Located about three-quarters of a mile north of the city limits at today's intersection of Bowery and Grand Street, the Bowery Gate was the main landward entrance into occupied New York.

British-occupied New York was an uncomfortable place, to say the least. The outflow of pro-rebel civilians was more than matched by an inflow of Tory refugees fleeing repressions of "inimicals" in whatever outlying areas the British could not keep under occupation. Added to the refugees were the soldiers and the hordes of camp followers that trailed every eighteenth-century army, all squeezed into a town that, however small it had been before the war, was now even smaller, having lost about a third of its housing stock in the "great fire" that broke out shortly after the American troops left. Whoever, if anyone, started it, the great fire had left nearly everything west of Broadway, including Trinity Church, in ashes. The area became known as "canvass town" for the crude shelters made by rigging pieces of sailcloth over the remains of basements and cellars.

Little new housing could be built, for no lumber was available. Indeed, there was hardly any firewood to be had in the city. Manhattan was soon stripped of whatever trees could be chopped down, and wood-cutting parties sent into New Jersey ran afoul of armed rebel militia, at times requiring the dispatch of up to five thousand British soldiers to guard the woodcutters.

From September 1776 to the end of the war in November 1783, the number of British troops on Manhattan fluctuated between three thousand and twenty thousand. The British stationed as many of their troops as they could up on the wild north end of Manhattan Island, but large numbers still had to be kept within the main defenses of the city itself. In the crowded camps that grew around the lower end of the Bowery, and the sprawling settlements of the army's camp followers and other "support industries," bad food and increasingly polluted water joined the mosquitoes from the salt marshes to raise the disease rates to frightful heights. One British military hospital buried 120 out of 200 patients over a period of five months.

Most of the British dead, and the dead American prisoners from the infamous Rhinelander Sugar House prison (down on what became Liberty Street) were buried in unmarked mass graves recorded only as being "near the Jews' burying ground" of Shearith Israel. The five-story stone sugar warehouse was the worst of the various jails and prison ships in which the American prisoners of war were kept, where overcrowding, neglect, and brutality produced a death rate of nearly 70 percent within a year and a half. Some American prisoners were buried along the north side of Trinity Churchyard, where the Martyrs' Monument would eventually commemorate their sacrifice, but most of the mass burials in Manhattan were entirely lost, and their remains may lie somewhere near the lower Bowery.

Relations among the occupiers themselves were not very good, and tensions increased as the war dragged on and morale declined, especially after the disappointing campaigns of 1777–78. British encampments were located near the Bowery's breweries and taverns, placing constant temptation before the eyes of the ever-thirsty British soldiers. Being paid only six pence a day on average (and sometimes not even that), the soldiers sought other means of gaining drinking money. The result was the Bowery's first crime wave that made the area dangerous to civilians and provoked complaints to the harried provost officers about the "constant robberies" taking place there. British soldiers tended to blame their German allies for this problem, it being well well-known disappointed the Hessian soldiers were when they discovered that, in British America at least, wholesale looting of occupied enemy towns was not an acceptable victory celebration. The Hessians, for their part, knew how many British soldiers were recruited from jails and the steps of the gallows, and muttered about their inherent criminality.

Soon it became standard practice to keep British and Hessian camps as far away from each other as possible to prevent the fistfights that might grow into skirmish-sized engagements. British officers also frequently quarreled with their Hessian counterparts, and numerous duels were fought in the fields along the Bowery outside the Bowery Gate. The usual solution was to park the Hessians up on the north end of the island, or else place them east of the Bowery out at Corlear's Hook. The British 17th Dragoons were kept on more or less permanent station at the very south end of the Bowery where they could serve as a mobile police force or a rapid reaction force in case of an enemy breakthrough at the Bowery Gate.

Sprawling around the British camps were the hordes of camp followers, mainly women with their children. British army regulations provided for a limited number of officially sanctioned women to be attached to each regiment, usually the wives of sergeants or corporals. Others might be temporarily "married" to private soldiers through a ceremony of jumping over a ramrod (or a broomstick). Both the recognized wives and the unofficial camp followers provided a wide range of support services for the soldiers. Drawing one half of a man's ration (and a quarter ration for each child), the wives made ends meet through laundering, sewing, and nursing. Denied rations and living in shantytowns among the tannery yards along the north shore of the Collect Pond, the unofficial camp followers survived as best they could, often through such means as prostitution.

Some of them were abandoned women, others the offspring of rootless destitution. The camp followers lived and died in squalor, and gave the Bowery its first scenes of wholesale human misery. Perishing of disease, exposure, and casual brutality, most of the women in the area north of the camps were buried unmarked and unnoted, except for one who had preceded them by a few months.

Charlotte Stanley had arrived in New York shortly before the war broke out, in 1774. The daughter of a Church of England clergyman and a distant relative of the Lord of the Isle of Man, she was seduced by a British army officer and, unaware that he was already married, came to New York with him.

Charlotte soon found she was an inconvenient woman, but her officer set her up in a small rented place at 24 Bowery Lane, near today's corner of Pell Street on the old Plough and Harrow tract. But when the onset of the war prompted him to abandon New York, he also abandoned Charlotte, and the penniless and pregnant girl was evicted and set to wandering the Bowery and the streets of New York in search of shelter. She was eventually taken in by a kindly, though unnamed, soul. But in December 1775, she died shortly after giving birth in his small house, which may have been on the outskirts of Bowery Village.

It was said that shortly before her death Charlotte was reunited with her clergyman father, who had come to New York in search of her, and who through his church connections was able to at least spare her the indignity of an unmarked grave. He instead arranged to have her buried in Trinity Churchyard before he returned to England with Charlotte's newborn daughter Lucy.

Charlotte gained posthumous fame in 1794 when Susanna Rowson published her story as the novel *Charlotte Temple*. In the novel, the fictional Charlotte was given a long and touching demise, plus an impassioned speech over her grave site by her now contrite seducer. A hundred years later, other fallen women on the Bowery would swallow poison and die on the sidewalks, unremarked and unremembered, but the story of Charlotte Temple struck a chord with a sentimental reading public. In 1800, Charlotte Stanley's daughter Lucy came to New York to reclaim her mother's bones for reburial in England, but, perhaps mindful of the impact the novel was having, she saw to it that a substantial monument was erected over the now empty grave. A flat stone mounted on four pillars bore a metal plaque with the arms of the house of Stanley and the name of Charlotte Stanley. The pillars would eventually break and the plaque was stolen, but the stone, with the name Charlotte Temple chiseled on the space left by the stolen plaque, would become a place of pilgrimage, with visitors leaving flowers, votive objects, and graffiti. The tombstone is still in Trinity Churchyard at the head of Wall Street, and can be glimpsed from Broadway. To this day, flowers still appear on the tombstone from time to time, placed by persons unknown.

The Revolutionary War dragged on, but the expected all-out American attack on New York City never materialized. After the surrender of General Cornwallis at Yorktown in 1781, the conflict sputtered through two years of inertia and negotiation until Washington marched triumphantly down the Bowery at the head of his troops to receive the official British handover of New York at the Bowery Gate on November 25, 1783. The American troops stood down outside the Bowery Gate while Washington retired to the Bull's Head Tavern to await the completion of the British evacuation of the city. Finally, the Americans marched through the Bowery Gate and continued on down to Fraunces' Tavern at Pearl and Broad Streets for the official raising of the Stars and Stripes. For years afterward, the day would be commemorated as a civic holiday every twenty-fifth of November, with reenactment parades on the Bowery, though later these parades were rerouted to Broadway. The Evacuation Day Parade remained an annual event until petering out in the 1930s, eclipsed by the Thanksgiving Day Parade.

4   Pleasure Gardens

THE BRITISH LEFT BEHIND A very different city than the one they had entered in September 1776. The old Dutch town was fast disappearing, and the English city of the "good old colony days," as seen across the gulf of eight years of war, was seemingly little more than a dim memory. Great changes had taken place, and more were to come, as New York grew to become an American city, and began its celebrated habit of reinventing itself every thirty years or so.

Symbolic of this change was the destruction of the old Stuyvesant mansion. Already over one hundred years old, the building caught fire in 1778 and burned to the ground. Whether it was accident or arson nobody could say, but a link with the past had been severed. A rumor spread that immediately after the fire, a strange figure with a wooden leg was seen poking about in the ruins.

Peter Stuyvesant, they said, had come back to witness the death of his old Bouwerie. The village was still there, of course, though in a much expanded version, and the little tavern at the crossroads had grown into a cluster of taverns on what was now the outer limit of the city. The war had disrupted the Bowery's role as a place of entertainment, but being on the entrance to a growing city, it would soon revive.

Stuyvesant's mansion was gone, and his beloved chapel wasn't much better off. His widow Judith had continued the private services there until her own death in 1687, but after that things fell off, as the children and grandchildren moved away from the old manse and built houses of their own on the easterly portions of the Stuyvesant lands. Judith Stuyvesant had neglected to arrange for an endowment to provide money for the chapel's upkeep, and it soon fell into decay.

In 1793, another Peter Stuyvesant, the great-grandson of the director-general, decided to do right by the old warrior's memory. He gave a parcel of land and $4,000 cash to Trinity Church in order to build a new church on the site of the old chapel. However good the great-grandson's intentions, he left Old Peter with another reason to feel restless in his vault: despite all his efforts on behalf of the Dutch Reformed Church, the family had long since turned Episcopalian. In honor of the church's origins, a pew was permanently reserved for the use of any visiting representatives of the Dutch government, but the services were now read from the Anglican *Book of Common Prayer*.

But that wasn't the problem. The problem was that Trinity's charter had named it as the only Anglican (or now, after Independence, Episcopalian) parish in the city of New York—all other Episcopal houses of worship could only be mere chapels, dependent on the original Trinity. But old Royal charters didn't carry much weight in the newly independent country, so Peter Stuyvesant II hired the lawyers Alexander Hamilton and Richard Harrison to establish the legal basis for his St. Mark's In-the-Bouwerie to become the first independent Episcopal Church outside Trinity.

The cornerstone was laid on April 25, 1795, and the building was consecrated on May 9, 1799. A larger building, it encompassed the site of the old chapel, and enclosed the Stuyvesant vault within its eastern wall. Its official name, the Church of Old St. Mark's In-the-Bouwerie, still causes some confusion. Although the building was new, the site was old, and in fact would become the city's oldest site of religious worship still in use today (Stuyvesant's old chapel had been built before Trinity Church was founded). "In-the-Bouwerie" referred to Peter Stuyvesant's farm and village.

The Stuyvesant family would add to the grant in 1803 by giving St. Mark's additional land for its churchyard, with the proviso that a section be set aside for the burial of any Stuyvesant family slaves or their descendants.

After the Revolution, a revitalized New York City resumed its northward growth, and confiscated Tory-owned lands along the Bowery were
sold off to developers. Oddly enough, many of the new streets laid out
along the Bowery would be named for the same Tory families that the
lands were taken from. James Rivington was rehabilitated once it was
discovered that he had been an American agent all along. But the Royal
Lieutenant Governor Broome also got a street named after him, as did the
Delancey family and their neighbors the Stantons. In fact, the Delanceys
got three streets named after them: in addition to Delancey Street itself,
Oliver Street was named for Oliver Delancey, and James Street was named
for James Delancey (and only coincidentally became the site of St. James'
Church). It was a family achievement not to be duplicated until 1794,
when Dr. Gardiner Jones got Jones Street named for himself, while his
brother-in-law Samuel Jones, not to be outdone, got both Great Jones
Street and Jones Alley.

As if to cover up the taint of Tory memories, the remaining streets
in the area were eventually named for American heroes in the War of
1812: Chrystie, Forsyth, Eldridge, Allen, Ludlow, Pike, and Willett were
dubbed in this fashion.

After the signing of the Constitution, it was decided to temporarily
locate the nation's capital in New York. New York's brief stint as the capital of the United States brought a much needed boost to its economy and
helped fuel the city's expansion. President Washington himself chose an
uptown address: on Cherry Street, about where the western abutment of
the Brooklyn Bridge now stands, within easy reach of his Secretary of the
Treasury, Alexander Hamilton, and various other members of the new
government.

With the new nation's government established and the economy rising, the Bowery became the scene of progressive experimentation. At the
north end of the Bowery, just above the Two Mile Stone, "Baron" Freder-
ick Charles Hans Bruno Poelnitz turned his twenty-two-acre estate into
a farm where he tested out such exotic crops as woad and madder, and
tried different species of grass that might be used for cattle pasturage. The
baron also operated one of the first threshing machines, tinkered with

various kinds of experimental plows, and even built a device that could measure the force needed to plow different types of soils.

Poelnitz's farm became an attraction to people making an excursion up the Bowery. George Washington paid a visit, was impressed by the baron's work, and ordered one of the baron's "Horse-Hoes" to be sent to Mount Vernon. But native New Yorkers are not as easy to win over as out-of-towners, and the eccentric baron became a laughing stock around the town. Not long after Washington's visit in 1789, he grew tired of the laughter and sold it.

Poelnitz's farm wasn't the only experiment going on along the Bowery in those days. In the summer of 1796, John Fitch braved the pollution (and the monster) of the Collect Pond to test out the world's first steam-powered boat, an eighteen-foot yawl that ran on a screw propeller and circled the Collect Pond at six miles per hour. What should have been a revolutionary event somehow failed to make a splash. Fitch went on to Philadelphia, where his steam-powered ferry boat also failed to make an impression. Eleven years later, Robert Fulton would win fame when his steam-driven *Clermont* sailed up the Hudson. By then the disappointed Fitch had gone to Kentucky and killed himself.

The coming of peace meant that the Bowery now resumed its former role as pleasure ground for the city. The old taverns remained, but pleasure gardens were the new thing, combining entertainment with a formal parklike atmosphere and an occasional bit of theater or public spectacle. Some early pleasure gardens had opened in New York before the Revolution, but they kept to the area of Broadway below the Commons, convenient to their genteel patrons, and didn't penetrate as far north as the more proletarian Bowery. But now the city itself was growing toward the Bowery, making it a more attractive venue.

Manhattan still had plenty of countryside, but with its woods, plowed fields, cow pastures, and salt marshes the countryside was suited more for carriage riding than idling about in. The city had little in the way of parks and open spaces. Only the tiny Dutch bowling green and the much-abused Commons were available, and so there was a market for private playgrounds where upscale families could relax and unwind.

The site of the old Bayard mansion on Bayard's Mount, scene of treasure hunts, Revolutionary War fortifications, and even for a while a bear-baiting pit, was chosen as the place for the New Vauxhall Gardens. An "old" Vauxhall Gardens had flourished further south for a while. But keeping with its famous namesake in London, a larger and grander place was needed. An uptown location was deemed more suitable as New Yorkers fled north from the Yellow Fever epidemic, even if the proposed new location for the gardens would unknowingly bring them closer to the salt marshes that were the cause of the epidemic in the first place. The New Vauxhall Gardens opened in 1798 south of today's Grand Street, featuring convivial entertainment as well as, in the manner of its famous London namesake, evening fireworks displays.

In 1805, the city decided to level Bayard's Mount and use its earth to fill in the increasingly foul and polluted Collect Pond, forcing Vauxhall Gardens to move again. The new place, located between today's Broadway and the Bowery, bound by 4th Street on the south and Astor Place on the north, had been a botanical garden set up by Swiss physician Jacob Sperry. Sperry's herbs joined the output of the nearby quinine-grinding windmill in supplying medicines for the many ailments New Yorkers were suffering from, and people off for a jaunt to the countryside found the gardens a pleasant and salubrious place to visit.

Manager Joseph Delacroix found it an easy matter to turn Sperry's de facto pleasure garden into the real thing. He installed sculptures featuring American patriots mingled with classical gods and goddesses, thus adding an edifying educational component. In the evening the place was lit by nearly two thousand hanging lamps, and there were, of course, fireworks displays.

This third Vauxhall Gardens was at first a slightly inconvenient distance from the town, so to bring patronage to the place, Delacroix provided a horse-drawn "shuttle bus" service. He also continued the spirit of Sperry's Botanical Garden and sold health-conscious visitors an herbal "Vauxhall Beverage" whose curative powers were said to come from the waters of a supposedly medicinal spring near Bayard's Mount. (This was the same spring for which Spring Street is named, and whose

healing waters occasionally flood area basements today.) For the cultur-
ally inclined, Delacroix opened up a summer theater on the grounds. The
1806 theater season at Vauxhall featured performances by Mr. and Mrs.
David Poe, soon to become the parents of Edgar Allan Poe.

As if all that were not enough, Delacroix made aviation history on the
Bowery. The first balloon ascent in New York was an "Aerostatic Ascension" on August 2, 1819, by Charles Guille, riding in one of the first
hydrogen balloons and ending the show with a daring parachute jump.

The Vauxhall's success soon drew competitors to the Bowery. In
1802, Christopher Tomlinson's Tea Garden and Tavern opened on Prince
Street just off the Bowery, and featured a bowling alley for playing Dutch
ninepins as well as a green for playing English skittles. It was apparent
that tea could be as much a pleasure beverage as beer, and that there was
money to be made in catering to the family trade. Benjamin Waldron's
Inn and Tea Garden opened the same year as the third Vauxhall Gardens,
and was located across the Bowery, on the north side of Stuyvesant Street.

Joseph Delacroix's son Clement got into the act too, and in 1819 went
into competition with his dad. His Apollo Gardens in the backyard of
his house at 37 Bowery sold the products of his distillery up the road at
258 Bowery, combining hard liquor with the new craze for ice cream. Ice
cream and whiskey didn't mix, and Clement closed up the place before
the year was out, substituting a French language school for a few years
before moving off to Philadelphia in 1823.

The new pleasure gardens were joined by a growing number of conventional taverns. Shortly after the end of the war, the city had given an
inadvertent boost to the Bowery's role as a street of taverns. Noting with
dismay the fact that the city already had 333 licensed drinking places,
the city tightened up the rules for tavern licensing, specifying that new
licenses would only be granted to such places as were "necessary to the
accommodation of travelers." As the Bowery was the main landward
entryway into the city, locating a tavern there made it easy to claim that
it was for the accommodation of travelers. Up at the crossroads between
Vauxhall and Waldron's was the Sign of Noah's Ark, and, perhaps picking up on a zoological theme, there was also the nearby Dog and Duck,

a place especially noted for its asparagus gardens. A bit further down was the Duck and Frying Pan at 287–291 Bowery, the Gotham Cottage at 298, and the first of New York's several Pig & Whistles at 131 Bowery.

New taverns also congregated at the lower end of the Bowery by the Tea Water Spring, though the quality of the water there wasn't what it used to be due to seepage from nearby tanneries. The Plough and Harrow, or the Farmer's Tavern, about where Doyers Street would join the Bowery, was a favored place for people in the cattle trade who preferred not doing business at the more raucous atmosphere up the road at the Bull's Head. The Black Horse Inn stood by the Kissing Bridge where Canal Street is today, with Van Ranse's and Spicer's Inns nearby.

Some of the drinks that were served in these taverns at the end of the 1700s might have given pause to many a latter-day Bowery pub crawler. Popularized by New Englanders, Flip was the great standby. There were various recipes for flip, but they usually involved a mixture of beer, molasses, and rum, mulled with a red-hot fireplace poker that was known as a "flip-dog." There was also calibogus, or simply bogus, a mixture of rum and beer, and there was mimbo, or mim, made of rum, sugar, and water. Blackstrap was concocted of rum, molasses, and water, with a dash of herb bitters. It was judged wise to mix your rum with something—New England rum was known as kill-devil, and not without reason. A brave man might mix the rum with hard apple cider to make stonewall, and there was always applejack, better known in those days as jersey lightning.

The city was growing, and the Bowery wouldn't run past open fields much longer. By the time the 1811 street plan was enacted, an increasing population had already pushed the developed area of the city up the Bowery as far as Houston and Great Jones Streets. Part of this change is documented by the work of the Bowery's first artist, William P. Chappel, who painted the local scene between 1805 and 1810. His 1810 painting of the intersection of the Bowery with Chatham Square shows low wooden buildings, and the only traffic is the stagecoach on its way to Tarrytown. A "hot corn wench" is doing business on the corner of Doyers Street. It was the brief transition period for the Bowery between the country road it had been and the urban thoroughfare it was about to become.

Development followed hard on the heels of the taverns and pleasure gardens. By the early 1800s, the Bowery contained a mixture of businesses. An early concentration of the city's shoe stores was an outgrowth of the leather tanneries located northeast of the Collect Pond. More general businesses were seen along the Bowery as well, including dry goods, bookstores, furniture, pharmacies, and jewelry. The buildings along the Bowery still had a quaint appearance, built of wood and seldom more than two stories tall. The goods offered for sale could be seen through small windowpanes on the ground floor; plate glass wasn't available yet. Here and there a business would have a wooden awning stretching over the sidewalk offering strollers shelter from rain and sun. The awning might also serve a more practical purpose: for a dry goods dealer it would keep sunlight from fading his stocks of vegetable-dyed cloth. On the other hand, businesses such as jewelry would want to invite in the daylight to make their goods sparkle, and so left their storefronts unsheltered.

Some of these businesses proved very durable, lasting clear through the Bowery's various downward spirals into the 1930s and 1940s. Olliffe's Pharmacy at 6 Bowery, founded in 1814, outlasted Cowperthwait's Furniture, founded in 1807, to become the Bowery's oldest living business concern by the 1930s. Benedict's Jewelry, founded in 1818 at 28 Bowery, lasted nearly as long, and was the precursor to the jewelry district that is still found today along the eastern reaches of Canal Street. The poet Joseph Rodman Drake ("My Beautiful Bronx") ran a pharmacy from 1816 through 1819 at 121 Bowery; although nearly forgotten today, he started a long and curious association of the Bowery with poets.

Joining the established businesses were the street peddlers. This was a tradition that dated back to the days of New Amsterdam (as did the agitation against street peddlers by established merchants), and street peddling in the area would eventually reach a climax in the early twentieth century along such streets as Orchard and Hester. The Bowery in the early 1800s also saw the beginning of New York's fascination with street food. Hot dogs and ice cream bars hadn't been introduced yet. Instead, the street food of the day was hot corn on the cob, sold out of a simmering pot and given a quick wipe with a butter-soaked rag; a rather messy business but one that proved popular for most of the nineteenth century, and which was at least slightly safer for the consumer than the other standard street food, raw oysters.

Traditional street cries and jingles were the means by which the peddlers advertised themselves; the cry of the hot corn girl was:

> Hot Corn! Hot Corn!
> Here's your lily white corn!
> All that's got money—
> Poor me that's got none—
> Come buy my white corn,
> And let me go home.

But they didn't always have a home to go to after the corn was sold. Hot corn was almost always sold by young girls between eight and twelve, and often younger. Like the newspaper boys of a later generation, these "Hot Corn Girls" were often the subject of sentiment and romance, but the reality behind the sentiment could be brutal. The charmingly ragged girls were more often than not abused, abandoned, or orphaned girls, destitute and only a step or two away from outright prostitution.

Adjoining the growing number of pleasure gardens and small businesses along the Bowery were several small cemeteries. There had been the old Shearith Israel cemetery and the Moravian Cemetery down by Chatham Square, and in the late 1790s a new Negro Burial Ground was established east of the Bowery between Stanton and Rivington Streets. Another cemetery was added in 1796 when the old estate of the local landowner Mangle Minthorne was dispersed to his heirs. This estate lay east of the Bowery above North Street (later Houston), stretching off to the marshy lands around where Tompkins Square would be built. Minthorne sought to divide the good and bad lands as best he could, and he apportioned the land into nine strips fanning out from a point on the corner of the Bowery and North Street. Part of this land lying along the Bowery was sold off to become the burial grounds known as The Bowery Common. Mangle Minthorne himself was buried at Old St. Mark's.

The Bowery Common was divided into several tracts serving different religious denominations: Dutch Reformed, Methodist, Baptist, Presbyterian, and, as if to tweak the spirit of old Peter Stuyvesant, Quaker. In this Quaker tract, the victim of one of the city's oldest and most notorious unsolved murders was laid to rest in January 1800.

The Yellow Fever epidemic of 1798 convinced the city it was time to secure reliable water supplies, and it chartered the Manhattan Water Company to supply fresh water to the city. Nobody then could say for certain just what caused the Yellow Fever, but the brackish water supply of Manhattan certainly did nothing for the health of the city. The Manhattan Water Company, founded by Aaron Burr, was unable to follow through on its initial plans to tap the Bronx River, and instead sought to exploit whatever water sources could be found on the lower end of Manhattan, including the Tea Water Spring, to fill a reservoir on Chambers Street. It also dug a number of wells, one of which was sunk in the Lispenard Meadows on the western end of Spring Street.

On the day after Christmas 1799, the body of young Gulielma Sands was found floating in the water of the Lispenard Meadows well. A coroner's jury found she had been murdered and dumped down the shaft. Being of a Quaker family from Cornwall, New York, she was buried in the new Friends cemetery on the Bowery in early January 1800, while the investigation of her murder continued. Eventually, Levi Weeks, a fellow lodger in her boarding house on Greenwich Street, was indicted for the murder, but a brilliant defense conducted by the legal team of Aaron Burr and Alexander Hamilton got Weeks acquitted. The murder was never solved, and a legend grew of the ghost of Gulielma Sands haunting Spring Street. Alleged sightings continue to this day, notably by a local artist who, in 1974, claimed he saw Gulielma's specter rise out of his water bed, festooned with strands of seaweed. The Friends cemetery would remain on the Bowery until 1904, long enough for its sidewalk to become the scene of additional tragedies.

Two more cemeteries were established near the Bowery in the 1830s, and these are still there today, little-known relics of the city's history. The Marble Cemetery was founded just east of the Bowery as an upscale private burial ground in 1830, planned to accommodate 156 family vaults. A notable early burial here was that of President James Monroe, who lived out his last years in a house at Prince and Lafayette Streets. (Monroe's body was eventually moved to Hollywood Cemetery in Richmond, Virginia.)

Two years later, another private burial ground was established down the street from the Marble Cemetery on the other side of Second Avenue. First named the Nicholas-Banker Burying Grounds, it was expanded and incorporated as the New York Marble Cemetery in 1832. Although it is not open to the public, an association of vault owners still meets periodically to attend to the upkeep of the place. John Erickson, builder of the Civil War ironclad the *Monitor*, is buried there, as is a prominent merchant with the unique name of Preserved Fish. The New York Marble Cemetery also took in an old piece of the city's history: the Dominies' Vault, originally located by Bowling Green for the burial of the Dutch Reformed ministers of New Amsterdam, was relocated there.

Though planned to be an exclusive resting place "for gentlemen" and their families, New York's development soon overtook the New York Marble Cemetery. Not long after it was founded, a brewery was built adjoining the cemetery, and when funerals were held, the brewery workers would stand in the windows and make fun of the high-society types in the cemetery. This became so obnoxious that the cemetery raised the wall adjoining the brewery to block out the catcallers. The high wall still stands in the rear of the cemetery, though the brewery has long vanished.

With so many cemeteries in the area, a number of marble yards could be found along the Bowery whose industry produced a generous supply of the marble chips that became a favorite projectile for nineteenth-century rioters. The last of these marble yards was still in business as late as the 1930s at the end of what was then called Robinson Crusoe's Alley (today Freeman's Alley) in back of the site of the Second Negro Burial Ground between the Bowery and Chrystie Street.

The Bowery's future was also shaped by a nearby industry. After the Erie Canal linked it with the Midwest in 1825, shipping and shipbuilding became major New York industries. The East River was the chief shipbuilding location, and the old Stuyvesant family lands east of the Bowery lying along the river became known as the "Dry Dock Neighborhood" for the shipyards and repair works located there. The Dandy Beach Shipyard began the trend when it opened in 1824, and eventually shipyards would line the East River from Pike Slip up to 13th Street. After being nearly forgotten, the name of the Dry Dock Neighborhood, or "Dry Dock Country," would be briefly revived in advertisements for the local Dry Dock Savings Bank in the 1970s.

The Bowery became a center for the early banking industry in New York, partly as an outgrowth of its cattle industry. The Bull's Head Tavern eventually spawned a Bull's Head Bank, which printed its own banknotes featuring a fine engraving of a bull's head. In 1830, the Butchers and Drovers Bank was established at 128 Bowery. Three years later, a group of local businessmen decided, as a philanthropic enterprise, to found a mutual savings bank where the laboring classes could safely keep their savings, and thereby learn the virtue of thrift. On June 2, 1834, the Bowery Savings Bank opened as a rent-free tenant on the premises of the Butchers and Drovers Bank.

Handling the sort of small savings accounts that the commercial Butchers and Drovers Bank wasn't interested in, the Bowery Savings Bank was open for business two evenings a week after the Butchers and Drovers had finished business for the day. The tellers were at first the founders themselves, volunteering their time to the enterprise, attending to depositors who often came directly from their jobs, fetching out soiled and crumpled banknotes from the cuffs of their trousers. The Bowery Savings Bank's funds and papers were kept in a leather-bound chest stashed in the vaults of the Butchers and Drovers Bank for safekeeping. Expanding into home mortgages following the disastrous fire of 1835, the Bowery Savings Bank soon began to overshadow its host, and in 1836 it purchased the Butchers and Drovers building and moved to a separate location on the corner of the Bowery and Grand Street, where today Stanford White's Bowery Savings Bank building is a designated New York City Landmark.

These two banks on the corner of Grand Street were the anchor around which other banks and insurance companies eventually set up on the Bowery. The Bowery and the Butchers and Drovers were joined by the New York Bowery Insurance Company across Grand Street, with the Citizens Insurance Company setting up at 167 Bowery and the Tradesman's Insurance down on Chatham Square.

An increasing role as a transportation artery brought other changes to the Bowery. As early as 1732, monthly stagecoach trips to Boston had departed up the Bowery, and the Bowery soon became the main drag for local stage lines connecting Manhattan with the mainland. In 1831, New York's first streetcar line began on the Bowery, with the New York and Harlem Railroad running horse-drawn cars from City Hall up the Bowery to 27th Street, where they were hooked up to steam locomotives and run all the way up to Harlem. By the time of the Civil War, three competing streetcar lines ran up the Bowery.

New styles of pleasure gardens moved in to replace the older places as the early 1800s wore on. The influx of Germans into the area east of the Bowery created a "Kleinedeutschland" (Little Germany) and also created a need for a new style of drinking establishment. The Germans preferred well-ordered places where the family could be brought on Sundays and where the drinking was done in silence, except for the oom-pah band or deep political discussions. The German Wintergarden at 45 Bowery was admired when it opened in 1845 for its magnificent cast-iron and glass rotunda, and its well-appointed dining rooms and galleries.

Unfortunately, the Wintergarden occupied the site later chosen for the Manhattan Bridge plaza, but its neighbor across the street at 56 Bowery proved more durable, lasting well into the twentieth century. The Atlantic Garden was considered the best German beer hall, and the standard of behavior at the place won grudging respect even from local English and Yankees who otherwise deplored the German fondness for lager beer, as well as the scandalous German habit of drinking it on Sunday. The Atlantic Garden sported a huge mural depicting a bucolic scene. The mural was actually a graveyard scene painted in fine detail, something the local temperance crowd never grew tired of pointing out. A small orchestra composed of a pianist, violinist, and a drummer performed from a box suspended from the ceiling, so everyone in the place could enjoy the music equally well. The nearby Volkstheater was a precursor to vaudeville, where singers and comedians took turns on the stage while the audience put away the cheese and beer.

The Bull's Head and Butchers and Drovers Banks served the needs of a still-growing cattle industry. An endless demand for meat at the Fly Market and the newer Centre Market joined with the needs of ships' provisioners along the East River (to say nothing of the consumption of sausages in Kleine Deutschland) to make the Bowery, still the main route by which cattle were driven to the city, a natural place for butchers to set up business, and that business soon grew beyond the small-scale abattoirs of the 1700s.

Even with the quickening pace of development in the early 1800s, the Bowery was still a quiet, if not a dull place during most of the daylight hours. Local memoir writer Felix Oldboy, recalled in the 1880s what some old-timers told him of life on the Bowery in those early days of the century:

> The Bowery has never been a place of sentiment or romance. Its life was largely passed out-doors; its people loved the street and its excitements. Those who are living and remember all about it, have told me of the crowd that daily gathered at 17 Bowery to see the Boston Stage, carrying the United States Mail, depart and arrive. It was a great event of the day. Those who traveled by coach down into the wilds of Massachusetts Bay were considered as a species of Argonauts, and indeed the journey by such mode would be a formidable one today.

It is often said of the Bowery, in reference to its colorful history, that it is the only major street in New York never to have had a church located on it. That is true, but only by a matter of a few yards in some cases, and a matter of definition in others. Most of the missions that would locate on the Bowery would of course hold religious services on their premises, but missions do not count as regular churches. In 1825, the Bleecker Street Church was built just around the corner from the Bowery. It eventually moved uptown to become the Fourth Avenue Presbyterian Church—shortly after the Bowery north of Astor Place had been renamed Fourth Avenue. And when in 1846 Grace Church was built on the narrow block separating Broadway from the Bowery at 10th Street, its doors were firmly and definitely installed facing Broadway. But, even lacking a church, the Bowery in time would gain a colorful religious history of its own.

The Bowery shared in the enthusiasms and sects that characterized religion in the new nation. One of the most interesting of these was the Millerites. An upstate preacher named Miller had predicted, based on some complex calculations he performed using numerical clues he derived from the Bible, that the world was going to come to an end on April 23, 1843. The prediction set off a wave of fervor and excitement beginning in the religious hotbed of the so-called "burned-over district" of upstate New York, and the movement soon spread itself far and wide.

The Millerite excitement soon spread to the Bowery, and a congregation formed at Chrystie and Delancey Streets. The merchants on the Bowery responded to this movement in various ways. One dry goods man, observing how the Millerites were suiting themselves up in angelic garb for the big day, saw in this a unique sales opportunity, doing a brisk business in "white muslin for ascension robes." By contrast, a Bowery shoe merchant chose to shed himself of the vanity of worldly goods, and gave away his entire stock of shoes, gaining himself cosmic credit while ensuring that his neighbors would at least meet their rapture well shod.

As is invariably the case, predictions of doom proved premature. The appointed date of April 23, 1843, came and went, but an unfazed Miller claimed that his calculations had been off by exactly six months, and so the end of the world was rescheduled for October 23. Excitement mounted across the country as the date approached. Prayer meetings were held in the street at Chatham Square, and the Millerite congregation at Chrystie and Delancey packed the house. As the sun went down on the evening of October 22, the Millerites on the Bowery and elsewhere donned their ascension robes and peered eagerly at the skies, often climbing onto rooftops or up trees in hope of getting an unobstructed view of the coming glory. A nonstop prayer meeting convened at Chrystie and Delancey, interrupted only by a brief panic when some local boys decided to hasten the fires of Armageddon by shooting off Roman candles.

But nothing happened apart from that, and a perplexed Miller went into hiding. Most of the Millerites dispersed and converted their ascension robes into nightshirts. The remaining Millerites founded the Seventh Day Adventist Church, a congregation of which is still located at the site of the original Millerite congregation at Chrystie and Delancey Streets.

The Bowery was the scene of other religious and charitable pursuits, some quiet and productive, others quite strange. In 1822, Margaret Prior set up a Methodist school for poor children at the neighborhood then called Bowery Hill around 10th Street, which flourished for some years. By the late 1820s, the neighborhood had become the place where a number of leading figures in New York's evangelical community lived.

In 1829, however, a Christian perfectionist society set up on Bowery Hill, formed of people who believed that ordinary humans could attain moral perfection on this earth—if only they tried hard enough. The new perfectionist community on Bowery Hill was called the Retrenchment Society, and was founded by Frances Folger with Sarah and Elijah Pierson. The Retrenchment Society sought perfection by shedding all worldly material vanity and living a life of studied simplicity. It rejected all adornments and luxuries, plus alcohol and tobacco, of course, and added to that a ban on coffee and tea. Even that wasn't quite enough, so they added cake, pastries, and even butter to the forbidden list. That is, when they ate anything at all; frequent and prolonged fasting was also part of the program.

Elijah Pierson soon organized a breakaway church for the Bowery Hill community, with himself as the preacher and his house serving as the church building. Congregants gathered in Pierson's house pursued devotions of unusual intensity, meeting as often as fourteen times in a single week, and on one occasion they kept a prayer meeting going for three weeks straight. Pierson and his wife Sarah also set up an asylum for the young prostitutes they rescued on forays down to the Five Points district at the south end of the Bowery.

Sarah's later death left Elijah deranged with grief. Renaming himself Elijah the Tishbite, he left Bowery Hill and set up an even more

radical sect in a house on 4th Street. There he met up with one Robert Matthews, a street preacher known as Jumping Jesus who walked
along the Bowery clad in an outlandish costume and announcing that
he was Matthias, an 1,800-year-old Hebrew prophet. Eventually, Jumping Jesus Matthias and Elijah the Tishbite moved with their followers
to Ossining, where their doings resulted in a murder trial and a sexual
scandal, as recounted by Paul C. Johnson and Sean Wilentz in their
book *The Kingdom of Matthias*. The evangelical community on Bowery
Hill passed out of local memory, though the locale became the site of
Grace Church in 1846.

Millerites, perfectionists, and prophets proved to be a passing thing
on the Bowery, but a couple of other religious and charitable efforts grew
into major institutions. Sailors' Snug Harbor, a charitable institution giving care and shelter to old sailors, had its origin in the twenty-two-acre
farm lying west of the Bowery just below Bowery Hill, once the experimental farm of Baron Poelnitz. Poelnitz had sold it in 1789 to Captain
Robert Richard Randall, who bequeathed it in 1801 as a home for old
sailors. Randall's intention was that the institution be located there, using
his mansion, but by the time the probate litigation among the heirs ended
in 1831, the trustees saw that the Bowery had become a much more raucous place than the good Captain had ever envisioned and decided to
lease out the lands to endow an institution located on the north shore of
Staten Island. (It continues today in North Carolina.) While Randall's
mansion was torn down in the 1860s, Randall's lands along the Bowery
remained part of the endowment. It was perhaps with this in mind that
the infamous saloon keeper John McGurk later named one of his Bowery
dives Sailors' Snug Harbor.

If Sailors' Snug Harbor (the charitable institution) remains today an
invisible presence on the Bowery, Cooper Union grew to become its major
landmark. Today one of the leading educational institutions of the city,
it rivals Massachusettes Institute of Technology for engineering prestige.
The school began in the upper room of John Coutant's house on the edge
of Bouwerie Village at the site of the present-day Cooper Union building.
A shoe store during the week, the house became an adult Sunday school

on weekends, when ministers from the John Street Church came up to teach adult converts.

Peter Cooper was a member of the church and had the idea of expanding the Sunday school, which was later formalized as the first Sunday school in New York, with Cooper as superintendent. But Cooper wanted to expand this effort into a regular educational institution. He went on to become an inventor, and ironmaster, and one of the leading industrialists of the 1800s, and as his fortune grew, so did his educational interests. In 1854, he endowed and built the present Cooper Union building on the site of the old shoe store and Sunday school, on the triangle where Third Avenue branches off from the Bowery.

Religious activities and educational foundations such as Cooper Union might have gently nudged the image of the Bowery toward dull respectability, but even as Peter Cooper organized his school on the old site of the Two-Mile Stone, more raucous and colorful activities were beginning to flourish farther down the street that would set the stage, literally, for years to follow.

5 Humbug

THE PLEASURE GARDENS DECLINED, BUT the Bowery developed a new life as an entertainment center when the theater came in the 1820s. Since the founding of the elegant Park Theater on Park Row and Broadway, the theatrical district had been inching its way up to the Bowery for some time. Midway between the Park Theater and the eventual site of the Bowery Theater, the Chatham Theater opened up in 1822.

Theater was still ill-regarded by many people in New York. Puritanical types regarded it as a frivolous diversion that distracted people, especially the young, from more productive uses of time, and moralistic sorts held an enduring prejudice, dating from Restoration London, that linked theaters with prostitution. Theatrical promoters in the new nation looked for ways to distance the theater from its old taint of immorality.

When the old Bull's Head Tavern moved uptown in 1826, Henry Astor, by now the owner of the site, decided to tear down the old tavern building and put up a theater in its place. To assuage public opinion, he saw to it that the new theater would not only look elegant but would have the support of the best elements of New York society. He persuaded Mayor Philip Hone to lay the cornerstone in June 1826, and in his speech that day Mayor Hone reminded his audience of the high-toned cultural purposes the new theater would serve. He spoke of the theater as being a positive force for society, something that would serve as a means of elevating the taste and morals of the town as well as "soften the manners of the people." He had no idea how ironic that speech would come to be, or how soon.

The Bowery Theater started out presenting conventional plays and light opera, opening prophetically with a play called *The Road to Ruin*. But within months of its opening, history would be made, and local moralists would be given confirmation of their belief that theater was inherently immoral, regardless of what Mayor Hone had said.

On January 15, 1827, the Bowery Theater brought something new to America: the ballet. The ballet of course was long known in Europe, and as a distinguishing touch the Bowery's manager, Charles Gilfret, brought in the noted French ballerina Madame Francisque Hutin to perform a *grand pas seul* titled "La Barege Coquette" in between the evening's performances of *Much Ado About Nothing* and a concluding farce.

Madame Hutin's costume of opaque tights and short skirt shocked the sort of people who clothed their piano legs in muslin and made a habit of referring to turkey legs as "drumsticks." Although Hutin was clothed from neck to toe in her skirt and tights, her outfit nevertheless brought down the house. According to one report, "the cheeks of the greater portion of the audience crimsoned with shame, and every lady in the lower tier of boxes left the house." The men in the lower tier were apparently made of sterner stuff, and lingered for a second look. Still, the reaction the next day was withering. Local artist Samuel F. B. Morse (not yet the inventor of the telegraph) railed in the newspapers against the "public exposure of a naked female," which must have left many who were not there that night wondering what they missed. The prominent abolitionist Arthur Tappan, no slouch in the prudery department, went on record as recommending a permanent female boycott of not just the Bowery Theater, but theaters everywhere. Caught in the middle of the uproar was Mayor Philip Hone, who, mindful of the fulsome speech he had given the previous June, was compelled to defend Hutin's performance as high art. After that first night, though, Hutin switched her costume to voluminous Turkish harem pants.

The enduring association of the theater with immorality would prove to be a self-fulfilling prophesy, as places such as the Bowery Theater were gradually abandoned by upper-class New Yorkers. Many upright types would have nothing whatsoever to do with the theater or with theatrical people. Harriet Beecher Stowe, for example, would refuse to adapt her novel *Uncle Tom's Cabin* as a play because she considered theater to be so inherently sinful that not even a work as moral as her own could lift it, nor would she besmirch herself by even writing a playscript. When her book was eventually adapted by another playwright, however, she could not resist checking it out; she attended the play's opening disguised in a shawl and thick veil.

Such attitudes shaped the career of the Bowery Theater and of the theatrical district that grew up around it as theaters, being market-driven businesses, played down to an ever-lower common denominator. The Bowery Theater eventually became known as "the Bowery Slaughter-house" for its rough-edged clientele and the wild and raucous productions they favored. New York's theatrical scene soon split into two districts, with the relatively respectable theaters clustering a block to the west on Broadway, leaving the Bowery as the domain for more popular entertainment. Surveying the theater scene in 1847, the physician Charles Smith noted that "the Park and Broadway are genteel and formal, the Olympic, bizarre and grotesque, and the Bowery and Chatham, sensual, bold and roistering."

Bold and roistering indeed. Melodrama and rough comedy soon became the standard fare on the Bowery, and the Bowery became the birthplace of a new style of acting. When the up-and-coming actors Edwin Forrest and Junius Brutus Booth came to the Bowery in the 1830s, they soon developed an acting style suited to their enthusiastic audiences. The "American" style of acting that developed on the Bowery was influenced by melodrama, and was characterized by athletic performances full of body language and bold posturing. This American style was applauded by the local "nativists" who contrasted its vigorous honesty with the too-subtle English, or "teapot" style of acting. When Forrest or Booth took the stage, local audiences found that Shakespeare could be great fun, and demanded more and more of it.

Their stars were happy to oblige. Forrest's portrayal of Macbeth would be the hallmark of his career, and lead to trouble later on. Junius Brutus Booth premiered his own hallmark performance of *Richard III* at the Bowery Theater, and later toured the country with it. Rumored to be mad, Booth was a consummate actor who sometimes became too caught up in the roles he was playing. On one occasion, he got so carried away doing a sword fight scene that he pursued his frightened opponent clear out of the theater and into a saloon across the street, where the alarmed clientele had to relieve the stage monarch of his sword before he produced a real-life tragedy with it.

It is hard to imagine nowadays, when theatergoing has become an expensive, upmarket entertainment, just how popular it was with working people in the 1800s. Its popularity was very much like that of movies a century later, and people went to the theater as often as they could afford. Playbills changed frequently; plays whose run continued for years were something unheard of back then. A run of sixty performances was considered exceptional; in the Bowery theaters, the bill would often change every week or so. Popular plays, though, would be frequently revived for short runs. A particular favorite at the Bowery Theater was the play *Charlotte Temple,* performed ironically within yards of the house where the real Charlotte Stanley had lived.

There aren't many scripts left from the glory days of Bowery melodrama. Indeed, many plays would hardly have a script at all. Melodramas were not treated with the strict formality of Shakespearean drama—the words and the plot could vary from performance to performance according to the whim, memory recall, or sobriety of the performers. More importantly, they changed according to the mood of the audience. "Interactive theater" is usually thought to be a late-twentieth-century invention, but on the Bowery back then performances usually were interactive, and the audience's will was not expressed by penciled ballots collected by the ushers. The "gallery gods" up in the cheap seats were quick to loudly express their displeasure with the acting or the turn of the plot, and if things were not soon set right, a variety of projectiles would rain down on the stage, starting with pennies, proceeding to rotten vegetables, and sometimes on to more serious stuff. A song of the period set to the tune of "Oh! Susanna" summed up a typical situation in the career of Dan Rice, one of the inventors of the minstrel show:

They posted placards all about to prove he was no clown,
His Shakespeare wit all common stuff, he couldn't dish it brown.
All this they said and plenty more, till Dan began to feel,
A little riled about the gills, and thought he'd have to peel.
Oh! Bill Spriggins, who heaved that last brickbat,
It didn't hit Dan Rice's head, it only smashed his hat.

It could have been worse; in San Francisco, audiences would throw lit firecrackers onto the stage. But the Bowery's audiences were rough enough, and they even attracted foreign comment. When in 1828 Frances Trollope visited New York, she took in the scene at the Bowery Theater and was duly shocked. The nearly universal custom among American men of chewing tobacco and spitting the juice in any direction in which it could safely land on the floor repelled Mrs. Trollope, as did the way in which they made themselves at home in the theater, draping their feet over the rail or the nearest empty seat. Their attitude, she wrote, was "indescribable," which didn't stop her from describing it anyway: "the heels thrown higher than the head, the entire rear of the person presented to the audience, the whole length supported on the benches." When her book *Notes on the Domestic Manners of the Americans* came out in 1832, many Americans were outraged. The audiences at the Bowery, however, began to rein in their manners a bit, and henceforth whenever someone was spotted hanging his feet over the gallery rail, the cry went up, "a trollope!"

Even with their feet on the floor, audiences at the theaters along the Bowery had their own laid-back norms of behavior. Dime novelist Ned Buntline, in *Three Years After*, described a typical scene in one of these theaters:

The audience was packed as close as it could be on low unbacked benches, and now began to express a desire that the performance should begin.

"Lift that 'ere rag, will yer!" shouted one, alluding to the curtain.

"Why don't yer strike up with yer piney forty?" [pianoforte] cried another.

Some of the b'hoys whistled, others yelled, some stamped with their feet, and others threw second-hand quids of tobacco from one side of the room to the other.

But all at once a pale shadow was seen to appear suddenly, as if he had been gathered together out of the smoke which filled up the room, and as he seated himself before the piano, the crowd gave one mingled scream of triumph and delight, and then became tolerably quiet. . . .

[And] having murdered Yankee Doodle and Lucy Neal, to the evident delight of the audience, who gave a voice-iferous, foot-iferous, and fist-iferous applause, he ceased, and the curtain rose, amid yells of, "Off hats in front? Sit that 'ere red-headed loafer down! Quit a spittin' yer baccy juice on my back or I'll lam yer from the word go!"

The Bowery Theater continued to make entertainment history. It was one of the first places in New York to host the new minstrel shows. Pioneered by Dan Rice in the late 1820s, the shows featured white performers wearing burnt-cork blackface performing what purported to be songs of the southern slaves, and doing dances that owed as much to Irish step dancing as they did to anything done on southern plantations. Mayor Hone was a bit irked to learn that Rice was performing nightly at the Bowery Theater doing "his balderdash song." It wasn't the sort of thing he had in mind when he'd laid the theater's cornerstone in 1826, but when he later met Rice in person he decided that Rice was actually "one of the most entertaining men I ever met in company." Minstrel shows became a standard item of entertainment before the Civil War, both on the Bowery and along Broadway. "Dixie," which songwriter Dan Emmett adapted from a song he'd collected from an African American family in Ohio, had its premiere in a Broadway theater a block away from the Bowery as a "walkabout" song that brought the performers onstage for a minstrel show. It then went south to become the unofficial national anthem of the Confederacy.

Other entertainments joined the theaters and pleasure gardens along the Bowery. There were animals and a bit of humbug, too. One of the more popular attractions was the Bowery Menagerie just north of Bayard Street. In December 1826, an interesting incident was alleged to have happened there. Two tigers broke out of their cage and were having the llama for lunch when the menagerie keeper happened to walk in. The female tiger went for the keeper, who was only saved when the elephant grabbed the keeper with his trunk and swept him out of harm's way. The lion decided to get in some points for himself too, and poked his paw through the bars of his cage and sunk his claws into the female tiger's back. The elephant and the lion stalled the tiger's assault long enough for help to arrive. The keeper, seeing a publicity opportunity, had an aquatint printed up depicting the incident.

The Bowery Menagerie was a popular attraction for many years, and animals of one kind or another would continue to be an entertainment staple on the Bowery well into the 1900s. The Menagerie's popularity was enhanced by the fact that its advertising and publicity was handled for a time by P. T. Barnum.

The genial, broad-framed figure of Phineas Taylor Barnum is familiar to many Americans as the most famous circus promoter and showman of the nineteenth century, even if his famous quote about the birthrate of suckers is one he swore he never said. What isn't commonly known, however, is that P. T. Barnum's career as "The Great Showman" had its start on the Bowery. His brief experience as the Menagerie's publicist showed him that there were possibilities in both the Bowery and the entertainment business. In 1835, he was the co-owner of a grocery store when the opportunity for a big score presented itself. The small-time showman Coley Bartram had been going around exhibiting Joice Heth, a blind and nearly paralyzed African American woman who Bartram claimed to have been George Washington's wet nurse. The fact that this, if true, would have made her age somewhere over 120 years only added to the appeal. Bartram had documentary "proof" for anyone with doubts; he showed Barnum her bill of sale dated February 5, 1727, and Barnum offered him $1,000 for the exhibition rights.

To the end of his life Barnum insisted that he was the one taken in, and that he really did believe that Heth was George Washington's wet nurse. He was certainly ready to convince other people. Even though Heth had previously been exhibited in Philadelphia, she was new to New York, and Barnum realized that with the proper presentation he had a potential moneymaker on his hands. He bargained with William Niblo, owner of Niblo's Garden Theater, to rent out a room in a coffeehouse Niblo owned in Chatham Square on the corner of Bowery and Division Street, and exhibited Heth there to great success in 1835.

When the attention died down, Barnum found he couldn't come up with a follow-up exhibition, and he returned for a while to a more conventional business selling shoe polish and bear grease hair dressing at a shop at 101½ Bowery. The Joice Heth episode was one of the most disreputable moments in Barnum's career, but in coming to the Bowery he had certainly chosen a propitious place to begin a career in humbug. In 1840, he reentered show business, taking over at the Vauxhall, Gardens as manager of the saloon and the entertainments. He promised "a combination and succession of novelty, variety and attractions perfectly unparalleled in this city." Barnum's expansive adjectives soon became the hallmark of the advertisements he put in the papers. At Vauxhall, he developed a format of two-part programs with as many as ten variety acts. The acts could be anything, as long as they were entertaining: music, drama, magic, ventriloquism, and more, all strung together without any overlying theme. Along with the German Volkstheater down the Bowery from Vauxhall, Barnum had become one of the coinventors of the vaudeville show, an American style of light entertainment named for a location in Normandy, France.

Despite his success at Vauxhall, Barnum soon grew tired of the venture. The Vauxhall was no longer the genteel sort of place it had been a generation before, and crowds of Bowery B'hoys and associated toughs were now the predominant element in its clientele. It was a bit too rough for Barnum, and when the opportunity came to purchase the American Museum down by the old Park Theater he jumped at the chance, and history was made. Or, rather, made up.

In the humbug business, Barnum actually was preceded by one of the greatest hoaxes in New York's history. The retired butcher "Uncle" John

DeVoe was a familiar character at the Centre Market on Grand Street in the summer of 1824 when he announced he had a major project in hand. He and a friend named Lozier had determined that the island of Manhattan was in danger of sinking from the weight of the city clustered on its southern tip. Anybody who doubted this fact could observe the pronounced downward slope of the land south of Chatham Square.

To save the city from this peril, DeVoe would saw the island free of the mainland at Kingsbridge, float the island out into the bay, and turn it around so that the city end would now be securely braced against the bedrock of Marble Hill. Lozier averred they had been in secret conference with Mayor Stephen Allen, and while Allen had given his go-ahead to the project, he wanted to keep it quiet, lest the public panic.

Uncle John then produced a huge ledger in which he began signing up prospective workers. Drawn by the prospect of good wages, more than three hundred men signed on for the job of cutting Manhattan free with giant steel saws, and rowing it out and back with great banks of oars. Uncle John, it seemed, had neglected nothing, making arrangements to have herds of cattle driven to Kingsbridge to feed the village of workers, as well as carpenters who would build the work camp and fashion the giant oars, and blacksmiths who would craft the giant saws.

Having everyone sworn to secrecy, Uncle John set an appointed day when everyone involved was to gather at Bowery and Spring Street and form up in a grand procession to the work camps at Kingsbridge, accompanied by fifes and drums and herds of lowing cattle. When the appointed day arrived, over five hundred people gathered at Bowery and Spring Street—but not Lozier and Uncle John. As the day wore on, it began to dawn on people that the whole business had been a hoax and that Lozier and Uncle John had flown the coop. Bands of men began to comb the Bowery looking for them, but they were safely gone. Embarrassed to think how smoothly they had been taken in, the crowd dispersed without any uproar or violence. When things had at last cooled down, Uncle John resumed his customary seat at the Centre Market.

The decline of the Vauxhall Gardens symbolized what many old New Yorkers were already describing as the decay of the Bowery, and the

Bowery's growing reputation as a wild and wide-open place was made worse by overly vigilant moralists who were eager to find occasions of sin. In 1829, the masquerade ball craze arrived on the Bowery from Europe. Masquerade balls had been going on in Europe for hundreds of years, but when they came to the Bowery and Chatham theaters it started a new fad.

The moralists were quick to condemn the phenomenon. Rumor had it that people used the balls as pick-up places and the disguises were a way of ensuring quick, anonymous sexual encounters. Perhaps these encounters were nothing more than a ride over the Kissing Bridge, but the fevered minds of the moralists were quick to see all sorts of possibilities. Perhaps recalling his embarrassment over the ballet affair, Mayor Hone promptly condemned the balls on the grounds of the "licentious privileges assumed by many under the protection of a fictitious modesty," and the New York City Common Council prevailed upon the state legislature to outlaw masquerade balls. The balls continued on the Bowery, however, with the theater and hall owners simply paying their fines as part of business until the fad died out. Masquerade balls would be revived on the Bowery from time to time in the future, serving different communities.

The tableau vivant was another example of how otherwise innocent art forms could sell tickets by pushing the boundary between art and salaciousness. Tableaux vivants—"living pictures"—became popular in theaters on the Bowery in the 1830s, again echoing a fashion from Europe. With no lines for anyone to remember or louse up, they were the simplest performances in the world, merely a group of actors and actresses dressed up and posed to impersonate famous paintings, sculptures, or historic scenes, displayed briefly with a bit of music or narration. For theater managers, it was the perfect short piece to fill in the space between the main features.

It wasn't long before backstage impresarios saw greater entertainment possibilities in tableaux vivants. The exhibition of Hiram Powers's statue "The Greek Slave" in 1843 showed them the way. The statue was the first major American sculptural work depicting nudity, and female nudity at that. It was a national sensation, and Powers eventually knocked off six duplicates of the statue that toured the country, often with a special "ladies' night" for women to view the statue demurely cloaked in a white muslin shift. Of course the nude girl in chains was really a very moral and uplifting work of art—the sculptor himself insisted, with a straight face, that it was her serene spirit, not her body, on display. "Clothed in sentiment" was how another critic put it.

Soon "The Greek Slave" was being performed as a tableau vivant, as part of Dr. Collyer's Model Personification at the New York Apollo Rooms a few months after the original statue was exhibited in the city. Dr. Collyer's model posed in flesh-colored tights, and the exhibition was approved by the newspapers. Dr. Collyer's success prompted a new wave of tableaux vivants in the Bowery theaters, each one a bit more daring than the last, and depicting such uplifting subjects as Venus rising from the sea, Susanna in her bath, and, inevitably, the Three Graces. The tableau vivant went on to become a staple of the extra admission rooms of Bowery dime museums, as well as a popular presentation piece in brothels, although it would have a more respectable revival in middle-class amateur productions around the turn of the century.

With their down-market audiences, the Bowery theaters soon acquired a close association with prostitution, and this at least was no legend. It was nothing really new, either—the association of theaters with prostitution went as far back as London in the 1660s, where the "orange girls" working the crowd had more than oranges to sell. The theaters in the mid-1800s served sexual purposes much as did some later-day movie houses. The upper tiers were a good place to solicit men out for a good time, and they were convenient places for the clients to bring their hired dates.

There were, however, some lines that could not be crossed. Traditionally, there were only two areas in the theater where prostitutes were allowed to appear, apart from the stage itself: the gallery, if they were accompanied and thickly veiled, and the uppermost, or third, tier. The custom gave rise to the euphemism "ladies of the third tier."

The unwritten rules were broached only at great hazard. In the 1820s, New Yorkers were shocked when one Jake Leroy had the nerve to appear with a known prostitute, Fanny White, in the second tier instead of the third. Prostitutes themselves knew better than to push their luck, and often enforced the rules among themselves to prevent a social scandal from erupting. In at least one incident, a brothel madam whipped two of her girls when she learned that they had shown themselves—and drunk, too—in the first tier of a theater. As time went on, some theater owners on the Bowery made things easier for everyone by installing a separate staircase to the third tier so the "chaste" (who after all bought the more expensive tickets) would not have to be offended.

The puritanical notion that theaters were inherently sinful—"vestibules of hell" was what one editor called them—was reinforced and confirmed in many people's minds by the way prostitution became virtually institutionalized at many Bowery theaters. And the institutionalization only helped make things worse in some places, even leading to specialization. The third tier of the Franklin Theater became in the 1830s a notorious hangout for exploited child prostitutes (and sometimes their child patrons as well). The children there were commonly as young as ten or eleven, and occasionally even younger.

Excess forced restrictive measures, and by the time of the Civil War the third-tier tradition was disappearing. Theater managers sometimes removed or closed off the third tier altogether, or else had the area closely policed by bouncers. By the time of the Civil War, prostitution had largely shifted away from theaters to venues such as the new "concert saloons" that combined light entertainment with food and drinks.

Growing out of its older role as the site of pleasure gardens for the well-to-do, the Bowery in the 1820s developed into an entertainment district that unabashedly catered to the democratic, antielitist spirit of Jacksonian America. As more elitist entertainments moved away from the Bowery to Broadway, the Bowery and its theaters became the playground for the Bowery B'hoys and their paragon, the Mighty Mose.

6 The Mighty Mose

BY THE 1830S THE BOWERY had developed a distinctive atmosphere of its own, along with a distinctive personality type inhabiting it. The Bowery was never a neighborhood in its own right, but rather served as the common meeting ground of several neighborhoods that bordered it, and it was from these that it drew its character and clientele. The lowest of these neighborhoods, both geographically and economically, was the Five Points.

Like the old African Burial Ground on the other side of the Collect Pond, the Five Points was a place beyond the pale, an improvised neighborhood that grew up on the northeast side of the old Collect Pond at the bottom of the Bowery. It took its name from the five corners formed by intersection of Anthony, Orange, and Cross Streets, where today's Worth, Baxter, and Cardinal Hayes Place meet behind the New York County Courthouse. Ignored and neglected, the Five Points became a spot where the poorest of the poor settled in shacks and slums among the smelly breweries and even smellier tanneries. Things were made even worse after the pollution of the Tea Water Spring forced the breweries that had clustered there to close down. One of these abandoned breweries, Coulter's Brewery, stood in the center of the Five Points and became the symbol of the urban degradation found there. Coulter's Brewery overlooked the ironically named Paradise Square, a tiny traffic island where the southwest corner of Columbus Park is today.

The Five Points became famous when in 1813 Collect Street (today's Centre Street) was built across the site of the filled-in Collect Pond and

connected the Five Points with the rest of the city. The Old Brewery was
the slum's slum, a rookery filled with otherwise homeless squatters eking
out a living as best they could by rag picking, petty theft, or violent crime.
Stories about the place grew with each telling, and it is hard today to
know how much to credit, but it was confidently said that over a period of
about fifteen years at least one murder was committed there every night.

By the 1840s, the Five Points had hit bottom, and could not be
ignored any longer. The appearance of the place enhanced its evil reputation. The filling in of the Collect Pond had done nothing to drain off its
underlying aquifer, and as the years passed the roughly built houses and
shacks had begun to settle into the marshy ooze, sagging and tilting surre-
alistically at all sorts of crazy angles. Ned Buntline, in his novel *Mysteries
and Miseries of New York*, described the scene in "the Points" through the
eyes of one of his characters:

> He gazed with wonder at the long rows of little wooden build-
> ings, their cellars sunk far below the swampy street, and, as he
> passed them, he gazed upon rooms filled with ill-dressed men,
> and painted, bloated women, who were drinking, dancing, shout-
> ing and carousing.

The New York traditions of "slumming" and "rubbernecking" tourists,
which became common activities on the Bowery in later years, began
in the Five Points. It became one of the places people arriving in New
York asked to be taken to. Even Abe Lincoln went to see it when he
passed through town in 1860. In 1842, Charles Dickens, international
expert in slum conditions, took a tour of the Five Points, and he recorded
his impressions in his book *American Notes*, which, like that of Frances
Trollope's ten years before, succeeded in irritating his American readers.
Dickens noted the "coarse and bloated faces at the doors," houses whose
"patched and broken windows seem to scowl dimly, like eyes that have
been hurt in drunken frays," and the "hideous tenements which take
their names from robbery and murder; all that is loathsome, drooping
and decayed is here."

Dickens made the Five Points the iconic slum of nineteenth-century New York. The "Points" would see a very long line of distinguished visitors tut-tutting about the place without anything concrete being done about it. And the place visited by the famous onetime tourist became in itself a tourist attraction: the dive in the Five Points that Dickens went into and described was later renamed "Dickens' Place" and became so famous that the name was retained even after the original building burned to the ground in the 1850s and had to be rebuilt from the ground up.

The reputation of the Five Points began to rub off onto the Bowery a few decades earlier, in the late 1820s, along with the activities of its street gangs. By the 1830s, the influence of the Five Points could be seen in the changed character of the Bowery's street life, epitomized by the emergence of the Bowery B'hoys. Street gangs were nothing new to 1830s New York. The first mention of them was as far back as 1728, with Smith's Vly Gang based at the Fly Market. By the mid–eighteenth century, the first gang by the name of Bowery Boys had appeared, competing with such groups as the Broadway Boys, and the African American gangs known as the Long Bridge Boys and the Fly Boys.

The Bowery came into its own in the 1830s and enjoyed its first heyday as a place of national fame. It was the age of Andrew Jackson, the age of the common man, and the age of a robust, self-assured democracy. And nowhere was that democracy so robust, or the common man quite so common, as on the Bowery. The Bowery had become one of those historic streets where things happened, a place that, like Carnaby Street or the junction of Haight and Ashbury, encapsulated in its very name the spirit of a particular time and place. And the Bowery's paragon in those years was the Bowery B'hoy.

Part butcher boy, part fireman, part street dandy, and part sailor, the Bowery B'hoy was one of those visible street characters, like the bikers, punkers, or teddy boys of a later age, that proved endlessly fascinating to the public and the press, who never grew tired of writing about them or describing them. The descriptive publicity in turn refined the image of the Bowery B'hoy, and his style evolved into a uniform.

The uniform of the Bowery B'hoy retained elements from several sources. At first he wore a long apron derived from the butcher trade, though as time went on that was discarded in favor of a long frock coat that signaled he was a gentleman of leisure, regardless of his actual occupation. Beneath the frock coat he wore a tight pair of pantaloons and a colorful vest, with an open-collared shirt. The shirt was a thick fireman's shirt of woolen flannel that served as protection from shooting sparks. The black leather plug hat, polished to a mirror shine, was also borrowed from the fireman's. It was originally a sailor's headgear, adopted by firemen as a rudimentary head protection, though by the 1840s the more modern style of fireman's helmet was coming into use. The Bowery B'hoy could also wear a carefully brushed beaver hat, but the important thing was that it be worn cocked forward in an insouciant manner.

His hair style reflected a sort of working-class dandyism—clipped close in the back and on top, the front sides were let to grow long, and were carefully rolled with either bear grease or (more economically) by soap, giving rise to the term "soap locks."

The Bowery B'hoy was also identified by his gait and general attitude. It was important to walk with a certain rolling swagger, rocking forward on the balls of the feet as if ready to start a fistfight, which was something every Bowery B'hoy was supposed to be ready for. If not moving, he couldn't simply stand there, but had to show the correct Bowery B'hoy attitude by reclining against something such as a lamppost, like the man of leisure that he was, cooly surveying the passing scene from behind a cigar held in the teeth at just the right upward angle. The Bowery B'hoy had his own distinctive mode of speech too, described by one observer as being somewhere between "a falsetto and a growl," and of course a distinctive slang vocabulary to go with it.

Needless to say, the Bowery B'hoy needed a Bowery "G'hal," most likely pronounced in a similar manner with a drawn-out aspirated vowel. Nineteenth-century standards of modesty and decorum crimped the style of the Bowery G'hal somewhat; there were simply limits to how far a woman could defy convention back then without being regarded as altogether "ruined." Still, the Bowery was the working-class playground where young women could meet with men on freer terms than anywhere else. But not too free—many Bowery B'hoys and associated loafers still held the attitude that an unaccompanied woman was free game for whatever they wanted to do, and instances of gang rapes of lone women were reported on several occasions.

The safest situation for a prospective Bowery G'hal, like a latter-day gun moll, was in being attached to a particular Bowery B'hoy, who could be depended to react violently and effectively to any untoward advances made to her. Once so attached, the Bowery G'hal developed a style of her own: a saucy and insouciant attitude, and a costume more colorful but no less modest than that of her more respectable sisters. In moving about at the side of her B'hoy, she imitated—as best she could under long skirts and petticoats—his rolling swagger.

The Bowery B'hoys were at once a street gang, a fashion statement, and an attitude. Newspaper accounts rendered "Boys" into "B'hoys" following a then-popular pronunciation whose sound is no longer known for certain. It was probably pronounced with a drawn-out, aspirated "o," sounding something like "buh-oys," though perhaps it may have had a vaguely Irish sound more like "byes." In any event, the spelling served to make the Bowery B'hoys distinct. The Bowery B'hoys took their image from two different working-class groups: the slaughterhouse workers and the volunteer firemen.

The original Bowery B'hoys were the "Butcher Boys," not a single gang but rather a generic term for groups of young men organized according to their places of employment in the slaughterhouses along the Bowery. These places of employment were the sources of group identity and a fierce loyalty. One butcher named Keyser was especially popular: "I kills for Keyser" was the boast of his employees. Keyser achieved a special far-reaching fame; story has it that one of his boys signed on as a sailor and taught the phrase to the chief of some reputed Pacific cannibals. The chief, believing it to be a ritual greeting of the Americans, used it to greet subsequent visitors to his island, occasioning no small degree of nervousness.

The image that every Bowery B'hoy aspired to was that of the volunteer fireman. Up until the Civil War, fire protection in New York was managed entirely by companies of volunteers, presided over and directed by a city-appointed Chief Engineer. These firemen, like their latter-day professional counterparts, were local heroes, daring fate to rescue lives and property from the frequent fires that endangered a largely wooden city. But unlike the modern-day version, these were lads who lived in the neighborhood that they served, and whose headquarters was the clubhouse for the locality's young male elite, along with hangers-on who hoped to become one of them.

In an age of hand-operated pumps, volunteer fire companies needed a large number of men to operate them, while their dashing image ensured that there was always a bountiful number of young men eager for the privilege of belonging to a company. Most of the men who "ran with the machine" were needed to operate the hand pump, or as the traditional command went, "man your brakes!" Working in carefully drilled teams, the volunteer firemen not only borrowed their leather hats from sailors, but the traditional commands they worked by were also drawn from nautical terminology: "vast playing" was the order to stop pumping, and hoses were referred to as "lines," as in "back your lines out" to deploy the hoses, or "take up your lines" to bring them back in.

The firehouse might be little more than a shed housing the engine, sometimes simply a conveniently situated carriage house belonging to a local home owner or livery operator. Men belonging to the company lived or worked in the neighborhood, and when the cry of a fire went up, these men could be relied upon to drop whatever job they were working on and join the engine in its race to the fire scene. Some volunteer companies had so many men attached to them that they could dispense with horses needed to pull the engine. Even after steam-driven pumps became available, most of the volunteer companies didn't bother buying one, as they could still rely on the camaraderie of the hand pumps.

Firefighting was an intensely competitive business. Strict territorial boundaries between neighboring fire companies were not observed, and when the cry of a fire went up companies would race each other to get to the scene first. Whichever company succeeded would not only get to be the heroes, they could usually depend on a substantial gratuity from the person whose property was saved. In fact, that was how the volunteer companies funded themselves, and it was generally a good idea to be generous with them in case you needed their services another time.

Another good reason to be first at the scene was to have the first crack at the closest fire hydrant. The farther away the hydrant, the more difficult it would be to draw water from it and raise pressure in the hoses with the hand-operated fire engines. On more than one occasion, rival companies arrived at the scene of a fire and fought over the rights to a disputed fire hydrant while the house burned down.

The racing of man-drawn fire engines was so crucial a part of the practice of volunteer firefighting that it became a frequently practiced technique with its own body of strategy and tactics, and it even became a sporting match between fire companies when there wasn't a fire going on. The last fire engine race was in the late 1940s, when the H. V. Smith Museum of fire engines was being prepared at the Home Insurance Company's offices at 59 Maiden Lane. To bring the antique engines from their warehouse to the new museum, groups of fire enthusiasts in long coats and fedoras formed up and raced the engines through the streets of the financial district—on a Sunday, of course.

One solution to the hydrant problem was to keep hydrants guarded. Each fire company had its gang of boys hanging about it, and it was an easy matter to enlist these boys to keep watch over key fire hydrants (where at least they wouldn't be hanging about the fire shed and making a nuisance of themselves) or to race ahead of the company and hang onto the hydrant before the engine arrived. The boys, honored at being assigned such an important task and anxious to prove their worth to their heroes, could be depended upon to guard the hydrants with their lives, if need be by violently fending off any rival company (or its gang of boys) who arrived on the scene behind them. Both future firemen and future gangsters often got their start as "butt-enders" guarding their chosen hydrants by sitting on them, or covering them with an empty barrel. It is partly in memory of this that when the professional Fire Department took over in 1865, one of the first requirements they laid upon new recruits was that they memorize the precise location of all hydrants in their district.

Peter Stuyvesant, here portrayed by an actor, leads a 1913 pageant in honor of a new playground. Some say his spirit still watches over his old Bouwerie Village. *Library of Congress*

New York City's oldest burial ground, Shearith Israel Cemetery remains tucked behind tenements near Chatham Square. *Library of Congress*

Located near the Collect Pond, the pure water of the Tea Water Pump was used for beverages other than tea. *Library of Congress*

On July 9, 1776, the Declaration of Independence was read to American troops camped along the Bowery. *Library of Congress*

A victorious American army paraded past the Bull's Head Tavern to reclaim New York City on November 25, 1783. *Library of Congress*

The newly laid out Broadway joined the Bowery in a still rural area that would become Union Square. *Library of Congress*

While people used the Bowery for Sunday horse races, animal shows were always popular at the Bowery Amphitheater. *Library of Congress*

The fiercely Democratic Bowery B'hoys were always ready for a "muss." *Library of Congress*

With his shiny top hat, red fireman's shirt, and carefully styled "soap locks," the actor
Frank Chanfrau portrayed the legendary Mighty Mose and epitomized the image of the
Bowery B'hoy. *Library of Congress*

Showman P. T. Barnum launched his career on the Bowery with the exhibition of a fraudulent "living curiosity." *Library of Congress*

Rumored to be mad, Junius Brutus Booth brought a manic edge to his performances at the Bowery Theater. *Library of Congress*

Anti-immigrant tensions culminated in the deadly 1849 Astor Place riot. *Library of Congress*

The Dead Rabbits took on the Plug Uglies in an epic 1857 street battle that included firearms and barricades. *Library of Congress*

The extravagant production of *The Black Crook* had little plot, but lots of pretty ladies. *Library of Congress*

"Tableaux vivants" were ever-popular presentations along the Bowery, not always in costumes. *Library of Congress*

Honor and competition came into play even on those occasions when fire companies cooperated with one another. When serious fires erupted, additional companies would join together to draw water from distant hydrants. Hand-operated pumps could only draw so much, so the practice was for one or more engines to connect themselves together and pump in unison to draw water from a distant hydrant. This was a test of the companies' brawn and pumping skills. The worst and most dishonorable thing that could befall a company was to be "washed." If the pumping of two companies fell out of synch, the faster pumpers would "wash" or flood the pumps of a slower crew in front of them. It was more than mere shame: it would disrupt the smooth flow of water in a situation where seconds counted.

Volunteer fire companies were a great thing to belong to, and for politicians an essential precondition of their electibility, even if it only meant belonging to a company as an honorary or retired member. "Boss" Tweed, for example, remained proud of his membership in the "Americus" company, whose emblem he got adopted as the Tammany Tiger. The fire volunteers even had their own parade and holiday. Beginning in the 1840s, the volunteer fire companies of the city held a parade every Washington's Birthday, when the companies got to show off both their disciplined numerical strength as well as the spit-shined splendor of their equipment. Beginning in 1856, the parade ended at the statue of George Washington, where the Bowery met Union Square, for a special wreath-laying ceremony.

Although Benjamin Franklin organized the nation's first volunteer fire company, for many years Washington was the only founding father with a statue in the city, so he was chosen for the honor. George did have his own connections with volunteer firefighting. It was said that as a youth he "ran with the machine" of an Alexandria, Virginia, fire company, and he retained an interest in firefighting through his adulthood. Before departing for Boston in June 1775, he purchased a pump for the Friendship Fire Company of Philadelphia, of which he became an honorary member while he was serving in the Continental Congress. The firefighting careers of Washington and Franklin got somewhat confused in the public mind: there are nineteenth-century ceramic figurines in the New York Fire Museum inscribed "Washington" although the rotund and bespectacled figure could be none other than Ben Franklin. But the enthusiastic and patriotic volunteers didn't care. So popular was the parade that it continued long after the volunteer companies were abolished in 1865—an association of ex-volunteers kept up the tradition every year, dwindling down to a handful of very old men who still made the annual pilgrimage into the 1920s.

The all-time classic model of the Bowery B'hoy was the legendary "Mighty Mose." The Mighty Mose was New York's version of Paul Bunyan and Davy Crockett, a gigantic figure of a Bowery B'hoy and hero fireman. The original seems to have been Moses Humphries, a printer at the *New York Sun* and a volunteer fireman who ran with the engine "Lady Washington" of Company 40 located at 174 Mulberry Street, around the corner from Hester Street. The Lady Washington engine, sometimes called "The White Ghost," was a marvel in itself. Described as one of the wonders of the world, it was painted all in white with gold leaf trim and sported portraits of Martha Washington.

The Lady Washington was a champion fire company, and Mose Humphries was its paladin. From these simple facts the legend of the Mighty Mose grew and flourished. Once, it was said, the boys of Company 28 arrived at a fire ahead of Lady Washington, but at the very sight of Mose, they gladly yielded the best fireplug. Mose was usually first to arrive at a fire—taking a shortcut by leaping over buildings—and being the first there he could always claim the post of honor, the man who held and directed the hose nozzle. But Mose was a good sport, and would graciously let other men take turns holding the nozzle. If need be, he could single-handedly take over the work of manning the brakes, normally the job of up to twenty men. And not only would he keep the water flowing, he would sing his company's fire song as he did it:

Huzza for brave old 40
Ever prompt at the fire bell's call.
Three Cheers for brave old 40

Huzza for firemen all!
When the red flames wildest flash
On the startled midnight air,
When the crackling embers crash,
Old 40's men are there.
Secure may the mother sleep,
With her babe upon her breast.
Brave hearts their watches keep,
To guard them when they rest.
When sudden fires alarm them,
In the dwelling where they be,
The fires shall never harm them—
Old 40's men are nigh!

What became of the real Moses Humphries and how he became transformed into the Mighty Mose is uncertain. Humphries vanished from the scene sometime in the early 1840s. Perhaps, as some accounts have it, Lady Washington was "washed" by one of its rivals, The Old Maid #15. Or Mose was rejected by his sweetheart, Lize. Or, in what seems the most likely story, Humphries was beaten up by Henry Chanfrau of the Old Maid #15 in an epic fight at the corner of Pell Street and the Bowery in 1836. Mose and Henry were the champions of their respective companies, and the fight developed into a general brawl between the fire companies and whatever bystanders happened to join in. In the end, Mose and the Lady Washington company were badly beaten. Mose retired in shame, fled the city, and, as some would have it, made his way to Hawaii, where legend says he organized a new fire company and spent his days putting out volcano fires.

By coincidence, Chanfrau won his fight at Bowery and Pell in front of the house he was born in. This frame building, known as "the Old Tree House," was also the same building that Charlotte Temple had been lodged in, having been transplanted from its original location a stone's throw down the Bowery.

Even though Henry Chanfrau won the fight, his fame would prove fleeting, as his kid brother Frank Chanfrau would immortalize the fallen

Mose in the play *A Glance at New York in 1848,* which premiered at the
Olympic Theater on February 15, 1848. The sketch was written by the
theater company's manager, Benjamin Baker, who, perhaps at the behest
of Frank Chanfrau, tried something new and different in using a volunteer fireman as a central character. A bit daring, too—volunteer firemen, like their associated Bowery B'hoys, were considered uncouth, and
it wasn't certain just how well their blunt manners and language would go
over, even to a Bowery audience.

As it was, the sketch was a smash hit, and grew into a full-length feature. Frank Chanfrau knew how to play the part, as he had been one of
the boys who hung around his older brother's fire company. The play
depicted some of the exploits of Mose, and ended up with his daring
rescue of a child from a burning building. This was supposed to have
been based on an incident in which the real-life Humphries rescued a
mother and her three children by reaching a third-floor window via a ladder perched atop eight stacked barrels.

Mose made Chanfrau's career and boosted him to a position as manager of the Chatham Theater. Knowing a good thing when he had it,
Chanfrau developed the Mose character into a series of plays, *Mose in California*, *Mose's Visit to Philadelphia*, *Mose in a Muss* (a fight), and even *Mose
in China*. The public simply couldn't get enough of Mose, and a series
of picture books were also published, showing Mose dashing about in a
sulky with his girl Lize, or off *Among the Britishers* viewing the sights of
London and introducing the English to the manners of the brash American democracy.

The exploits of the theatrical Mose blended into a set of urban legends that were still being told along the Bowery as late as the 1940s.
Mose grew into a giant with red hair, with a beaver hat two feet tall, and
who wore a fireman's helmet as big as a pup tent. With boots the size of
river barges, he could leap across the East River, swim the Hudson in two
strokes, or anticipate the Circle Line by swimming around Manhattan
Island in six strokes. He loved getting into a "muss," especially when the
"Plug Uglies" from the Five Points came around to contest the territory of
the Bowery B'hoys. When a fight broke out, he would plow in swinging

a hickory wagon shaft, often breaking it over the thick skull of a Plug Ugly.

Mose had a lighter side as well. Cherry Street was bare of cherry trees because Mose got hungry one day and uprooted the trees to have the cherries for lunch. Likewise the mulberries on Mulberry Street. A pioneer of urban rapid transit, Mose would often pick up a horse trolley in Chatham Square and stride its route up the Bowery with the trolley slung over his shoulder, a service not always appreciated by the passengers who fell out the open rear end of the car.

Mose had his companions, notably his faithful compadre Syksey. And Bowery G'hals too. A relationship with Linda the Cigar Girl never quite blossomed, even after he rescued her from a burning building. Mose's real love was Lize. Seeking to convince the reluctant Lize to marry him, Mose went off to the California goldfields where he panned for gold using a pan the size of a bathtub, then bounded across the continent back to New York bearing seven kegs of gold under his arms while Syksey and Lize looked on in wonder from the West Side docks.

The merry adventures of Mose bashing the Plug Uglies concealed a very real darker side to the Bowery B'hoy culture. As the 1840s progressed, an increasing amount of gang violence and criminality began to predominate along the Bowery.

7   Dead Rabbits And Plug Uglies

THE LIGHTHEARTED ESCAPADES OF MOSE the fireboy concealed a growing social decay along the Bowery and in the neighborhoods that surrounded it. Politics and poverty were combining to change the scene on the Bowery, and the colorful Bowery B'hoys were increasingly overshadowed by such violent street gangs as the Dead Rabbits and the Plug Uglies.

The Bowery was shrinking as well. The opening of Broadway north to connect with the old Bloomingdale Road put an end to the Bowery's position as the main thoroughfare in and out of the city, and Broadway began its ascension over the Bowery as the place where the "better elements" of society shopped, worshiped, and sought entertainment. Soon the Bowery would no longer even lead out of town. When Union Square was created in 1845, the Bowery's northern segment connecting with the Bloomingdale Road and with the Old Boston Post Road vanished beneath the tulip beds of the new park. The Bowery now abruptly ended at 14th Street, and the traces of the old Boston Post Road north of Union Square began to vanish beneath the precisely surveyed blocks of the city's 1811 master plan that submerged Manhattan's old farm lanes, watercourses, and vagaries of terrain beneath a rigid, evenly spaced street grid. Beginning at 1st Street above North (Houston) Street, the grid marched inexorably northward to 155th Street, leaving an unaltered Broadway to now be Manhattan's chief thoroughfare.

As if to compensate for the loss of its northern end, a southern extension of the Bowery was carved out running south from Chatham Square to link up with Pearl Street. As the New Bowery was being built, it cut through the tenements lining so-called "Jews Alley" and brought the nearly forgotten Shearith Israel cemetery to light again. But the name of New Bowery never caught on, and the street's name was eventually changed to St. James Place.

Construction now boomed along the Bowery as the city spread and houses and tenements were hurriedly thrown up in its neighboring wards to accommodate the increasing immigrant population. The city's 1811 master plan sprang forward, burying the remaining landscape of rural Manhattan under the streets of the ordained grid. The construction caught up with the old Bouwerie Village, and, except for Stuyvesant Street, all its streets were surveyed out of existence, and the new streets laid out over where they had been.

All but vanished from the map, the old Bouwerie Village managed to hang on to its separate identity until the end of the 1830s. Local resident Michael Floy's diary, written during the 1830s, described a village that still considered itself a part of the countryside—New York was still "the town" to the villagers. Bouwerie Village was a quiet sort of place where people tended to show up late to prayer meetings, and city people coming up to the village thought its inhabitants were "a harmless set and know nothing." But by the end of the decade the city's development would march all the way up the Bowery and overtake the memory of Bouwerie Village.

All this growth and change disturbed a lot of old-time New Yorkers, and if they complained that the noise was enough to wake the dead, they were quite right, or so it seemed. At first, a strange tapping sound was heard coming out of the Stuyvesant vault. Later, as construction crews wrenched the streets of Bouwerie Village into oblivion, an ancient gentleman in old-fashioned knickerbockers and white lace—and a wooden leg—was reported to have been seen around the construction sites, often angrily glaring at the construction workers. On one occasion, his stare proved so unnerving that he spooked the crew right off the work site and into a convenient tavern.

The ghost of Peter Stuyvesant, they said, had come back, and he wasn't happy at seeing New York City engulf his Bouwerie Village. But he really lost his temper when Second Avenue was constructed. Slicing through the old streets of Bouwerie Village at a 45-degree angle, the new Second Avenue cut right through the middle of Old St. Mark's graveyard, leaving the eastern portion of the cemetery isolated and marooned in the middle of a block, soon to be enclosed by tenements. The graves that lay in the path of Second Avenue had to be hurriedly dug up and transplanted to the remaining part of the yard near the church, where to save space the remains of entire families were interred in single vault shafts.

Old St. Mark's had been changed too. As if to emphasize the switch over to Episcopalianism, an elegant front porch and a belfry were added in 1828. But it was the violation of the graveyard that proved to be too much for the spirit of Peter Stuyvesant. Shortly after the construction of Second Avenue began, he appeared in the churchyard one night and threatened the sexton with his cane. The sexton was the man responsible for looking after the graveyard, and he had failed in his duty by allowing Second Avenue to plow through the consecrated ground. Stuyvesant could do no more than shake his cane, so the frustrated ghost disappeared into the locked church and began frantically ringing the bell, as if sounding the alarm for the death of his Bouwerie Village. The badly shaken sexton rounded up some helpers, and together they entered the church. The bell immediately stopped ringing, but they saw that the bell rope had been cut in half, with no sign of where the lower half of the rope had gone to. The next day, someone thought to open up the Stuyvesant vault, and sure enough, the missing half of the bell rope was down there, lying atop Stuyvesant's coffin. This legendary incident seems to have been the end of Peter Stuyvesant's musical career, but the old church bell can be found today, set up in the churchyard of Old St. Mark's just a few feet away from the Stuyvesant vault, as if daring the old man to come out and ring it again. As time went on, he would have plenty of provocation.

Peter Stuyvesant was not the only irate character walking the Bowery in those years. New York was a booming city, engendering various social tensions as part of its growing pains. In the 1840s, it would become very much an immigrant city, with large numbers of Germans and Irish moving into the neighborhoods surrounding the Bowery. The Germans formed the first wave of these new immigrants, with substantial immigration underway in the 1830s and reaching its stride in the 1840s. In the second half of the 1840s came the great waves of Irish, fleeing the failure of the potato crop back home. The potato blight, which actually appeared in Germany three years before it did in Ireland, spurred a great wave of German immigration as well. It didn't result in the mass epidemics and starvation in Germany that it did in Ireland, but when grain prices tripled and quadrupled it spelled economic ruination for many German artisans and laborers, and they gladly sailed for New York in the holds of Bremen tobacco ships.

The dominant Anglo-Saxon element in New York had long since forgotten they had been interlopers in the Dutch colony two centuries before. As early as 1692, a "native" New Yorker was writing to his relatives in England complaining that, "our chiefest unhappiness here is too great a mixture of nations." In the 1840s, they reacted to the influx of new immigrants at first with bemusement, then with contempt. The Germans got off somewhat easier, as many of them were skilled and semiskilled workers who could be fitted into such expanding New York industries as furniture and shoe making. Besides, since Germany was the land of Martin Luther, people assumed that all Germans were Protestants, even though a majority of the German newcomers were in fact Catholic.

The greatest contempt of the "native Americans" (as the Anglo-Saxons were now terming themselves) was reserved for the Irish. Coming from a Celtic culture that many Anglo-Saxons found more alien than that of the Germans, the new Irish immigrants of the 1840s were usually Catholic, and mostly agricultural laborers, without the sort of industrial skills that were sought after in the New York economy. With two strikes against them at the start, the Irish were left to seek their livings in such pursuits as the docks, street construction, or other such public works projects as the construction of the Croton Aqueduct.

Although the economy was generally expanding, labor tensions were already a part of the New York scene when the new immigrants arrived. The first of many riots in and around the Bowery in those years happened on the new Lafayette Street, which had been cut through the back of the old Vauxhall Gardens to connect with Astor Place. The construction of the colonnaded houses of La Grange Terrace, whose remains are today a designated landmark, caused a riot by local stonemasons whose workshops were located around the Bowery. Word had gotten out that the stone used in the buildings had been quarried by convict labor at the new quarries up the Hudson at Sing Sing, and the Bowery stonemasons descended on the site and tried to shut it down.

Even before the massive waves of immigration following 1845, the "native Americans" had been organizing themselves to try and preserve their fantasy of an Anglo-Saxon arcadia from the incoming hordes of the unworthy. Several secret oath–bound societies were formed that eventually got lumped together under the term "know-nothing" for the reply the members were expected to give to any official inquiries. New York had already seen some notable anti-immigrant riots around the Bowery in 1833 and 1836 before the chief know-nothing organization, the Order of United Americans, was founded in 1845. Its New York headquarters was on the Bowery, in the New England Hotel on the corner of Bayard Street. It was a well-chosen location—the Bowery B'hoys, now the name of an organized gang, were militantly nativist, and their headquarters was two doors up at 40 Bowery.

Tammany Hall, so often associated with the stereotype of the Irish politician in later years, was exclusively nativist in its early days. The transformation began with a riot at its first "wigwam" on the corner of Chatham and Spruce Streets in 1817 when over two hundred Irish supporters descended on the place to demand the nomination of Dr. Thomas Addis Emmet to run for Congress. Emmet was a prominent refugee from the failed Irish uprising of 1798, and the brother of Robert Emmet, executed by the English for fomenting his own revolt in 1803. In spite of the efforts of the old guard, by the 1830s Tammany had taken in a significant Irish Catholic element.

Ethnic tensions between old-timers and newcomers occasionally crossed with tensions over the growing question of slavery. On July 10, 1834, an anti-abolitionist riot nearly wrecked the Bowery Theater. A document critical of the institution of slavery had been issued by a group of concerned people in England, and this had been reported in the New York newspapers. Despite their ancestral affinity, the American nativists were as violently anti-English as they were anti-Irish. England may have been three thousand miles away, but the manager of the Bowery Theater was an Englishman, and that fact made the theater a suitable target for nativist rage that night, and the Bowery B'hoys arrived in force to shut it down. The rising American actor Edwin Forrest was on stage when the audience erupted, and he braved a shower of marble chips to plead with the rioters to return to order. Ironically, Edwin Forrest would be at the epicenter of a much more violent nativist riot fifteen years later.

Unnoticed and unremarked, nativism's own poster girl was distractedly wandering up and down the Bowery right past the Know-Nothing and Bowery B'hoys' headquarters. Maria Monk had come to town to become famous, working with a New York publisher to bring out a lurid account of what she said were her experiences in a convent in Montreal. When *The Awful Disclosures of Maria Monk* came out in January 1836, it was a bestseller, a salacious account of predatory sex, sadism, flagellation, and more going on behind the walls of a convent in Montreal. That her own mother went on record as saying Maria was a congenital liar made no difference to enthusiastic readers. The book appealed both to Protestant bigotry and to the repressed sexuality of her readers, and Maria went on a speaking tour around the country and even brought out a ghost-written sequel claiming yet another round of bondage and shame, this time in a Philadelphia convent. A huge number of people chose to believe her absurd fabrications, and *The Awful Disclosures* earned a permanent place in the arsenal of nativism. It is still reprinted by various back-alley publishing houses today. But fortune proved elusive for Maria, and as her already unstable grip on sanity crumbled for good, she found herself walking the Bowery as an anonymous prostitute.

Ethnicity and neighborhood became the organizing points for a new violent generation of street gangs that appeared in New York in the 1840s. The nativist Bowery B'hoys held sway over the Bowery from their headquarters down by Bayard Street, but they were frequently challenged by such foreign gangs as the Five Pointers, the Plug Uglies, and the Dead

Rabbits, among others. One curiosity of the period was a nativist gang, the True Blue Americans, composed of American-born Irish kids. They existed on the Bowery under the tolerance of the Bowery B'hoys, as their chief activity was to wear stovepipe hats and long frock coats buttoned to the neck while holding forth on street corners and in saloons, preaching the imminent violent destruction of the British Empire and all things English.

A more dangerous group was the Forty Thieves in the Five Points. The city in 1825 legalized grocery stores—previously people could only buy food in established markets—and these grocery stores became—like candy stores in the 1950s—the rallying points for local youth gangs. Especially since, unlike candy stores, the grocery stores often sold liquor in the back room. The Forty Thieves established themselves in Rosanna Peers' grocery store by Anthony and Worth streets. Several other gangs soon organized in Five Points grocery stores.

The gangs named Plug Uglies and the Dead Rabbits came to dominate the Five Points scene. The members of these groups were renowned street fighters, but unlike the straightforward fisticuffs of the old-time volunteer fire companies, the new youth gangs included clubs, knives, and eye gougers in their arsenals, and thought little of beating and stomping someone to death. The name of the Plug Uglies came from their headgear: an oversized leather plug hat, or "ugly," that was stuffed with padding. When a fight began, the hat would be pulled down low over the ears to serve as a sort of skull protection from flying bricks and flailing clubs.

The name of the Dead Rabbits boasted an even more interesting origin. In the street lingo of the day a "rabbit" was a sharply dressed street dandy, and "dead" was a superlative adjective (like "cool" in the twentieth century). Like the latter-day Teddy Boys, the Dead Rabbits were proud of their appearance, and adopted their name to advertise it. In one of their early street fights their opponents, intending a joke or an insult, snatched the carcass of a rabbit from a butcher shop and flung it at them. Rising to the challenge, one of the Dead Rabbits took the carcass, stuck it on the end of a pole, and carried it into the fray like a Roman eagle standard.

From that time on, the Dead Rabbits invariably went into battle with a standard bearer carrying a dead rabbit aloft on a long pole.

The emerging gangs on and along the Bowery existed for years and made for themselves a complex local history of wars, truces, broken treaties, shifting alliances, and transfers of territory, all against a background of rising criminality and an increasing scale of violence. That violence would be brought to the public eye in a spectacular way in 1849 in the great eruption known as the Astor Place Riot.

The theatrical and personal rivalry of two actors combined with volatile nativist tensions to produce one of the bloodiest riots in New York history. Edwin Forrest was a long-established American actor who had appeared at the Bowery Theater in his early days. Specializing in Shakespearean roles, he had long since moved up in the theatrical world, but the Bowery was still his home base, and his old fans among the Bowery B'hoys idolized him as one of their own. But in the late 1840s, his dominance on the stage was challenged by a restrained English "teapot" actor named William Macready.

Despite the fact that his own father had been born in Scotland, and despite his own marriage to an Englishwoman, Forrest early on adopted the nativist attitudes of his Bowery B'hoy fans, and had made a secondary career for himself as a much-sought-after speaker at nativist meetings. His rivalry with Macready was thus as much an ethnic conflict as a personal one, and Macready served as the personification of everything the nativists and Bowery B'hoys hated. As the idol of the Bowery B'hoys, Forrest wasted no opportunity to let his detestation of Macready be known, even going so far on one occasion as to hiss at him as he performed on the stage in London. In New York, their festering rivalry came to a head in May 1849 when Macready was booked to perform *Macbeth* at the Astor Place Opera House on the night that Edwin Forrest was playing the very same role at the nearby Broadway Theater.

It was too much a challenge to ignore: Macready's appearance at the Astor Place Opera House would bring him within sight of the Bowery and onto Edwin Forrest's old turf. The competition between the American-born Forrest and the English interloper Macready was taken up as an issue by the Know-Nothing elements in the city, who determined to secure the purity of the American stage by driving the Englishman away. But there was yet another personal rivalry at work that would turn the tense situation into something truly explosive.

In the spring of 1849, one of nativism's staunchest defenders in New York was the heavyset Elmo Z. C. Judson, better known by his pen name of Ned Buntline. Buntline was no stranger to conflict; he had arrived in New York in 1846 after having killed a man in Nashville in an altercation over Buntline's alleged improper attentions to the man's teenaged bride, and Buntline had only narrowly been rescued from the traditional lynching party that followed.

In New York, however, Buntline set himself up as a moral crusader, and found plenty of material. Although his main crusade was temperance (in spite of an intermittent drinking problem of his own), he soon expanded his range to include issues of crime and prostitution. He was particularly taken with the story of Charlotte Temple, and made a point of visiting her grave in Trinity Churchyard. His researches led him to write a set of fact-based stories, *Mysteries and Miseries of New York*, in 1848.

The success of *Mysteries and Miseries* boosted his career, and enabled him to launch his own newspaper, *Ned Buntline's Own*, in July 1848. The newspaper would be the platform from which he could expound on issues of moral reform and, increasingly, nativism, despite the fact that his wife, too, was from England. But his explorations of the seamy side of Gotham led him to conclude that immigration was the leading cause of crime in New York, with two out of three criminals, by his account, being foreign-born. "We have plenty of room in this country," he wrote in *Mysteries and Miseries*, "for immigrants, if they would seek the unsettled parts; but it is to be regretted that most of the new comers lack the means or the inclination to go to the interior, and thus become a burden to the inhabitants of the sea-port towns."

Buntline, from his office at 2 Astor Place, soon became a well-known figure to the B'hoys along the Bowery. He became a "Generalissimo" of the Order of United Americans, and a leading member of the United American Mechanics, both hard-line nativist organizations. Buntline used his newspaper to keep nativist tensions simmering, and was delighted to find an opportunity to combine his two interests of moral reform and nativism when he set out to attack James Gordon Bennett of the *New York Herald*. Bennett was not only a "base born Britisher," but he was a Catholic as well. And worse still, he was guilty of carrying advertisements in his newspaper for a book titled *The Married Woman's Private Medical Companion*, whose frank medical advice to women made it an intolerable scandal to such defenders of feminine purity as Ned Buntline.

The feud between Buntline and Bennett came to a head in April 1849 when Buntline printed certain allegations about the moral character of Bennett's sister, Georgiana C. Crean. If Buntline expected Bennett to show up at his office offering a traditional frontier brawl with horsewhip and bowie knives he was disappointed. Bennett, instead, had Buntline arrested for slander, and it took $2,000 to bail him out of jail. In a sour mood and eager to lash out at what he saw as a foreign conspiracy, Buntline returned to his office to learn that, as if to add insult to injury, the Englishman Macready was scheduled to perform in two weeks at the Astor Place Opera House, right within view of Buntline's office window. Apart from its convenient location, the Astor Place Opera House would be an excellent target for Buntline's rage—its part owner, William Niblo, was an Irishman.

Buntline was not alone, however. He enjoyed the support of another Bowery character who could be relied upon to rally the B'hoys. Mike Walsh was a fellow journalist, the publisher of an even more rabid nativist newspaper called *The Subterranean*. He was both a self-made journalist and a self-professed tough guy—he made a habit of sleeping rough in Tompkins Square Park and other places, and would stroll along the Bowery in midwinter without an overcoat. By the 1840s, he was an important figure among the Bowery B'hoys as well as the leader of the Spartan Gang, which was known for attacking Irish gatherings and that once even stoned the house of Archbishop Hughes. Walsh was also one of the last nativists in Tammany Hall, giving venomous speeches against the rising influence of the Irish, all in spite of the fact that he himself had been born in Ireland. With the support of Mike Walsh and the Spartan Gang, Ned Buntline would do whatever he could to see that Macready's provocative performance would not go unopposed.

Something was definitely amiss on the evening of May 7 when the manager of the Astor Place Opera House found the audience filling up with Bowery B'hoy types, not normally the sort of people who attended Shakespearean drama at the prestigious Opera House. They remained reasonably orderly as they awaited the curtain raising, apart from making rude gestures at the well-dressed people staring down at them from the boxes. The people in the boxes, increasingly nervous, noticed what appeared to be hand signals being flashed around among various parts of the crowd, as if a prearranged plan of action was awaiting a signal to begin. As the time for the curtain raising approached, a low but rhythmic foot stomping was heard throughout the theater, the classic get-on-with-it demonstration by Bowery Theater audiences impatiently waiting for the management to " hoist that rag!"

The signal for action was to be the appearance of Macready. When Macready came out and began to speak his opening line, "So foul and fair a day," the crowd erupted with a roar and a volley of rotten eggs. Macready tried to brazen it out, but was drowned out by the noise and hit with another round of rotten eggs. Some more scientifically sophisticated B'hoys uncorked chemical stink bombs and rolled them down the aisles. Macready wisely quit the stage and fled the theater by a back entrance, and the crowd dispersed without any further violence.

That would have been the end of the matter, but for Macready's announcement a few days later that he was going to return to the stage and play out his performance. Now placards appeared along the Bowery:

Workingmen!
Shall Americans or English Rule in this City?
The crew of a British steamer have threatened
all Americans who shall dare to offer their
opinions this night at the
English Aristocratic Opera House.
Workingmen! Freemen! Stand up to your
Lawful Rights!

The placards were signed by the "American Committee." It is not certain who printed and posted those placards, but Buntline in his newspaper went into editorial overdrive, comparing the impending showdown with Macready with the embattled farmers' stand against British tyranny at the battle of Lexington in 1775. As evening fell on May 10, Buntline, sword in hand, harangued the gathering crowds in front of the Astor Place Opera House, even repeating the famous quote from Lexington, "If they mean to have a war, then let it begin here!"

This time around, the ticket sales had been closely controlled, and the crowds of Bowery B'hoys who showed up at the theater found themselves booked out of the house and kept out by a line of policemen. They milled about and stoned the Opera House instead, while a small band of nativists inside planned to rush the stage. But the police inside the theater already knew their signal, and pounced on them the moment they arose and threw them out of the building.

The knowledge that Macready's performance was defiantly still going on inside the theater threw the crowd into a frustrated frenzy. As the crowd grew, the situation grew more menacing, and finally Macready was persuaded to exercise the better part of valor and quit the theater by a rear door. Robert Emmet Jr., the nephew of the Irish revolutionary, took the Englishman to his home for safekeeping. The crowd, ignorant of Macready's exit, surged forward against the line of police and prepared to assault the Opera House.

Clearly the situation was growing out of hand. The militia was called in, and, accompanied by a troop of cavalry, they came up Broadway and entered Astor Place via 8th Street, taking up positions in front of the theater. The crowd met their arrival with a shower of paving stones and marble chips. The militia stood their ground, with one-third of the men injured. Called upon to open fire, General Hall of the cavalry refused to do so without a direct order from Mayor Woodhull. The mayor wasn't there, but General Sandford of the militia took the permission of the New York County Sheriff J. J. V. Westervelt as good enough authority, and ordered his men to prepare to fire.

Meanwhile, General Hall and Colonel Duryea tried one more time to calm down the crowd, warning that the troops were going to shoot. This impressed nobody, and the crowd gave even more attention to the militia. General Sandford's sword arm was disabled by a paving stone, with the crowd shouting "fire and be damned!" One rioter, a dramatist himself, boldly stood up before the muskets of the militia and shouted, "Fire if your dare—take the life of a freeborn American for a bloody British actor!"

With Sandford down, Hall now had his troops elevate their guns and aim over the heads of the crowd, but without opening fire. This didn't impress the crowd either. The word was going around that the troops had only blank cartridges and leather flints in their guns.

Hall now ordered his troops to face the Bowery and open fire for real, aiming low to cause leg wounds rather than fatalities. Still, it took three commands from Hall and Duryea before a full volley erupted. The crowd fell back for a moment, then rallied and surged forward again. The police, who had been keeping track of Buntline's position in the crowd, took advantage of the momentary retreat to dive into the crowd and nab him. They took him into the theater and locked him up in the barroom, an ironic predicament for the professed temperance crusader.

As the crowd surged forward, another volley caused the crowd to fall back, and Hall ordered a final chasing volley to drive them away for good, directing half his troops to fire down 8th Street and the rest firing down Lafayette Street into the retreating mob.

The final toll was twenty-two killed outright, and another thirty wounded. (Some accounts give the toll as high as thirty-four killed.) The horror of it rocked New York, and the nativists called for a rally the following evening in City Hall Park. After speeches and demands for vengeance, the crowd spilled out of City Hall Park and marched on the hated Opera House, only to find Astor Place completely cordoned off. Nine hundred policemen (virtually the entire force) were backed up by a thousand soldiers and another thousand special deputies in blocking the Bowery and all other approaches to Astor Place. Confronted this time by a large and well-armed force, the crowd melted away, and a second bloodbath was averted.

There would be some curious echoes of the Astor Place Riot over the years. The Astor Place Opera House never lived down the tragic reputation it acquired that night, and struggled on for just three more years before closing for good. General Sandford would go on to face the much worse Draft Riots in 1863. Notwithstanding his grandfather's rescue by the son of an Irish revolutionary, William Macready's grandson would, in 1920, command British troops in the Irish War of Independence. *Macbeth* acquired a renewed reputation as a bad-luck play, one that was never to be quoted in a theater outside of an actual performance or rehearsal, nor even to have its name mentioned out loud, being referred to only as "The Scottish Play." After serving a short jail sentence, Ned Buntline moved on to St. Louis, where the following year he organized a bloody anti-German riot. He would eventually return to the Bowery in far more peaceful circumstances.

The Bowery itself would pay for being the scene of a riot by having yet another piece lopped off it. In the immediate aftermath of the Astor Place Riot, the more affluent residents of the upper Bowery petitioned the city to rename the stretch above Astor Place as Fourth Avenue. From that point onward, the truncated Bowery would be seen more and more as a place apart from the realm of normal society, and the Seventh Regiment Armory was placed on the east side of the Bowery just below Astor Place by way of keeping the cork in the bottle. More than a century later, in 1972, an enigmatic black cubic sculpture by Bernard Rosenthal called "Alamo II" would be erected in Astor Place reportedly in commemoration of the bloodshed that took place there in 1849. (Still a landmark on Astor Place, the pivoted sculpture can be rotated, to the delight of muscular visitors.)

The Astor Place Riots focused attention on the growing scale of violence and criminality in New York. Ned Buntline in 1848 had estimated that there were some five thousand "thieves, pocket-book droppers, burners, watch-stuffers, hack-bucks, mock-auction men, gamblers, dance house keepers, grog-shop keepers, pick-pockets, & c." running loose in New York. Things rapidly got worse. By 1855, there were estimated to be about thirty thousand boys and men in the city owing some degree of allegiance to a gang—about the same number, by some counts, as there were prostitutes in the city.

The street gangs thrived as functionaries of a corrupt political machine. The association of the Know-Nothings and the Bowery B'hoys in 1849 had shown the profitability of such an arrangement. Alliances were now cultivated between street gangs and ward politicians for their mutual benefit. The ward bosses could shelter the gang members from the worst punishments of the law. In return the gangs served the ward bosses as ready-made strong-arm squads, which, by not being direct members of the political parties, preserved for their patrons a safe degree of deniability if things got too out of hand.

On election days the gangs went to work. With no secret ballots, intimidation of voters could work very well—within their neighborhoods, the gang members pretty much knew who was who, and who should be kept away from the polls. There also were those whose vote had been paid for in one fashion or another—favors owed, etc.—and someone would be needed to keep tabs on the polls and make sure these individuals voted the way they were supposed to. Or, if not, the gangs would make note of the fact and inflict retaliation, whether immediately or later.

Then there was the business of repeat voting—voting early and often, as one famous wag put it. Gang members were needed to help organize squads of "repeaters" and usher them from one polling place to the next, and, by their menacing presence, keep any election watchers from making a fuss if they suspected repeat voters were present. The intimidation worked so well sometimes that the repeaters could afford to be quite brazen. In one instance, a repeater gave the name of the Bishop of Manhattan. When one poll watcher said he doubted that the scruffy fellow was really Bishop Doane, the repeater replied, "The hell I ain't!" and voted anyway. Outright thefts of ballot boxes could also be resorted to in desperate cases.

The gangs thrived not only because of political patronage, but because the forces of the law, such as they were, were for a time divided against themselves.

New York had set up and managed its own municipal police force in 1844, but by 1857 the graft and corruption on this force had grown so great that the state legislature had stepped in and passed a law removing police powers from the city and passing them directly to the state legislature. The state legislature then set up its own force, named the Metropolitans. New York's mayor, Fernando Wood, wasn't going to let his police force get taken away just like that, and he fought the law through the courts, in the meantime simply refusing to follow the legislature's instructions to dissolve the municipal police force. While the case rattled through the courts, the city spent a two-year period with two rival police forces that not only acted in competition, but denied each other's legal right to exist. The situation culminated in a literal "police riot" in front of City Hall in June 1857, with the two rival forces fighting each other when the state tried to enforce the recent decision of the state supreme court affirming the legality of the legislature's actions.

Two weeks after the police battle at City Hall, on July 4 and 5, 1857, the street gangs of the Bowery and the Five Points came together for an epic showdown of their own. It started on the fourth with what was to be a preemptive strike by the Dead Rabbits and Plug Uglies on the headquarters of the Bowery B'hoys and associated Atlantic Guards at 40–42 Bowery. After a short, hard fight, the Bowery B'hoys drove off the Five Pointers. The Dead Rabbits fell back to their base in Paradise Square to regroup.

The two-day battle that followed became famously known as the Dead Rabbits Riot. Across the Hudson in Hoboken, Henry S. Backus, the "Saugerties Bard," immortalized it in a popular ballad: "At last the battle closed, but few that night reposed/For frightful were their dreams accordin'/For the Devil on two sticks was marching on the bricks."

Reinforced by the Roach Guards, the Dead Rabbits returned to the Bowery in the early hours of the following morning to strike at another Bowery B'hoy hangout, the Green Dragon Saloon at the corner of Bowery and Broome Street, four blocks north of the Bowery B'hoys headquarters. They smashed the place to smithereens, even taking the trouble to tear up the boards of the dance floor, and either drank or poured out every drop of liquor in the saloon.

Learning of this, the Bowery B'hoys and Atlantic Guards tumbled out of their berths, mustering their remaining members and any other gang who owed them allegiance as they raced up the Bowery to intercept the Dead Rabbits. The two forces collided at Bayard Street, and a massive street brawl began. "Pull off the coat and roll up the sleeve," the ballad sang, "For Bayard is a hard street to travel." The Bowery B'hoys took the worst of the initial impact and were driven around the corner of Bayard to Elizabeth Street. There, they hastily assembled a barricade of dray wagons and fought the Dead Rabbits to a standstill. Dozens of fighters swelled into scores, then hundreds. They fought with the street fighter's arsenal of clubs, brass knuckles, knives, brickbats, and fists, backed up with an occasional pistol or musket fired from a rooftop. "Like wild dogs they did fight, this Fourth of July night/Of course they laid their plans accordin'/ Some were wounded and some killed, and lots of blood spill'd."

With the long-awaited gang showdown in progress, secondary fights flared around the vicinity as various other gangs set out to even old scores. The Kerryonians, a small but fierce gang of Catholic Irish kids from the Five Points, whose members could all trace descent to the County Kerry, sought out the nativist Protestant Irish Orangemen for a sectarian show-down along Little Water Street. Other minor gangs in the vicinity of the Bowery combed the streets in search of enemies.

In the eye of the spreading storm, time-out was called in the ferocious free-for-all on Bayard Street when a force of Metropolitans charged up the Bowery to stop the fight. The gangs suddenly found common cause and together fought the police, invading houses and buildings lining the Bow-ery in order to hurl projectiles from the rooftops. The Metropolitans were driven off, and that might have been the end of it, as the Dead Rabbits had been taking it hard and were inclined to call it a day. But their girls from the Five Points had come along to watch the fun, and they egged on the reluctant Rabbits with various taunts concerning their courage and manhood.

The fighting resumed, as further reinforcements came up from out of the Five Points and from the neighborhoods around the Bowery. By early afternoon, between eight hundred and one thousand men and boys were battling it out around the Bowery and Bayard Street, fighting with whatever weapons could be found to hand, from pistols to pitchforks.

Additional combats swirled around the edges of the main fight, as various other street characters sought to take advantage of the disorder and rob nearby houses, whose owners appeared with muskets and shotguns and added additional fire to the spreading confusion.

The Metropolitans were not about to give up either. They repeatedly returned to the fray with as many forces as they could muster, but they could barely make a dent in the situation. No sooner would they make a foray and nab some prisoners than the fighting would resume as soon as their backs were turned. As the day stumbled on toward evening, it was clear that the situation was getting worse. Fires were now being set along the fringes of the battlefield, and the possibility of a conflagration forced the authorities to take desperate measures. Remembering the disaster at the Astor Place Opera House eight years before, they hoped the police alone would be able to handle things without having to call in the muskets of the militia. But it was clear that although the Metropolitans were giving a very good account of themselves, they were overwhelmed by the sheer numbers of the united gangs. The militia was at last called out, and came down the Bowery about 9:00 p.m., just in time to scatter the last exhausted remnants of the sidewalk warriors.

The exact toll of the Dead Rabbit Riot remained uncertain, but at least eight men were killed and over a hundred injured, about fifty of them seriously. Though none of the worried citizens of New York knew it that night, open gang warfare in New York had reached its peak. A relative peace from exhaustion settled down over the Bowery for a while, with only small-scale raids and fights over the next two years. The greatest civic violence in New York history lay just five years in the future, but the Bowery would see little of it.

8　Dear Friends And Gentle Hearts

THE COMING CIVIL WAR CAST its long shadow across the Bowery. In the winter of 1860, Abraham Lincoln came to New York to address the Young Men's Republican Union in the Great Hall of the new Cooper Union building. Politically astute people in town sensed that this speech would be something important, and the evening was a sellout, packing 1,500 people in the hall at twenty-five cents each. Lincoln's speech that night indeed proved to be something important: with its famous quote, "let us have faith that right makes might," Lincoln effectively launched himself as a presidential contender, and editors and politicians, led by Horace Greeley, elbowed their way behind the stage to offer Lincoln their congratulations and get a closer look at the unknown tall fellow from Illinois. New York was just as unknown to Lincoln; before he left town, he went to Brooklyn to hear the famous abolitionist Henry Ward Beecher preach in his Plymouth Church, and then took the obligatory tour of the Five Points.

By 1860, New York had become the economic hub of the nation, with a population that had passed half a million people. It was increasingly a manufacturing center, with iron foundries and factories clustering east of the Bowery, and a new factory district growing up above Canal Street. Immigration had scarcely slowed since the great wave of the 1840s, and scarcely a generation later the Bowery was lined with immigrant neighborhoods, mainly Irish and German. The factories and foundries they worked in made goods for both the North and South, and likewise the shipping industry served both parts of the nation. Despite a significant pro-abolitionist sentiment, the city stood to lose a lot of business in the event of a civil war, and few businessmen or laborers looked forward to it.

Other shadows of the irrepressible conflict followed Lincoln to the Bowery. In October 1860, the Southern "Fire-eater" William Yancey spoke at Cooper Union; within six months of his speech, he would pull the lanyard of a mortar in Charleston and send the first shot of the Civil War arcing through the sky toward Fort Sumter. The next day, President Abraham Lincoln would call for seventy-five thousand volunteers to put down the "rebellion."

As Election Day 1860 approached, the Republican "Wide-Awakes" in New York organized a famous torchlight parade up Fifth Avenue, a parade that was widely commented upon and illustrated in the press. Less well-known to history is the anti-Lincoln parade that followed. More than thirty thousand marched against the election of Lincoln, moving up Broadway to Union Square, then turning around and marching down the Bowery. The uniform of the evening was Mose's old Bowery B'hoy red shirt. Marching past enthusiastic crowds lining the Bowery, the spectacle was too good to bring to an early end, and so it went on up and down the Bowery in a massive street party lasting into the small hours of the morning and accompanied by the shooting off of Roman candles and other fireworks.

New York City was very much a southern city, "the northernmost city in the Confederacy." With much of its economy linked to the South, secession and war were bound to be bad news for the New York economy, as William Yancey had pointed out in his speech at Cooper Union. New York was a center of the cotton trade, the location of many of the factors and middlemen who handled the trade between the cotton fields of the south and the textile mills of New England and Europe, as well as the bleaching and dying "finishing" mills that depended on textiles woven of Southern cotton. New York shipping firms, using ships built in New York, handled the lion's share of the cotton traffic.

Not only did New Yorkers traffic the cotton, but some New Yorkers trafficked the enslaved labor force that produced it. Despite the slave trade being outlawed in the early part of the century, the port of New York was the home base for many of the nation's "blackbirders" who ran a clandestine slave trade, shipping enslaved Africans to Cuba and the South. One of these "blackbirders," Nathaniel P. Gordon, would be the subject of New York's last public execution in 1862.

New York City, as usual, voted Democratic that election year of 1860. When the results were in there were, just as in the South, a lot of angry men dismayed at the election of the "Black Republican" Abe Lincoln to the presidency. Shortly after the election, an angry meeting was held at Brooke's Hall on Broome Street around the corner from the Bowery. With the Secret Service not yet in the business of keeping tabs on such things, the crowd there felt little need for restraint, expressing open threats of violence to stop the inauguration and freely expressed desires that someone would assassinate Lincoln before he made it to the White House. Lincoln's stopover in New York in March 1861 included no tours or speeches. Instead, the closely guarded president-elect was quickly hustled through town on his way to Washington.

New York's reaction to the outbreak of the war was a mixture of enthusiasm and reluctance. Despite a good deal of pro-Confederate sentiment, many young men, anxious for the adventure of a lifetime, rushed to enlist for the Union once they learned that the flag had been fired upon. One Bowery entrepreneur reacted to the war in characteristic Bowery fashion. Cloaking himself in patriotism, he advertised that his shooting gallery would offer "free" shooting instruction by "accomplished professors" to prospective army recruits. The instruction might have been free but the ammunition and targets no doubt still had to be paid for at a hefty markup.

The Bowery's position amid working-class German and Irish neighborhoods made it a center for the recruitment of the North's volunteer army. The Irish in particular had by now established a strong institutional presence along the Bowery—the Ancient Order of Hibernians had their headquarters down by Hester and Baxter, and the Hibernian Hall at 42 Prince Street was the recruiting place for the soon-to-be famous 69th Regiment.

One of the chief leaders of the Irish community, Michael Corcoran, lived on the corner of the Bowery at 5 Prince Street, and he became the colonel of the 69th. There was an unspoken understanding between the Union authorities and the leaders of the Irish community that enabled the rapid recruitment of Irishmen despite the misgivings many Irish felt about the political purposes of the war. Many Irish leaders were members of a revolutionary organization, the Fenians, dedicated to launching an uprising against English rule in Ireland. The Fenians undertook the recruitment of Irish units, with Fenian officers, seeing an opportunity to create a trained, battle-hardened Fenian army to liberate Ireland after the war. The authorities acted as if they knew nothing of this hidden agenda, even though the 69th had a well-known reputation for Irish nationalist politics. Under Corcoran's leadership, the 69th had refused to parade in honor of the visiting English Prince of Wales in 1860, and had nearly been disbanded as a result.

But with the coming of the war in 1861, the Union authorities were desperate for organized units of men and gladly received a still-unrepentant 69th into the federal service while pretending to know nothing of the unit's Fenian agenda. The 69th marched out and gained early combat experience by starting brawls with the 79th New York, a regiment of Scottish Americans clad in tartan kilts. The men from the Bowery and nearby Mackerelville (east of First Avenue and below 14th Street) gained their glory in the otherwise disastrous Battle of Bull Run on July 21, 1861, where Corcoran was badly wounded.

Other Bowery lads from the volunteer fire companies signed up in the red-shirted New York Fire Zouaves, who had a brief but colorful career of their own. Composed of Bowery B'hoys and fire laddies, the Fire Zouaves were renowned for their rowdiness and hard drinking. Their fame spread as far as France, where a lithograph was published depicting a Fire Zouave merrily draining a bottle beneath a temperance poster. Enlisted under the charismatic leadership of the young Colonel Elmer Ellsworth, the Zouaves won applause in Washington when they put their old skills to work in putting out a fire in Willard's Hotel. Some of the glamour went out of their soldiering when Colonel Ellsworth was shot on the staircase of an Alexandria, Virginia, hotel after taking down a Confederate flag, and they were routed at Bull Run when they became the unlucky recipients of Jeb Stuart's first cavalry charge. Despite all that, when the Fire Zouaves came home at the end of their three-month enlistments in July 1861, they were given a hero's welcome, joining the returning members of the 69th for a big event at Hibernian Hall and a parade down the Bowery.

But the Bowery was already feeling the economic pinch of the war. In June 1861, the Union Defense Committee had set up its headquarters on what was now Fourth Avenue just above Astor Place. A Union private's pay being a less-than-munificent thirteen dollars a month, the committee sought to give relief to impoverished families of volunteers by handing out grants of three dollars a week. They didn't foresee the surge of applicants that came out of the neighborhoods of Mackerelville and Kleinedeutschland, and the numbers soon forced a reduction of the grants to two dollars a week.

In 1860, New York's Mayor Fernando Wood had hoped to steer the city out of the economic dislocations of the coming war by having New York City itself secede from the Union as the free city-state Tri-Islandia, free to carry on its customary trade between the North and South. The idea never caught on, and in 1862 Wood came to the Bowery, where he pulled no punches in appealing to the fears that gnawed at the minds of his listeners. He accused the Republicans of wanting to free the slaves so they could migrate to the North and drive down everybody's wages. "They will get," he declaimed, speaking at the Volksgarden at 45 Bowery, "Irishmen and Germans to fill up the regiments and go forth and defend the country under the idea that they themselves will remain at home to divide the plunder that is to be distributed."

The idea may not have been original to Wood, but his speech helped deepen a festering economic and racial paranoia that within months would result in New York's greatest bloodbath ever. New York's shipping industry was sorely disrupted by the outbreak of the war and the interruption of the southern cotton trade, and war industry at that stage had not quite grown enough to fill the gap. The exploits of the Confederate commerce raiders did further damage to what shipping industry remained, sinking so many ships and driving so many of those still afloat to foreign flags and ports that depression conditions prevailed on the New York docks. In August 1862, the Confederate raider *Tallahassee* sailed boldly up the coast and sat right outside New York harbor off Sandy Hook. It coolly destroyed or damaged over thirty outbound ships before leisurely making off for Nova Scotia. The working-class neighborhoods lining the Bowery relied on longshoremen's work to a great extent, and the collapse of this industry left many people fearful of what the next week would bring.

In June 1863, a longshoremen's strike against pay cuts brought episodes of violence, mainly directed against the few African Americans still remaining on the docks, who were being recruited as strikebreakers. Eventually, the government rounded up a force of army convalescents and had them guard the loading of army transports under fixed bayonets.

And then the draft came along to throw kerosene on the embers. The Militia Act of 1862 had defined all able-bodied men between eighteen and forty-five as eligible for military service, never mind the families they might be trying to support on what were already inadequate incomes. Enrollment began in 1862, and in August 1862 army provost marshals entered departing passenger ships to arrest any able-bodied men caught trying to leave the country.

With the initial enthusiasm for the war having left with the first bands of volunteers, rising casualty figures, listed every week in newspaper columns, left little incentive for seeking glory on the battlefield. The war especially hit home to the Bowery when the 69th, along with the rest of the Irish Brigade, was cut to shreds in a futile assault at the Battle of Fredericksburg in December 1862. At the army barracks on Park Row a lockup called "the Pen" swelled with deserters and AWOL soldiers that the marshals had picked up in the city. The fifteen-by-twenty-foot room held as many as seventy-seven men at one time. Strollers down Park Row at night could see the spectacle of prisoners chained to trees on the sidewalk so the others could have enough floor space to lie down and get a few hours of sleep.

The 1862 draft hadn't even been put into effect when a tougher 1863 law caused a sense of desperation to sweep throughout working-class neighborhoods. There were legal means of avoiding the draft: You could pay a commutation fee of $300, about a year's worth of wages for the average unskilled laborer. You could provide a substitute, if you were lucky to find someone dumb enough to volunteer to take your place at a price you could actually afford. Or you could go to the lawyer on Centre Street making a name for himself as "Habeas Corpus Howe," who was quite successful in getting people out of the army on a writ of habeas corpus and then discharged on some legal pretext, but that cost money, too.

Disenchantment with the war was everywhere. It is easy today to see that the Union victories at Vicksburg and Gettysburg were the turning point of the war, but at the time that fact wasn't apparent to the man on the street. Indeed, Northern morale took a nosedive when Lee invaded the North for the second time in June 1863, and for all anyone knew, he was heading for New York. Even the aftermath of the battle of Gettysburg did little to lift anyone's spirits; to the average newspaper reader, the unsuccessful pursuit of Lee's army meant only that a record number of lives had been wasted for little gain.

On June 3, 1863, exactly one month before the climax of the battle of Gettysburg, a massive "peace meeting" packed the Great Hall of Cooper Union. Opposition to the war had by now grown into a political movement, with the war's opponents sporting on their coat lapels copper Liberty heads cut from pennies, giving them, with a passing reference to the venomous snake, the popular name of "Copperheads." Copperhead politicians like Clement Vallandigham had been breezing into town and making antiwar speeches for months, helping to raise the political temperature. The keynote speaker at the Cooper Union Peace Meeting was Fernando Wood. Working the other end of the Bowery, this time after his speech to the workingmen at Atlantic Garden, he expounded a theory that the prosecution of the war by the federal government was both illegal and unconstitutional.

With tensions rising to a fever pitch in New York that summer of 1863, the odd thing was that when the Draft Riots finally exploded on July 13, the Bowery was actually one of the quietest places in town. Sparked by anger over the imposition of a military draft, and by the fact that the wealthy were allowed to purchase exemptions, the violence began uptown with the burning of the draft office at Third Avenue and 46th Street, and soon spread to other parts of the city.

The anger in those July days was carried outward toward the draft offices, toward the wealthy, and toward the African American community on the West Side, rather than to the Bowery itself. The four days of intense rioting, arson, lynching, and pitched street fighting with firearms and cannon left a number of casualties that even today is uncertain, but there may have been as many as one thousand dead and wounded.

The violence involved people from the Bowery's neighborhoods, and at times it scraped close to the Bowery itself. The Brooks Brothers store on Catherine Street near Chatham Square was looted by rioters. They did not get to loot the Lord and Taylor store over on Grand and Chrystie Streets, whose employees barricaded the place and stood guard with loaded guns. A. T. Stewart likewise guarded his famous department store. Stewart was an Ulsterman and bore no love for the impoverished Irish Catholics whom everyone agreed were leading the riots. As he issued rifles to his nervous employees, he made it clear that a shoot-to-kill policy was okay by him. A. T. Stewart's personal showdown with the rabble didn't happen; the rioters in his vicinity were more bent on seeking out pro-war editor Horace Greeley of the nearby *New York Tribune*, and gladly bypassed the fortified portals of Stewart's department store. But his anti-Irish opinions on this and other occasions would gain him many enemies in New York and would come back later to disturb his eternal rest.

As New York burned, nervous authorities called out whatever reinforcements they could get. The police performed sterling service, aided by an innovative telegraph system they had recently installed linking the precinct houses with central headquarters, and a number of courageous officers were injured or killed trying to face down the angry mobs. But the situation was clearly beyond their means—it was the Dead Rabbit Riot multiplied by twenty. Beyond the provost marshal's guard and some convalescent detachments, there was little military force in the city; most available troops had been pressed into service to deal with Robert E. Lee's invasion of Pennsylvania. Eventually, five regiments were detached from pursuing the Confederates retreating from Gettysburg and rushed back to New York to deal with the urban insurrection.

On the last day of the riots, a mob fought a pitched battle with the police defending the elegant townhouses on Gramercy Square. The residents in Stuyvesant Square on 15th Street and Second Avenue, casting a wary eye on the nearby Bowery, borrowed a hundred muskets from the police department and patrolled their neighborhood. Relief came before the rioters did—when the 152nd New York Regiment arrived on the scene, they were sent to camp out in Stuyvesant Square, and the grateful residents sent their servants out to feed the troops tea and sandwiches served from silver trays.

The city remained under military occupation for some time, as many people doubted that July 1863 would be the last of the trouble. But the city was exhausted. When the 1864 elections rolled around, General Benjamin Butler was sent in to handle things. Known as "Beast Butler" for his heavy-handed management of occupied New Orleans, Butler was a general who knew how to apply the iron hand. Expecting trouble from Mackerelville, Butler requisitioned additional troops, but kept them out of sight in ships hovering offshore. The expected trouble didn't happen, and the Confederate agents who launched a clandestine attack on New York that autumn failed to spark another uprising. Armed with chemical incendiary devices, their plan to burn New York City resulted only in a few, quickly contained fires in hotel rooms, though they did succeed in burning down Barnum's Museum.

The Bowery during the Civil War was a place in decline, and the rowdy theatricality of the 1830s was a fading memory. The efforts of missionaries and urban reformers down in the Five Points had made some headway in clearing the worst aspects of a place that had once outraged Dickens, but in cutting the heart out of the Five Points they only spread the poverty eastward. By the time of the Civil War, the lower end of the Bowery was engulfed in slums, and the area was already acquiring a reputation as a place of the unfortunate, a street of the forgotten. The transition from the older Bowery to the new was in some places very obvious. The Howard Mission, the first of many the Bowery would eventually see, was opened in 1861 at 40 Bowery, the former headquarters of the Bowery B'hoys, who along with their rivals had long since aged out of the street gang lifestyle and dispersed. Secondhand clothing stores began to congregate on the lower Bowery in the late 1850s, establishing the tradition of "Cheap Johns" that would last into the 1960s and increase the area's appearance of general seediness. Boarding houses and cheap hotels began to cluster in the area, catering to a growing number of down-at-the-heels transients.

The most famous of these transients boarded at 15 Bowery. In 1860, Stephen Foster arrived in New York, having made a name for himself as the composer of some of America's most popular songs. The handsome and soft-spoken Foster was to many people the very image of the prewar Kentucky gentleman, even though he was from Pittsburgh. "My Old Kentucky Home" was indeed one of the several popular songs to his credit, and he had done well up to that point, averaging some $1,300 a year from his songwriting. Exactly what prompted him to move to New York is unclear, though most likely it was a desire to move into the music business full-time, as the city was the center of the music publishing industry.

Whatever his motives, Foster arrived in New York in August 1860 already showing signs of the chronic ague that would plague him for the last three years of his life, which he spent in and around the Bowery. The exact nature of his illness is unknown; it might have been recurring malaria, or it might have been tuberculosis.

Foster's unhealthiness created a legend that he lived on the Bowery as an alcoholic, and that he died of drink. Foster, like many other gentlemen of his generation, was fond of drink—in his Bowery days he favored a sort of ersatz rum made of grain alcohol flavored with molasses and brown sugar, which he bought in the back room of a grocery store/saloon on the corner of Hester and Chrystie streets. Still, his close friend during those years, George Cooper, later insisted that he never saw Foster drunk, and Foster's growing illness and weakness may have had more to do with malnutrition and tuberculosis.

Foster first lived at a boarding house at 83 Greene Street, and later stayed in places on Hester Street before moving into his final location at a boarding house at 15 Bowery. Though most certainly a "no frills" living arrangement, this place was far from the worst place one could stay on the Bowery, costing twenty-five cents per night—not exactly the Fifth Avenue Hotel but by no means a five-cent flophouse either. The building, across the street from where Charlotte Temple had lived, remained standing until the 1970s, when it was torn down to make room for Confucius Plaza.

Foster came to New York to make a living as a songwriter, his career petered out in bitter disappointment. His contract with the publishers Firth Pond & Co. at 547 Broadway was eventually terminated, perhaps involving a dispute over the terms of the contract, or perhaps simply because of the declining quality of his work. Contrary to legend, Foster's Bowery years were, in terms of sheer quantity, the most productive of his career, accounting for more than half of his lifetime total of 105 published songs.

Quality, however, was another matter. Few of the songs he wrote during his Bowery years became classics: the war song "We Are Coming Father Abraham, 300,000 More" and "Beautiful Dreamer," published after his death, are the best known today. Foster "published" quite a few songs after he died, as a number of publishers were eager to cash in on his reputation. He was even credited with a campaign song for the 1864 presidential campaign of George B. McClellan, a clairvoyant achievement if true, since McClellan wasn't nominated until six months after Foster died.

As time went on Foster's health deteriorated, and he became a well-known, though shabby, figure along the Bowery. He sold a lot of songs to minstrel shows, but in an era before broadcasts and recordings, it was difficult to make a living by songwriting alone. Unless one made a career performing his own compositions, sales of sheet music were the only sure way of making money from music. Many people, however, picked up the tunes by ear without buying the sheet music, especially with the easygoing melodies that Foster wrote. Publishers often didn't want to get involved with fussing over royalties and copyrights, and would usually offer a composer a onetime fee to purchase the music outright.

By the winter of 1863, Foster had become a very ill man. Miss Parkhurst Duer, a clerk at one of Foster's occasional publishers, Horace Waters on Broadway, was shocked at his ill and pathetic appearance when she met him for the first time. She befriended him as best she could, to the amusement of the other clerks in the establishment, who had grown accustomed to making the shabby Foster their laughing stock. Parkhurst Duer would later raise money to place a plaque in Foster's memory at 15 Bowery.

By now, Foster was making the rounds of publishers, theaters, and music halls, selling as much music as he could. His creativity still worked when he needed it to. Whenever a flash of inspiration hit him, he would write down a song on whatever came to hand, even a piece of brown wrapping paper. Composed without the aid of any musical instrument, the song would be dashed off in a single draft and sold outright for cash at the door of a theater. Wood's Minstrels at 514 Broadway was a dependable customer. How many songs were written and sold in this manner, and thus completely lost to posterity, is unknown.

The circumstances of Foster's death created more legends that would dog his memory. For one, he did not actually die on the Bowery. On January 10, 1864, the fever and ague caused him to collapse in his room at 15 Bowery. Foster had been having these fainting spells for some time; a few days before, he had collapsed and upset a pan of boiling water, leaving a livid and untreated burn across his thigh. This time he collapsed over a porcelain washbasin. He broke the basin as he fell, and the jagged edge left a gash across his face and neck, giving rise to the rumor that he had attempted suicide. His friend George Cooper got him to Bellevue Hospital, where he died on January 13. His wallet contained all of thirty-eight cents and a scrap of paper with the words "dear friends and gentle hearts."

9　Women In Tights

CONCERT SALOONS WERE AN ENTERTAINMENT innovation born on the Bowery during the Civil War, and in many ways they set the tone for the Bowery's continued career as an entertainment district that lasted past the turn of the century.

The innovation of the concert saloons lay in their combination of sex, booze, and music. The first ones sprang up in 1859, and by the eve of the Civil War they were already being proclaimed a "mania." It is easy to see why. A concert saloon sported a small stage, on which ran continuous musical and dance entertainment, often of a dubious quality. But that wasn't the real entertainment. The main attraction was the "waiter girls" who worked the crowd selling watered drinks on a commission basis. This was at a time when women working in any retail business were still a novelty. The waiter girls of the concert saloons wore short skirts and low bodices, and were sure to bend low over the table when distributing the drinks, affording their customers the sort of quick peek that would ensure many return orders.

Many concert saloons were located in basements, prefiguring the speakeasy, but some could be rather grand establishments. The largest and grandest was the Canterbury, just over on Broadway between Houston and Prince. The Canterbury provided an extra attraction in the form of large wall mirrors that not only gave an illusion of space and grandeur, but permitted discreet ogling of the waiter girls as they made their rounds. The concert saloons on the Bowery catered largely to sailors coming in from the docks in need of optical as well as liquid refreshment after dreary weeks at sea, and their names proclaimed it: Sailor's Welcome Home, Flowing Sea Inn, the Jolly Tar, and the Sailor's Retreat, to name a few.

Such a blatant marketing of sex appeal soon drew the fire of newspaper editors and moralists. The *New York Post* proclaimed the concert saloons a "portico to the brothel," perhaps not an entirely inaccurate description of the nature of the business. The young women themselves, often said to be women on the downslope of an acting career, came in for a lot of criticism as well. The writer James McCabe wrote of them in 1872, "They are beastly, foul-mouthed, brutal wretches. Very many of them are half-dead with consumption and disease. They are in every respect disgusting. Yet young and old men, strangers and citizens, come here to talk with them and spend their money on them."

The rising tide of moral indignation prompted many Bowery concert saloon owners to belatedly try to clean up their act. One tactic was to host a weekly "ladies' night" during which drinking and smoking were forbidden. But in places like the concert saloons, getting by on the door admissions and sales of food alone just wasn't a winning proposition, and most places kept up a ladies' night only to maintain appearances. It wasn't enough, however. In April 1862, the New York State Legislature passed an Anti-Concert Saloon Bill that sought to render such places illegal. While it took the edge off the popularity of the concert saloons, the bill became only another milestone in the Bowery's growing tradition of creative evasion of moralistic legislation. Many owners got around the law by ceasing to charge admission. By offering the entertainment for free and charging only for food and drink sold, the concert saloons were transformed from theaters into restaurants, and thus became establishments outside the scope of the new law. City business directories from this time on would list an absurd number of "restaurants" along the Bowery.

The Bowery after the Civil War still hosted a large number of "respectable" businesses, survivors from the days when it was still a fashionable thoroughfare. Two fellows from the German neighborhood Kleinedeutschland east of the Bowery named Hammacher and Schlemmer opened up a modest hardware store at 213 Bowery, and the business continues on in the city today as one of the more upscale retail establishments. Kleined-eutschland was maturing into a stable community, and was already draw-ing a fringe of Jewish immigrants. At the lower end of the Bowery, the Atlantic Garden became the anchor around which a German Theater District grew up, with the Stadttheater, the German Volksgarten, and Lindenmuller's Odeon putting on plays and mainstream performances in German. Further up the Bowery was the Steuben House at 291–93 Bow-ery, and there was Walhalla Hall over at Orchard and Grand. By the cor-ner of the Bowery and 5th Street Beethoven Hall opened in 1870, just a few steps away from the French Jewish Synagogue.

Although a cluster of small German restaurants and basement-room beer "stubes" on St. Mark's Place featured low-bodiced *fraulein*, most German saloons along the Bowery were quiet, even staid places. Usu-ally located above the sidewalk traffic on a second floor that discouraged casual walk-in trade, these German saloons, called *lokale*, each devel-oped their own group of steadies, gathering together on a basis, more often than not, of politics and philosophy, discussed and argued at great length amid beer steins and long-stemmed pipes. The Steuben House, later renamed the Germania, became one of the largest and most popular of these places. The word "local" continues on today as a New York term for the neighborhood bar.

On occasion, the German establishments would resound with patri-otic fervor. One such occasion was the German victory in the Fran-co-Prussian War of 1870. Reporter W. O. Stoddard described the scene in the Atlantic Garden when the news of the German triumph came in:

> Ordinarily the crowd was so quiet over its beer and wine to seem almost stupid. But you should have been here on Saturday night, September 10 [1870] . . . when the details of the great French overthrow at Sedan were being brought in here by telegraph office. They sang the German's Fatherland and Luther's Hymn . . . until they were hoarse, and hardly could get breath to drink the health of "Unser Fritz" and Von Moltke and everybody else.

Nobody was drunk and one could not help feeling that a part of the "Fatherland" was here for they had brought it with them in their hearts.

The politics and philosophy of Kleinedeutschland often spilled out onto the Bowery. The German community in post-Civil War New York included a large proportion of refugees from the failed revolts of 1848 as well as other liberal political types for whom Bismarck's Germany was becoming an uncomfortable place. The politics of the community was expressed in the popular German term for the United States: the land of *Kein Koenig Da* (No King There). The German community developed a huge infrastructure of social and political organizations. The Bowery saw frequent processions by these various *vereins*. Although they were located on the east side of Manhattan, they often held their picnics and other functions over in New Jersey, necessitating a trip across Manhattan to get to the Hudson River ferries. In the best Germanic fashion, the *vereins* would form up in a parade outside their headquarters and make a procession across town with bands and banners to the ferry piers, and then again in the evening when they returned home.

There were more serious parades as well. On June 10, 1872, the Eight Hour Day Parade was organized by the Eight Hour Day League, based on the then radical notion of limiting working hours. The League's main base of support was in Kleinedeutschland, and appropriately the parade formed up at the Germania Assembly Rooms and proceeded down a Bowery lined with cheering crowds before ending up in a mass rally at Tomkins Square Park. The League's effort scored a limited success in reducing working hours, only to have the gains abruptly rolled back once the Panic of 1873 hit town.

The old Bowery Theater was still in business after the Civil War, and would make one more piece of theatrical history when Buffalo Bill made his first stage appearance there. The event also marked the return of Ned Buntline to New York. After leaving town in the wake of the Astor Place Riots, Ned Buntline had continued his career as a novelist, journalist, and all-around rascal. He came back to New York during the Civil War posing as a Union colonel—he had been dishonorably discharged as a sergeant—but he nevertheless had himself photographed in colonel's uniform at Matthew Brady's studio on Broadway, making a point to sit in the very chair in which Abe Lincoln had his picture taken.

Traveling out west after the war, Buntline smelled opportunity when he met a colorful and engaging character by the name of William F. Cody, at that time busily doing his part in driving the North American bison to the brink of extinction. Buntline promptly made "Buffalo Bill" famous through a fictional serial he published in the *New York Weekly*. The stories were soon adapted into a play by Fred Meader, and Buntline brought Cody to the Bowery Theater to attend the world premier of the play on February 21, 1872. He made sure that someone in the crowd would spot Cody, and the enthusiastic audience mobbed Cody and lifted him to the stage to make an impromptu speech. It was the very first of Cody's many appearances before an audience, and he liked it. Buffalo Bill was soon starring as himself as the play toured the country, and Buntline had the play rewritten, this time with himself as a character giving a temperance lecture midway through the performance.

The Bowery could still witness the birth of an overnight sensation, but nobody could conceal the fact that the Bowery was slipping further and further down the social scale. The admonishing expression, "Don't act like you were born on the Bowery," had started in the 1840s and by the 1870s had become a New York cliché. Even Ned Buntline could see how the street had declined from the place he had known twenty years before, and when the rewritten Buffalo Bill play, now titled *Scouts of the Plains*, returned to New York after its national tour, it was clear that it needed a more upmarket venue than the Bowery Theater. It opened instead at Niblo's on Broadway, and Buntline swallowed his nativist pride to appear on a stage belonging to an Irishman whose Astor Place Opera House Buntline had once tried to have destroyed.

Things had changed a lot since the 1840s and 1850s. The Bowery B'hoys had faded away, many of them into Civil War cemeteries, and the volunteer fire companies from whom they had taken their image were gone too. The city, disturbed by the prominent role taken by some companies in the Draft Riots in 1863, decided it was time to professionalize the force, and abolished the volunteer companies in 1865. Their last call was answered on August 31, 1865, to put out a minor stable fire on Mulberry Street.

The passing of the Bowery B'hoys did not mean the passing of the criminal scene on the Bowery, and new gangs arose to contest the territory. The Rag Gang held sway along the lower end of the Bowery, the Dutch Mob held the section between 5th Street and Houston, and the Boodle Gang had its base at the Centre Market, where police headquarters would eventually be located. Paddy Quinn's saloon, Island No. 10, named for a Civil War battle, was located over on Catherine Street, and became a notorious criminal hangout. Most significant was the Whyo gang, originally from the Five Points, who moved into the vacuum left by the collapse of the old gangs after the Civil War. Their favorite hangout was a Bowery Saloon known as the Morgue, named for the resemblance of the liquor served there to embalming fluid. The Whyos would outlast other gangs formed after the Civil War partly because they developed for themselves a secure economic base. They pioneered the involvement of organized crime with gambling, promoting and monopolizing games of stuss, a relative of the card game faro that was developed in Kleinedeutschland and which was often called Jewish Faro.

Stuss was not the only criminal novelty going on along the Bowery in the 1870s. A unique kidnapping episode took place in 1878 when the body of the recently deceased department store pioneer A. T. Stewart was snatched from its vault in the churchyard of Old St. Mark's In-the-Bouwerie. The crusty Ulsterman's open disdain for Irish Catholics had won him few friends by the time he died in 1876. After an earlier attempt was thwarted, the church tried to fool the body snatchers by relocating the lid of the vault away from the actual shaft. But since the body snatchers already knew the location of the vault, they could hardly be put off by such a cheap trick, and a few nights later they returned and hoisted Stewart's carcass over the iron fence. Peter Stuyvesant, reposing a few feet away, offered no comment.

Stewart's unpopularity among the Irish community ensured that the snatching of his body was much talked about along the Bowery, but not talked about to the police. It wasn't the first time that a body had been stolen in New York, but when a ransom note for Stewart's corpse was delivered to his family, it made history. As a money-making criminal venture, however, the kidnapping of a corpse left something to be desired. After all, there wasn't much the body snatchers could threaten to do with a hostage already dead, and so the negotiations dragged on without the usual sense of urgency. After the case had continued on long past the point of public boredom, Stewart's body, or what remained of it, was eventually handed over on a lonely road in Westchester for a disappointingly small ransom. A. T. Stewart didn't return to Old St. Mark's; instead, he was sealed in a marble vault in Garden City, reputedly equipped with an alarm system.

It would be said in later years that it was the coming of the elevated railroad that destroyed the Bowery. If it didn't destroy the Bowery outright, the coming of the Third Avenue Elevated hastened the changes that were happening there, and the shadows cast by the El would help define the Bowery for the next major phase of its existence.

The memory of the Bowery's early role as Manhattan's main transportation artery was maintained by the continuing development of urban mass transportation. First, there had been the stagecoaches, later the first streetcars, followed by the New York and Harlem Railroad's horse-drawn cars. Opening on November 26, 1832, the first horse-drawn passenger railway in the world ran up the Bowery from Prince Street to 14th Street, with speeds running as high as eight miles an hour.

This pioneering railway not only ran on the Bowery, but it was made there as well. The first car, the "John Mason," was built in the Elizabeth Street workshop of the Irish-born coachmaker John Stephenson, whose successful stagecoach-building business positioned him to build the cars for the horse-drawn railway. He kept apace as streetcar and railway technology developed, and the Elizabeth Street workshop eventually grew into the John Stephenson Company of railroad car manufacturers.

The horse-drawn railway had done a lot to speed the development of the Bowery and the Lower East Side, and when city planners began to look toward newer forms of mass transportation after the Civil War, the

Bowery was high on the list of places considered. The question of improving urban mass transit in New York had been on people's minds for some time without much progress being made. In a notable case of analyzing the obvious, detailed traffic studies had been done on lower Broadway in 1852, which duly reported that the traffic situation was impossible and something had to be done.

The growth of the city had overwhelmed the horse railway running up the Bowery. The *New York Herald* reported in 1864 that "people are packed into them like sardines in a box with perspiration for oil. Passengers hang from the straps like smoked hams in a corner grocery." In 1867, the obvious was stated once again when the state engineer reported that the horse railway was at the limit of its carrying capacity.

Transportation alternatives were widely discussed. An elevated railway had been proposed as far back as 1845. Inspired by the example of London, the idea of an underground railway had been around since at least 1864, only to be defeated in the state legislature by "Boss" Tweed's "Black Horse Cavalry" acting to protect Tweed's interests in surface transportation lines. The chief drawback of underground lines was the problem of ventilation caused by coal- and wood-burning steam engines, the only power source at the time. In London, they tried to solve the problem by convincing people that the sulfurous smoke was good for them; in New York an inventor tried to solve it by building a clandestine three-block-long subway on lower Broadway that ran on compressed air. Opening in 1870, the Pneumatic Railway was an acclaimed novelty, but the Tweed Ring saw to it that the legislature extended no backing.

Elevated railways seemed the only workable alternative. The Tweed interests tried to forestall this idea as well. Working behind the scenes, they helped put out a completely unacceptable proposal for a "Manhattan Viaduct Railway" atop forty-foot-high masonry piers that would have smashed right through the middle of the residential blocks of Kleinedeutschland and Mackerelville. But in 1867, Charles T. Harvey opened his West Side and Yonkers Patent Railway. The "Railway on Stilts" ran on elevated tracks along Greenwich Street, and when the rickety-looking structure didn't fall down it was hailed as a success. The ambitions of the line were wrecked in the stock market collapse of "Black Friday" 1869, but plans were soon afoot to grant franchises and build elevated railways throughout Manhattan.

Conceived in idealism, the Third Avenue Elevated Railroad came to the Bowery as the result of a swindle. One of the most enthusiastic pushers of the elevated railroad idea was an ex-army surgeon named Rufus Henry Gilbert. After serving as medical director for the Union Army's XIV Corps during the Civil War, Gilbert made a midlife career change and became assistant superintendent of the New Jersey Central. Still a medical man at heart, Gilbert was convinced that elevated railroads would be a great boon to the health of the metropolis—if they were done right. His idea was to avoid using the smoke-and-cinder throwing steam engines of the day and instead build an elevated railway that propelled trains through pneumatic tubes carried above the street on graceful wrought-iron structures. This idea, which he spent six years developing, would have the advantage of enabling people to move out of the unhealthy and congested slum districts and allow them to commute to their jobs without choking in the process with coal smoke.

It was an elegant-looking solution, but there were a lot of doubts about how well such a system would work for anything more than short distances. After taking his plans to a set of business backers competing for one of the city's franchises, the unhappy Gilbert was swindled out of his shares after being persuaded to temporarily change the plans to a coal-burning system to assuage skeptical investors. Once Gilbert was out of the way, the temporary alteration was made permanent. He had been tricked into designing the very kind of system he never wanted.

The newly formed Rapid Transit Commission of 1875 awarded Gilbert's Metropolitan Company the Sixth and Ninth Avenue routes while the Second and Third Avenue routes went to the New York Elevated Railway Company, the successor to Charles Harvey's West Side and Yonkers company. The Third Avenue Line was to run right up the Bowery.

As soon as the plans were announced, a storm of protest and dismay was raised against the proposed elevated railways on the Bowery and other places. Businesses on the Bowery campaigned against the proposed line, displaying large drawings in their shop windows illustrating the effects the "El" would have on pedestrians along the street: silk hats burned through by falling cinders, and expensive white dresses ruined by oil drippings. They also fought the plan through the courts, where they managed to hold up construction for a year, getting various physicians to testify against the destructive health effects of riding on the El, ranging from insomnia and meningitis all the way to moral perversions. "The business population," argued the *Scientific American*, whose editor had once backed the short-lived pneumatic subway, "on some thoroughfares will be troglodytes—dwellers in dark and shaded caverns." For the Bowery, at least, it was a prophetic statement. Backers of the El confidently asserted that it would eliminate transportation overcrowding, and make straphanging "pass into history."

In the end, the Bowery merchants only succeeded in shooting themselves in the foot with their propaganda campaign, ensuring that their middle-class and affluent customers would be panicked into abandoning the Bowery even before the El started running, exacerbating the Bowery's alienation from mainstream society.

Despite all the protests, construction on the El began in 1877, and on August 26, 1878, operations began from South Ferry to Grand Central. The line was extended to 129th Street in 1879, with a short branch running from Chatham Square to City Hall beginning in 1880. Extension of the line proceeded in stages, eventually reaching White Plains Road in the Bronx in 1920.

Being the broadest of Manhattan's avenues, the Bowery had ample room to fit an El into, and the trains ran on two widely separated tracks, each of which sat directly over the sidewalk curb, leaving a wide gap in the middle. A third line of tracks for express service would be added in 1916.

The trains were pulled by steam locomotives, with handsome cars painted a deep maroon with gold trim. While the El didn't quite bring about the Vesuvian rain of oil and cinders the merchants had predicted, the soft coal burned by the locomotives did drop some ash and cinders onto the streets below, realizing people's fears about the trains and helping to drive away from the Bowery the few well-dressed people who had remained. Reactions to the El were mixed. People in second-floor apartments were dismayed to find trains going by with people looking into their windows. Some prostitutes along the lines saw a business opportunity in this. They rented out second-floor apartments adjoining the El, and would display themselves and flash placards to the male straphangers going by. A few people thought it great fun to take potshots at the trains with revolvers as they went past their windows, but luckily this particular fad died out before anyone got killed.

Dreams of easy commutes were not to be realized, however. The city was growing so quickly that whatever transportation slack was gained by building the Els was soon filled up, as the neighborhoods in the east 40s and 50s quickly developed without greatly relieving crowding on the Lower East Side, which still claimed the most congested blocks in New York. Soon people were complaining of overcrowding and poor service on the El just as they had complained of the streetcars. The situation was soon made worse when the two elevated railroad companies were merged into a single entity in 1879, making it convenient for Wall Street operator Jay Gould to take over the whole thing in 1881. After 1881, the Third Avenue El became famous for poor service while its funds were milked for various stock manipulations, and maintenance was allowed to slide.

The Third Avenue El's woes continued throughout its history, and it often seemed as if nothing right could ever be done on the line. Electrification was planned to replace the sooty steam engines around the turn of the century, but the project turned into a boondoggle once Tammany Hall got into the act, and it nearly destroyed the El for good. A contractor had been brought in with an agreement to be paid 7½ percent of the labor payroll with no commission on materials, only to be replaced with a Tammany-approved contractor who charged 15 percent of the labor payroll plus a 10 percent commission on materials. The labor force was featherbedded by Tammany hacks and no-shows, and the materials were also supplied by Tammany-connected firms at a hefty profit.

Driven to the brink of bankruptcy, the Manhattan Elevated Railroad Company was happy to give up its 999-year lease of the Third Avenue El and pass it on to the newly formed Interborough Rapid Transit

Company in 1903. The IRT in turn would be burned by the terms of the lease, which required a fixed, guaranteed rental of 5 percent on the $60 million valuation of the property, nearly canceling out the profits it was then making on the subways. The IRT would do everything it could to rid itself of the El or the lease, meanwhile cutting maintenance to the bone. In 1927, IRT president Frank Headley reported that "I saw a car with clean windows today, and when I got back to the office I raised hell to find out who had cleaned those windows and spent all that money."

10 Suicide Hall

UNDERNEATH ITS RATTLING EL THE Bowery evolved a new persona. "No other city in Christendom possesses a street comparable with the Bowery," one commentator wrote, "It is the only noble and important thoroughfare which is foreign to the city and the country which possesses it."

And the Bowery was becoming more foreign still. As the 1880s dawned, the Irish and German neighborhoods lining the Bowery were being joined by a growing Chinese neighborhood by Chatham Square. There had been a Chinese presence in New York since the 1850s, a tiny community living in the Five Points, formed of visiting sailors and the stranded members of a bankrupted performing troupe. Chinese men in New York found themselves assigned an occupation as sidewalk cigar sellers, especially around City Hall Park. By 1880, the community had grown to about seven hundred, nearly all of whom settled in along Pell and Doyers Streets.

Whatever lurid tales were told of the Bowery, even more lurid tales were told of the Bowery's extension, Chinatown. The early Chinese immigrants were nearly all unmarried men, and as they settled into the old Irish neighborhood along Mott and Pell Streets they sometimes married Irish girls. Sexual jealousy gave rise to stories of "white slavery" of European women by rapacious Chinese. This was unfair, but the growth of "bachelor society" Chinatown did create a certain market for vice. The one-time farm cartway of Doyers Street, commonly called "Shinbone Alley," was reputedly lined with brothels full of European prostitutes serving a

Chinese clientele. More often, the prostitutes in Chinatown were in fact Chinese women—"Sing Sing Girls" smuggled in by the tongs, Chinese protective associations then engaged in a variety of both legal and illegal activities.

By denying citizenship to the Chinese, the Chinese Exclusion Act ensured that Chinatown would develop into a closed, insular society. Denied any opportunity for integration, the Chinese kept apart from the *lo faan* (barbarians) and regarded themselves as foreigners in a foreign country. Emphasizing their disassociation from America, the ceremony of *Jup Gum*—"the Picking of the Gold"—was frequently practiced, by which the bones of their dead were disinterred, cleaned, and sent back to China for reburial, in order to keep the ghost from forever sorrowing in an alien land.

Adding to the exotic mystery with which many *lo faan* regarded Chinatown were the tongs, tales of which provided a staple of sensational nonsense for Sunday newspaper supplements for generations. The tongs were real, though. The On Leong Tong (Peaceful and Virtuous Association) was founded by Chinese merchants, while a more working-class group formed the rival Hip Sing. On Leong controlled Mott Street, and the Hip Sing held Pell Street—with Doyers Street a sort of neutral ground amid a number of smaller associations. From 1900 through the early 1930s a series of brutal "Tong Wars" flashed in Chinatown, all fought within a three-block area at the low end of the Bowery. Much of the bloodshed took place along Doyers Street, where the crook of the old farm lane made it an excellent ambush site for "hatchet men." The hatchet men were reputed to do their assigned killings by means of a sharp hatchet concealed in newspaper, but in fact the hatchet men more often used revolvers, like any other sensible killer. The frequent ambushes gave the crook of Doyers Street the popular name of the "Bloody Angle," after the much-fought-over redoubt on the Civil War battlefield of Spotsylvania. Apart from "hatchet man," Chinatown's Tong Wars contributed another memorable phrase to the English language: getting "whacked" in a gangland assassination.

Apart from tong wars and prostitution, opium was the Chinatown commodity that most fascinated outsiders. There was also plenty of gambling in Chinatown, but the operators of the gambling dens then as today were too smart to admit Europeans, knowing that cultural misunderstandings could add a lethal aspect to an already tense activity.

Opium smoking, however, was accessible, and in its early days not illegal either. There was a much greater consumption of narcotics in the late nineteenth century than is often realized, and which may come as a surprise to many who assume that the "drug problem" is a creation of the 1960s. The hospitals of the Civil War had discharged large numbers of morphine addicts, and many patent medicines contained narcotics, often prescribed by physicians for various "female" problems they didn't care to deal with. Heroin was even an ingredient in a popular cough syrup.

Recreational drug use was a growing phenomenon being pioneered among the avant-garde artistic set, the so-called "bohemians" of the late 1800s. The fascination with opium smoking probably had as much to do with its complex rituals and exotic paraphernalia as it did with the dreamy intoxication it induced. As its popularity grew, opium consumption became more down-market. A young freelance reporter named Stephen Crane wrote about it in 1896. Describing in great detail the rituals involved in preparing and smoking the brass pipe assembled of links called "joints," Crane wrote:

> Perhaps the ordinary smoker consumes 25 cents worth of opium each day. There are others who smoke $1 worth. . . . The $1 smokers usually indulge in "high hats" which is the term for a large pill. The ordinary smoker is satisfied with "pin-heads." "Pin-heads" are about the size of a French pea. . . . There were at one time gorgeous opium dens in New York, but at the present time there is probably not one with any pretense to splendid decoration. The Chinamen will smoke in a cellar, bare, squalid, occupied by an odor that will float wood chips. The police took the adornments from the vice and left nothing but the pipe itself.

Many people viewed opium smoking as harmless recreation. But there was a more troubling underside to the business, namely chemical dependency and human degradation. As time went on the practice became popular with upper- and middle-class women seeking relief from boredom and nervous tension, and often already introduced to the narcotic habit by various medical prescriptions. The coming together of European women and Chinatown opium dens raised all sorts of sexual fears, and provided many sensational stories in such publications as the *Police Gazette*. Opium, it was commonly said, was the means by which European women were drawn into white slavery, a concern that was growing into a mania as the century ended. Still, there were plenty of things going on to be disturbed about. Chuck Connors, the local character newspapermen dubbed the "Mayor of the Bowery," gave tours of Chinatown for visitors in which he showed them a fake "opium den" complete with one or two languid "addicts." But the reality behind the sensational image disturbed him more and more as time went on. Speaking of opium smokers who came to Chinatown from outside the neighborhood, he later recounted,

They make three or four trips and the first thing they know they're living in a furnished room, smoking hop and rushing the duck. After a while the red goes out of their cheeks, and they be putting the paint on, and from drinking beer they get to putting away the booze.

It don't take long for a girl to get old in Chinatown, and the older they get the more desperate they get, and there ain't nobody [that] ever goes back to where they come from, excepting they go in a box, and that's the last trip they make anywheres.

They make believe that they're happy as long as the rent's paid, and there's enough in the house to buy a shell of hop, a can of beer, and a pack of cigarettes. They sing songs and hand out the old jolly, but they don't laugh on the level. They laugh like a nuckle-pusher in the ring [who's] getting licked when he's trying to make the other bloke think he likes it—it don't go no further than the mouth.

These bundles don't like to be alone, 'cause then they get to be thinking too much, and that's the reason they pal together.

But I have seen 'em when they was acting as if their hearts was broken and wishing that they had never seen Chinatown.

If opium smoking was the rage in Chinatown, beer was the true lifeblood of the Bowery. The building of the El accelerated the decline that had set in with the Panic of 1873, and the Bowery was becoming a place for drinking and cheap, rough entertainment. Much of its clientele was drawn from the other "bachelor society" that was growing in the European neighborhoods, with the new influx of Italian immigrants and the upsurge of Irish immigration following the hard agricultural times in the mid-1860s. Many of the new immigrants were unattached—either young men striking out on their own, or else married or engaged men coming over by themselves and planning to save up enough money to bring over the rest of the family in due time. And added to that was a steady stream of young men leaving family farms in search of success on the urban frontier, and the transient population of sailors on stopovers between berths.

The result was the dominance of a "saloon culture" that resulted in the most raucous and colorful period in the Bowery's history, one that would be attacked and deplored by many reformers and moralists, but still fondly remembered by many long after the Bowery had collapsed into a shell of its former glory.

What passed for beer on the Bowery was often a matter of opinion. Made quick and cheap in local breweries, Bowery beer wasn't a connoisseur's tipple, nor did it need to be. Junius Henri Browne noted of the local brews in 1868:

It is undoubtedly the worst in the United States—weak, insipid, unwholesome, and unpalatable; but incapable of intoxication, I should judge, even if a man could hold enough of it to float the [ironclad ship] *Dunderberg*. It is impossible to get a good glass of beer in New York, and persons who have not drank it in the West have no idea what poor stuff is here called by that name.

Good beer or bad, hard drinking was the main activity in Bowery saloons. Some places, evolving out of the concert saloons, attempted to supplement the drinking with some kind of rough entertainment. In many other places the ambience was in itself the entertainment, and to come through a night in such a place without being robbed blind or having your teeth knocked out of your head was a manly accomplishment to be proud of, the mark of the true Bowery boulevardier.

The new wave of Bowery saloons came close on the heels of the elevated train. The Sultan Divan at 241 Bowery was the pioneer, opening the same year as the El, in 1878. The Sultan Divan appealed to the roving male trade by specializing in barmaids that were worth looking at and hosted a "Grand Barmaids' Show" every evening from 7:00 p.m. till 1:00 a.m.

The Sultan Divan was quickly joined by other places with a rougher trade. One of the worst of these places was the one belonging to Owney Geoghegan. Geoghegan was the former leader of the Gas House Gang, which operated out of the Gas House District at the East River end of 14th Street, about where the Stuyvesant Houses are today. He was also a loyal and well-connected Tammany Hall worker and ward heeler, as well as a former bare-knuckle boxer. He put all his various skills and experiences to work when he became a saloon owner. Owney Geoghegan's place at 105 Bowery had various names. Commonly called Geoghegan's, it was also known as the Summer Garden, but its official name was The Old House at Home. It was certainly like no home anyone had ever come from. Among its varied patrons were a notable number of professional beggars, who stowed the props of their fake afflictions before spending the evening there. If Geoghegan's was too rough, one could always go next door to the Windsor Palace at 103 Bowery, where shortchanging was so commonly practiced that patrons in the know always carried exact change to pay for their drinks.

Geoghegan's packed in two separate concert saloons into a two-story building, decorated throughout with pictures of prizefighters. The main event was on the ground floor, where Geoghegan had a regular prizefighting ring set up in the middle of the floor. His waiters were all ex-prizefighters, and thus not men to be trifled with. But by putting up a five-dollar purse, a customer could watch any two of these waiters engage in a regular prizefight in the house ring. Quarreling customers were also strongly encouraged by the waiters to settle their disputes in the ring, where fighting each other was much better than trying to fight the waiter.

The fights that went on in Geoghegan's weren't put-on affairs, either. Befitting his professional status and his enduring interest in the sport, Geoghegan insisted on serious fights in his establishment. If any of these nightly prizefights displeased the audience, or displeased Geoghegan, one of the bouncers would step up to the ring to encourage more vigorous action by blasting the fighters' bare shins with blank revolver shots.

Those evenings in Geoghegan's were well remembered by those who survived them, and there were often contests between famous retired professionals. In later years, Chuck Connors would recall, "Up in Geoghegan's there was a ring for three rounds and no decision, and any knuckle-pusher [that] came along would always get a fight off the reel, with such blokes as Johnny Sheridan, Paddy Lee, Paddy Gorman, Funny Cooke, Tommy Evans, or Fiddler Neary."

Owney Geoghegan became a well-regarded personage on the Bowery. He was always neatly dressed in formal black and was considered by most people a pleasant person. When he died, his funeral procession became a memorable Bowery event when two different wives of the dead Geoghegan showed up in carriages, each of them considered themselves rightly deserving of the place of honor. As the procession set off, the two carriages bumped and jostled one another, jockeying for precedence all the way to Calvary Cemetery.

If Geoghegan's had the best fights, Billy McGlory's Armory Hall had the most publicity. Opening in 1885 at 158 Hester Street just around the corner from the Bowery, McGlory's Dancing and Variety Hall, as it was officially named, became known as the "lowliest resort in Gotham." It certainly had the liveliest dance floor of any place on the Bowery, where unattached men could go for a swing with equally unattached women who might be available for other activities later on. The dancing was important to McGlory, who went to the unusual length of hiring a band that could play decent music, even if the announcer was nicknamed "Poison-Face."

While the music was decent, many other things about McGlory's were not. Though reputed to be the worst dive in New York, it probably was not quite as dangerous as some other places, but its infamy ensured that it was the place for New Yorkers to go and impress out-of-town friends with their temerity and intimate knowledge of the evil city. Part of the fascination was that McGlory's became a destination for the early gay and transvestite scene in New York. Many of the waiters were gay, and there were curtained compartments for intimate same-sex encounters.

Knowing that he was treading the thin edge of legal and public tolerance, McGlory kept a tight rein on the nightly doings in the Armory Hall, and brooked no nonsense from anybody. "If you was all right you could stay," Chuck Connors recalled, "but if you wasn't a bottle over the coco would put you out of business, and give you a headache the next day."

Harry Hill's, known as "the best of the worst places," was over on the corner of Houston and Crosby. On Harry Hill's dance floor, wild and vigorous dancing was the norm, with some acrobatic moves that anticipated the dances of the swing era. The fastidious Hill was as proud of the range of cocktails his bar offered as he was of the dancing. A signboard outside the establishment promised "Punches and juleps, cobblers and smashes/To make the tongue waggle with wit's merry flashes." It was a range of mixed drinks not to be found in the ordinary Bowery dive, and Hill made sure his customers partook of them. "All men must call for refreshments as soon as they arrive," one writer noted of the rules of the house, "and the call must be repeated after each dance; if a man does not dance he must leave."

As the 1880s went on it became a matter of opinion which was the worst place on the Bowery. There were plenty of contenders, and where you went depended on what diversions, or depravities, you were most interested in. Paddy Martin's saloon down on 9 Bowery had an opium den in the basement, while across the street at 12 Bowery Dan Moos had a pit with weekly, or even nightly, cockfights.

On a street of dangerous dives, the World Poolroom at 19 Bowery was something else again. By the early 1890s, it was known as a place haunted by "peter players," a term of obscure origin meaning a gang that knocked out drinkers with drops of chloral hydrate and robbed them, sometimes leaving them stripped of their outer clothes, which could be quickly sold to one of the nearby "Cheap Johns" used clothing stores. The victims didn't always wake up—overdoses of chloral hydrate could have a lethal effect. If the peter players didn't get you, there was the Pretzel Gang who also hung out at the World. They were a street gang of local Germans, but if anyone asked, they'd be told they were all hard-working bakers. Fatty Flynn's on Bond Street was another infamous dive where an unwary stranger could be taking his life in his hands. Theodore Allen, often known as just "The Allen," had a place on Bleecker Street that was especially dangerous; it was reputed to be a popular gathering spot for members of different street gangs, with whom The Allen was on friendly terms.

Bismarck Hall on Pearl and Chatham had cubicles underneath the sidewalk housing a cheap bordello, where the outside light filtering through purple glass deadlights set in the sidewalk overhead gave the activities a special lurid glow. Bismarck Hall was also the haunt of one of the Bowery's more interesting characters in those years. Ludwig the Bloodsucker was the Bowery's own vampire. Little is known about Ludwig, except that he was a swarthy, black-haired German who liked to drink blood—usually cow blood from a nearby slaughterhouse, but rumor had it he drank that only when he couldn't get the human variety.

The dives seemed to get worse the further down the Bowery you went, and by the time you reached Chatham Square you pretty well had hit bottom. The places there had no colorful quirks to distinguish them, and only their names give a clue to their characters: the Fleabag and the Hell Hole were joined by the Doctor's, the Plague, the Harp House, the Cripple's Home, and the Billygoat.

The most tragic place was the Mug at 295 Bowery, hosted by John McGurk. A longtime Bowery veteran, McGurk started out at 267 Bowery with a place named the Mug, which was known as a "schooner house" where waiters would slip knockout drops in the drink and then carry out and rob the unconscious customer in a back alley.

The Mug was closed down by the authorities in 1887, whereupon McGurk opened up another dive a block down the street at 253 Bowery which he named Sailors' Snug Harbor, perhaps with a knowing smirk at the endowed lands across the street that supported the home for aged sailors. Sailors' Snug Harbor and its sister venture the Merrimac over on Third Avenue were bad enough, but McGurk reached the ultimate depths when he opened a new version of the Mug at 295 Bowery in 1895.

The Mug had a steady stream of customers, many of them sailors drawn by the trade cards that McGurk gave out to other sailors and which were tacked up in ports around the world. Sailors shipping out from Hong Kong or Liverpool would often be planning a night at McGurk's before their ship cleared the harbor. With sailors arriving from all over, the Mug was a tough guy's kind of place, with even tougher waiters and bouncers. "Shortchange Charlie" the headwaiter had a temper as short as the change he gave out, and he was not the sort of man anyone cared to argue with. Only the magician Harry Kellar could ever beat him at his game; Kellar once managed to palm back the balance of his change, while at the same time drawing some allegedly stolen jewelry from Charlie's person. Luckily for him, Kellar's fame ensured a rare sense of humor that night from Charlie, for at McGurk's, stolen jewelry was a sensitive issue. Although thousands of people would be robbed there, McGurk managed to maintain the reputation of an honest place. The Mug was a popular fishing ground for female pickpockets, but McGurk's ironclad rule was that if they were caught in the act they were to return the goods without argument and quickly exit the premises without having to be asked.

They usually did exit, because nobody in their right mind wanted to attract the attention of chief bouncer Jack "Eat-em Up" McManus. McManus was the star celebrity of the place, an ex-boxer just past his prime who had been a well-known character on the Bowery before McGurk hired him, and who would continue to have a lively career on the Bowery long after McGurk had passed from the scene. As brutal as he was effective, the unbeatable "Eat-em Up" McManus was perhaps the only bouncer on the Bowery to have a song written about him. Although he is not directly named, the song "I Put Him on the Cheese" was a popular number in the music halls for some time, and it was generally understood that the narrator was Eat-em Up McManus. The song described one of his typical evening's exploits:

A fresh guy came in the restaurant
And ordered a kidney stew,
"And keep your fingers out!," he said
"And get on a hurry too!"
He was looking for trouble, he wanted a row,
Says I, "You might say please;
Don't get gay with your sassy play
Or I'll put you on the cheese!"
"Kick his slats in," cried the gang,
And quickly gathered round.
I'm always perlite, I'm a favorite,
They wouldn't see me downed.
The omnibus slipped me a pair of knucks,
But I had no need of these;
I gave him a swipe with a piece of lead pipe
And it put him on the cheese!

What finally put McGurk's on the cheese was the series of deaths that earned it the nickname of "McGurk's Suicide Hall." How many died there is not known, but about fifty suicides in the space of its five-year career is a fair estimate. Although not actually a brothel as many people believed, the upper three floors of the building were rented out by McGurk to small-time pimps for use as a "crib," where they housed their exploited streetwalking prostitutes. This was the lowest and most brutal form of prostitution, one that quickly left its victims burned out mentally and physically. "There are very rough people that go to McGurk's," one of these women, Emma Hartig, would later testify to the investigating Mazet Committee, "Very rough men indeed . . . some of the girls live over McGurk's. . . . There are quite a number of such men hanging around McGurk's saloon and watching the girls and making them work for them."

Some of these women, at the end of their rope after three or four years on the street, chose to end their lives where their downfall had begun by taking poison with their beer in the downstairs saloon at McGurk's. It isn't known exactly how many suicide attempts, successful or otherwise, took place at McGurk's, but the ongoing suicide epidemic soon became well-known on the street, and the resulting notoriety drew even more patrons. A few men also made their way to McGurk's to take their fatal swallow.

While not entirely unhappy with the increased business, McGurk was nervous about the legal implications of the suicides raging out of control under his very nose. Knockout drops had caused him enough trouble when he was at 267 Bowery, and this was far more serious. Inquiring reporters were summarily ejected from the establishment after hearing McGurk vehemently deny that he had ever encouraged either prostitution or the suicides. McManus and Charlie soon had their instructions. They kept a sharp eye on the crowd, and if they spotted anyone either taking poison or nodding off they would organize the waiters and bouncers into a squad, roughly snatch her up, and make straight for the door, where they would unceremoniously drop the dying girl on the sidewalk. That way, anyone who died didn't do it in McGurk's establishment, and whatever happened on the sidewalk outside was no concern of his.

It didn't work perfectly, however, and like many of its erstwhile patrons, McGurk's Suicide Hall was doomed to a short life. The young Emma Hartig survived her suicide attempt in 1899, and was called to testify before the Mazet Committee investigating the various corruptions of New York City. Hartig's testimony shone an uncomfortable light on both street prostitution trafficking and McGurk's. "The police never arrested me before I took the poison," she told them. "I was one of the girls that got tired and took poison, at McGurk's, and then of course I was arrested, and that resulted in my changing my life."

It changed McGurk's life also. Prodded by another investigative committee, the Lexow Committee, Police Inspector Alexander "Clubber" Williams was ordered to mount a raid on McGurk's with fifty patrolmen. No doubt tipped off about the raid, McGurk ensured that the raid was a largely futile exercise, but the writing was clearly on the wall for him. Having accumulated a fortune of about $200,000, McGurk closed up the Suicide Hall in 1900 and retired to California, hoping that his reputation would not follow him there.

For those not interested in instant oblivion, the various dives and dumps along the Bowery also offered the means of committing slow suicide. Adulterated drinks were an old Bowery technique in places catering to the lowest end of the social-economic scale, and they never lacked for business either, as there were more than enough people roaming the Bowery who were too poor and too far gone to care.

In Stephen Foster's day there was the ersatz "rum" made of raw grain alcohol flavored and colored with molasses and brown sugar. By the 1880s, some places served fermented turnip juice charged with carbonic acid gas and served to customers as "champagne." In places called "barrelhouses," whiskey meant the lowest grade of rotgut alcohol cut further with prune juice and water, with a dash of cayenne pepper to give it some kick. Barrelhouses were the next-to-last step from the absolute bottom—they commonly sold stale beer straight from the barrel without the benefit of a glass or any drinking vessel. The customer would pay a penny and be handed the end of a rubber hose leading from the barrel. He then could drink all he could drink until he had to stop and draw breath, at which point the barkeep would snatch the hose away. Some people inevitably would inhale stale beer into their lungs while trying to get one extra gulp in for their penny.

Like many mainstream saloons, some barrelhouses had a specialized clientele. On the east side of the Bowery on the block opposite Chinatown was a row of barrelhouses that catered to the mendicant trade. Here the beggars of the Bowery came to spend their day's gains, often taking off their casts and other props as they came in and storing them in cubicles set aside for this purpose. For a price, they might also be allowed to spend the night sleeping on or under the tables before collecting their props and fanning out to their customary stations throughout the city the next morning. Beggars in search of fake props could also rent them in these places. Whatever you needed for a convincing sympathy-inducing appearance was available: crutches, casts, bandages, and even children could be hired by the day or week.

At the very bottom were the basement "doggeries." The doggeries ran their own recycling program—the stale beer remaining in the used kegs saloons left on the sidewalk for pickup was carefully siphoned out, touched up with various drugs and other chemicals, and sold in the doggeries for one or two cents a glass. The oblivion produced by doggery beer sometimes included permanent brain or organ damage.

Not all the saloons on the Bowery were low-down and dangerous places. Many of them hosted the sort of atmosphere that in later years would be looked upon with nostalgia as part of the colorful Gay Nineties of gaslight and shiny brass bar rails. The Bowery had a large number of "sporting men," fellows either living by gambling, or men with an intense interest in the sports world of the day. Their newspaper of choice was the *Police Gazette*, and their headquarters on the Bowery was Nicholl the Tailor's at 147 Bowery. Nicholl built up a clientele as the tailor of choice for local swells and Tammany Hall types; very often the young ward heeler's first step up the social ladder was a visit to Nicholl's for a smart and stylish suit. Like a barbershop, it was a popular place to hang around and pass the time of day, talking of baseball and horse races. Nicholl obligingly put up a sporting bulletin board, on which he posted the latest baseball scores and race results.

Old-time Bowery types found a refuge in the Hauser Beer Garden, started in 1885, and which kept up the genteel atmosphere of the old-time German Beer Halls, now something fading from memory along the Bowery.

If one didn't care for beer, there were places other than Harry Hill's where one could indulge in the newfangled fad of mixed drinks. Legend has it that cocktails became popular during Prohibition, as a means of making bad liquor drinkable, but the fashion was well underway before the turn of the century, and much of it was going on along the Bowery. Maybe not all the cocktails were invented with the most honest intentions in mind. In the 1870s, one New York publisher advertised a *Hotel and Barkeeper's Guide to Mix Drinks* [sic] that seven hundred recipes in 250 pages advised bartenders on how to "manufacture, adulterate and doctor liquors." The best place to seek the latest cocktails was the Little Jumbo on 119 Bowery, where famed bartender Harry Johnson ran the house. Johnson was an inventor of cocktails and the author of a respected bartender's manual. At the Little Jumbo, over one hundred cocktails were offered, among them the Gin Fizz and the Tom Collins.

Drinkers not interested in beer or cocktails could head for the Feser Brothers Wine Room at 269 Bowery, a wine bar with a German clientele. Or they could go up to Brubacher's Wine Garden up by Union Square. The fun at Brubacher's wasn't confined to the fine wines offered there. The place overlooked a curving stretch of tracks where the trolley lines went past Union Square, and the drivers for some reason were convinced that they had to take this curve at maximum speed to avoid losing their catch on the cable. The high speed and the deceptive curve ensured that so many pedestrians were hit by trolleys that the stretch became known as "Dead Man's Curve." Drinkers at Brubacher's would look out and take bets on the survival of individual pedestrians competing with the trolleys. As much as the (then) adjacent statue of Washington, the casualty rate on the street below inspired Brubaker's nickname of the "Monument House."

There was even one place on the Bowery that specialized in fermented apple cider, a drink that most hard-core urban types of the day dismissed as fit only for country "jays" and upstate "apple knockers." Arnold's Cider Mill at 222 Bowery sat right across the street from the Salvation Army Headquarters (in fact, the building had originally been the Salvation Army Headquarters), and the drinkers there could watch the apple cider being made fresh, as apples were mashed by a mill powered by a huge St. Bernard dog on a treadmill.

The better class of Bowery saloons, such as they were, had their own customs and rules that had to be followed. In saloons in those days a man could order drink by the bottle, but when he did so he was expected to pour himself a "gentleman's drink" of about a half a glass, by way of indicating to the watching barman that you weren't there to get blasted in a hurry and become a problem. If a man poured himself more than that, the barman would tersely ask him, "Will you be needing a towel, then?"

The "free lunch" was one of the legendary amenities of old-time saloons, but free lunch, too, had its rules and limitations. High-end places like the Hoffman House offered magnificent spreads, but in most saloons the free lunch was no more than cheese, crackers, and sometimes bean soup. Sometimes other items such as chopped liver or hard-boiled eggs were to be had, and everybody ate with the same fork, dropped into a glass of greasy water between customers. The precise rule granting access to the free lunch varied from place to place, and it was wise to know the law of the house before trying to help yourself. You had to order at least one five-cent beer, in some places two beers, and in other places it was preferred that you brought in a new customer, at least once in a while.

A big part of the bouncer's task in a Bowery saloon was guarding the free lunch counter. The expression "bum's rush" was invented to describe what happened to people who tried to make an unauthorized meal of the free lunch counter. Usually, this was done by coming in at a busy moment, waving in the direction of an already distracted bartender as if you were ordering a beer, and then make a dive at the free lunch, fill up, and exit without having bought a drink. Bouncers were wise to this maneuver, which had grown old the day after it was invented, and would quickly move to intercept the interloper and give him the "bum's rush" right out the door. Sometimes this was described as the "Spanish walk"; as the target had his arms pinioned behind him by the iron grip of the bouncer, this forced him into a sort of jerky quickstep thought to resemble the motion of a man "walking the plank" in pirate stories.

Most of the "restaurants" listed on the Bowery were nothing of the sort, but one place to go in search of real food was Mike Lyons' restaurant at 259–261 Bowery. From its opening in 1871 until its closing in 1907, the place was never closed for a minute, being open twenty-four hours a day seven days a week, holidays included. The food was good, even if the menu was somewhat limited, but one thing could be relied upon: there was always corned beef and cabbage. In its heyday, everyone on the Bowery went to Mike Lyons', and it was a gathering place for all sorts of people—artists and intellectual types shared the corned beef with criminals and politicians. It was the sort of mixture that the "downtown scene" would be made of in later years.

Under the noisy El, the Bowery's unique life flourished. Even though it seemed to be more and more a solidly male environment, the Bowery still

held out some of the freedom it had offered to women back in the 1830s.
While in most saloons throughout the city women were not allowed,
they were still welcomed in many Bowery saloons, except for most of the
German *lokale* and of course John McSorley's, which famously held its
no-woman policy until 1970.

Although most of the women who would appear in a Bowery saloon
were hard-nosed types, not all were. Beginning in the 1880s, the outreach
social workers known as "Salvation Army Girls" became a fixture working
the saloons and the sidewalks of the Bowery. They took quite a bit of flak
at first, but their courage and sincere dedication soon won them respect in
most places. Some of the most cynical and callous Bowery barmen liked
to believe that they still had a spark of decency remaining, and they laid
down the rule that nobody was to ridicule or hassle a Salvation Army Girl
appearing in the saloon, on pain of being ejected from the place.

Like Elijah Pearson in the 1830s and the Methodists in the 1850s,
the Salvation Army women struggled with an old problem as they tried to
catch young women at the beginning of a downslide into sexual exploita-
tion. By offering support, the organization provided an alternative to a
life of degradation. One of the most energetic of these Salvation Army
women, Carrie Joy Lovett, had a quiet understanding with many of the
Bowery barmen, who would often tip her off about girls on the brink of
the pit.

Since the days of the Bowery Theater's Third Tier, prostitution had
been a steady part of the Bowery scene, due to the Bowery's large floating population of unattached men, and the social mores that denied a living wage to unsupported women while condemning victims of rape or
seduction as "ruined." While brothel districts moved about the island, the
Bowery remained a place more known for streetwalking. Contacts made
on the Bowery, or as the century progressed, on Bleecker and 4th Street
between the Bowery and Broadway, were usually consummated in nearby
tenement rooms.

Streetwalkers along the Bowery became known as "hookers." Often
assumed to have begun with General Joseph Hooker in the Civil War,
the term actually originated years earlier at Corlear's Hook in lower

Manhattan, a marginal district where in the early 1800s a number of houses of ill repute clustered along Walnut Street (today's Jackson Street). Angling southward from North Street (today's Houston Street), Walnut Street was itself sometimes referred to as "the Hook." The word "hooker" was in use by 1845, and during the Civil War waggish soldiers honored their playboy general by referring to the swarms of prostitutes hanging about the campsites as "Hooker's Corps."

Walking the Bowery, prostitutes would often stop at shoe-shine stands to have their shoes shined while displaying their ankles—in those days a significant sight—or perhaps claim a customer by hooking her right arm around his left, making it appear that they were demurely strolling arm-in-arm. This maneuver, known as "hooking," is an alternate explanation of the origin of the term "hooker."

There were more creative ways of making sexual encounters along the Bowery. Personal columns in the newspapers were often used by strangers to make contact with each other. A man attracted to a woman he saw on the street would brush by her and whisper the word "personal" along with the name of a newspaper. He would place an ad in the personal column of the paper the next day, and the woman, if interested, would pick up the paper and see where she might make contact. "Lady in Grand Street car," read one typical ad, "Saturday evening 7:30—had on plaid shawl, black silk dress; noticed gentleman in front; both got out at Bowery; will oblige by sending her address to C. L., Box 199." The women responding to such ads wouldn't necessarily be streetwalkers, but prostitutes too played the personals game to get business from men too inhibited to proposition them on the street. The more upmarket types even advertised their business or change of address under the guise of a discrete "Social Notice": "Miss Gertie," a typical ad might run, "will be pleased to see her friends at . . ."

As the new entertainment district known as the Rialto opened up along 14th Street east of Fourth Avenue in the 1880s, the streetwalking moved uptown with it. In time, Union Square and Stuyvesant Square became known for both male and female streetwalkers. The anarchist Emma Goldman, then living by the site of the Stuyvesant Pear Tree on Third Avenue and 13th Street, tried streetwalking one day along the

Rialto in order to raise money for her lover Alexander Berkman, in jail
for trying to assassinate steel magnate Henry Clay Frick. As she recalled
it in her memoirs, she found the experience both degrading and nerve-
wracking. Her first customer took one look at her distressed state, sized
her up as an amateur, and simply handed her ten dollars and told her to
go home. She never tried it again.

As an early gay scene developed in New York in the late 1800s, one
of its chief places was on the Bowery, at Columbia Hall on 5th Street and
the Bowery. Dubbed "Paresis Hall" after the medical term for syphilitic
insanity, the saloon became known as a resort for male prostitutes. Paresis Hall, though, wasn't so much a venue for male prostitutes as it was
the chief location for New York's transvestite scene. It hosted a regular
organized club of transvestites, the Cercle Hermaphroditis, which rented
the room above the saloon as a place where its members could store their
clothes and change into drag before spending the evening downstairs.
Many of these men were from mainstream neighborhoods and occupa-
tions who commuted to the Bowery to pursue their secret hobby.

Other gay places opened in the vicinity of the Paresis. Little Buck's was
across the street, and there was Manila Hall, the Palm Club on Chrystie
Street, and the Black Rabbit over at 183 Bleecker. Billy McGlory's Armory
Hall gained an early reputation as a gay resort, and it would also host an
occasional transvestite ball. Long after Paresis Hall was defunct, the victim of Rev. Parkhurst's reform crusade in 1894, an annual drag ball was
held in the Little Beethoven Assembly Room, next to the old Beethoven
Hall across 5th Street from the site of the Paresis. The Walhalla Hall
began hosting gay and lesbian balls in the 1890s, though by the turn of
the century the action had shifted to the Sharon Hotel and Billy's Hotel
on Third Avenue above 14th Street.

Like everything else on the Bowery, the emerging gay scene had places
ranging from middling to awful. The worst dive on the Bowery gay scene
(and a contender for title of worst dive in New York) was Frank Stevenson's place at 157 Bleecker Street called the Slide. In the slang of the day, a
"slide" was a place where transvestite homosexual prostitutes solicited gay
men (though the word "gay" at this time referred to a female heterosexual

prostitute). Frank Stevenson made no effort to conceal the nature of the business in his place, and his choice of the name the Slide was about as blatant a piece of advertising you as could find. It even got written up in a lengthy *New York Herald* expose series in 1892. At the Slide, homosexual waiters sang suggestive ditties in falsetto and joined the customers at the tables.

The action at Paresis Hall and the Slide eventually drew a stream of insensitive spectators who came to watch those they deemed degenerates. But voyeurism was by no means confined to those places. As the 1800s drew to a close, the Bowery became a sort of permanent carnival midway for New York, where human diversity served as public spectacle.

11 Living Curiosities

THE PRESENCE OF SAILORS FROM the nearby East River docks led to the development of the lower Bowery as a center for tattooing after the Civil War. Back in the time of Julius Caesar, the Celts had been known for tattooing themselves, but the custom had largely died out in European culture since then. It was reintroduced to the West through contact with the South Pacific islanders in the 1840s. (The word itself is Polynesian in origin.) P. T. Barnum brought tattooing to New York in a big way in the 1850s with his exhibit of the first "tattooed man," one Captain Constentius, who, according to the story, had been tattooed all over his body as a torture after he was shipwrecked and captured by some South Sea islanders.

Tattooing became a fad among sailors, and in 1846 New York's first professional tattoo artist, Martin Hildebrandt, set up shop on Oak Street (present-day Rutgers Street) down by the waterfront. Curious customs were soon attached to tattooing among sailors. Many got tattoos to celebrate such accomplishments as crossing the equator, while some went to the trouble of having a crucifixion scene or similar religious subject tattooed across their backs, on the theory that they would thereby escape a flogging, as the bo'sun wouldn't want to commit the sacrilege of lashing the figure of Jesus with the cat o' nine tails. It didn't work. In later years, a notion got around that tattooing was a cure for syphilis, based perhaps on the fact that the red pigment used was mercuric sulfide. That didn't work either.

It wasn't only sailors that headed to Chatham Square for tattoos. Around the 1890s, it briefly became fashionable for society debutantes to have a small rose tattooed on one ankle as a sort of rite of passage. Superstitious landlubbers came down too; some believed that a tattooed red "x" in a circle was a charm against automobile accidents.

Tattooing in the early days was a painful business, which was part of its appeal to the hardened sailors who started to acquire tattoos both as evidence of their far travels as well as their manly ability to endure pain. Tattooing by hand was not only painful, but the slow speed of the process limited the range of designs that were possible. A Maori warrior could afford to spend weeks getting an intricate tattoo done, but a sailor on shore leave didn't have that kind of time, or money to spend. This changed when the first electric needle was introduced on the Bowery in the 1890s and revolutionized the tattooing industry.

The electric needle was originally an "electric pen" invented by Edison as a device for cutting duplicating stencils. It wasn't a great success in that role, but in 1891 Samuel F. O'Reilly made a few modifications and patented the device as the electric tattoo needle and made it available from his shop at 28 Cooper Square. The device punctured the skin at a precise and steady speed of over two thousand times a minute.

The device made all sorts of artistry possible, and a distinct "New York style" of tattooing developed. Much like the way the new "American style" of acting confronted the English "teapot style," the New York style of tattoos rejected the drab and restrained English motifs in favor of large and elaborate designs, bold colors, and heavy black outlines that made the tattoos stand out from a distance. The New York style eventually became the standard "American" style, and after World War II it became the worldwide standard of tattooing, with artists in such places as Singapore and Hong Kong following designs first pioneered on the Bowery. The Chatham Square artist Lewis Alberts is sometimes credited with perfecting the New York style.

Tattooing equipment was portable and required little space, but tattoo artists gravitated to permanent establishments on Chatham Square, and sailors lacking the exact address of any particular artist knew they

only had to head for Chatham Square to find a tattoo parlor. Tattoo artists displayed another Bowery innovation, the "flash"—a cloth banner or
a folding set of cards that could be hung in a window or by a door that
displayed the designs they had in their repertoire. A prospective customer
would take some time walking about Chatham Square and studying the
flashes before he settled on a particular design.

Armed with his new electric needle, O'Reilly, now called "Professor"
O'Reilly, went into the tattoo business in a big way. He was outshone by
his onetime apprentice Charlie Wagner, who inherited O'Reilly's business
when the Professor died. Wagner improved on O'Reilly's electric needle
and patented his own version in 1904, setting up a small "factory" at 208
Bowery to manufacture the needles while he kept a "studio" in the back
room of a barbershop at 17 Chatham Square.

Wagner, acclaimed the "Michaelangelo of the needle," remained a
fixture on Chatham Square for over sixty years. He specialized in tattooing circus freaks. Barnum's pioneering display of Captain Constentius
revealed an enduring public interest in full-body tattoos, and from then
on no circus freak show was complete without a "tattooed man" or (better still) a "tattooed woman." His most successful masterpiece was the
seventeen-year-old Betty Broadbent, who came to the Chatham Square
studio in 1926 to begin a program of full-body tattoos carried out by
Wagner and his assistant, "Sailor Joe" Van Hart. Their artistry was seen
on Betty's skin by an awed public throughout her forty-year career with
Ringling Brothers.

Competing with Wagner was the lady tattooist Mildred "Millie" Hull,
who kept a parlor at 16 Chatham Square. The sign on her wall made matters clear: "If you don't like tattooing you are in the wrong place. Don't
slam the door as you go out." Slamming doors were something tattoo-
ists didn't need when they had a needle buzzing in their hands, especially
Millie. Her specialty was women's cosmetic tattooing: tattooing in the
pencil-line eyebrows and beauty spots that were fashionable in the 1940s.

As a tattooing center, Chatham Square lasted from the 1880s up until
the late 1940s, when the business began to disperse as the old practition-
ers died out. By the time the city health department banned tattooing in

November 1961, reporters had to go over to a place on Eighth Avenue in search of indignant comments.

Tattooing flourished on Chatham Square because there it was conveniently situated to serve two different sets of clients: the sailors coming in from the waterfront and the freak shows in the dime museums that began to cluster along the Bowery in the 1880s.

The dime museums of the late 1800s were the embarrassing outgrowth of an educational movement that began with the best of intentions. Promoted by Charles Wilson Peale, who built his own museum in Philadelphia after the Revolutionary War, museums were intended to be beacons of culture and learning, bringing before the public collections of paintings, sculpture, scientific specimens, and archeological artifacts. "Natural History," Peale wrote, would "promote the national and individual happiness."

That may have been the intention, but it wasn't long before Peale's and other museums were in financial trouble from lack of public interest, and newer museum promoters saw clearly that they would have to sensationalize the exhibits to draw ticket sales.

New York's American Museum down at Broadway and Ann Street dated back to the Tammany Museum founded in 1798, but by 1841 it was in financial difficulties and was sold to P. T. Barnum. With his Bowery venture of displaying Joice Heth fresh in his mind, Barnum knew what would sell tickets to a museum. He also knew that, however sensational the displays of "humbug" might be in his establishment, it was wise to keep calling it a museum, never mind what Charles Wilson Peale might have thought. Lingering puritanical norms made many New Yorkers leery of going to such entertainments as theaters or menageries, so by calling his place a museum, it kept an educational veneer that enabled respectable people to visit it without guilt. After Barnum, every sensational display in New York, however ridiculous or outrageous, would be called a "museum."

"The good museums," Chuck Connors recalled of the many dime museums that set up along the Bowery, were "as thick as pan-handlers in a sleeping crib on a rainy night. . . . Every joint had a tattooed bloke, a bundle with white hair, [that] they used to call albino, a horse that was supposed to be a camel, or some other wild animal, and a back room where the tricks used to come off. There was always a strong arm guy at the door to choke the suckers in case of a holler, and to hand out the old gasoline."

In its classic form, the Bowery dime museum was a stationary circus sideshow, or rather a collection of sideshows, with a small theater for music and live performances. Outside the brilliantly lit doorway stood the "ballyman," also called the "outside talker," whose job was to keep up a constant stream of spiel to entice customers to come in. (These men never allowed themselves to be referred to as "barkers.") The outside talker doubled as the admissions man, admission usually being a dime, and he supplemented his income by the ancient Bowery art of shortchanging customers. It was said that some outside talkers weren't paid at all, but made their entire incomes through shortchanging.

The ballyman's spiel hinted at all sorts of marvels and wonders that could be beheld for the price of a thin dime. They knew how to read their prospective customers. To some, they would emphasize the educational aspect of what could be viewed inside, to others they would hint at sights of a more titillating nature.

Once inside the door, the customers would be in the hands of another character known as the "inside talker," or more commonly the "professor," who would guide them around the exhibits with a constant stream of commentary. The professor's spiel and expansive vocabulary was as important a part of the experience as the work of the outside talker; his explanations would help make the most banal, ordinary, or otherwise disappointing displays look like something significant indeed. Once the customers were quickly steered through the exhibits they were steered toward the theater, whose performances the professor advertised in the same expansive way, while noting that the performance, or concert, required the additional admission of a nickel: "Now you've seen our wondrous wares/Next is the big show given downstairs/You'll see a drummer most intense/The stars they'll cost you but five cents."

With such a concentration along the Bowery, the dime museums were an intensely competitive business, and each one sought to outdo the others with unusual attractions. Huber's Museum, at the top of the Bowery on 14th Street and Fourth Avenue, was considered one of the best and most respectable of the museums. For example, Huber's program for October 25, 1902, featured J. M. Moore's Minstrels, Mme. Jucca lifting a horse with her teeth, the seven-foot six-inch giantess Leah May, Del Kanon breaking handcuffs, Wohena the Indian Princess, Derkia the Magician, and in the Curio Hall, Debonair's Punch and Judy Show. The theater featured a performance of "The Champion Liar" by the Huber Stock Company, and a vaudeville show in the casino.

Huber's could always be counted on to book the unusual. It even managed to make an exhibit of a man who was famous for what he did *not* do. In the summer of 1880, the town was bemused by the record-setting forty-day fast of Dr. Henry S. Tanner, who engaged in the publicity stunt partly to promote his theory of fasting as a key to health. The fasting doctor was an overnight sensation, and Huber's put him on exhibit for an unheard-of admission of fifty cents. The exhibit lacked dynamism, somehow, and didn't last for long.

There were other beings in the house who did like to eat. Huber's menagerie included an African lion who was fed with scraps from Luchow's Restaurant next door. The lion may have been from Africa, but he soon learned to appreciate German cuisine. Story had it that one day the lion escaped from his cage, only to head straight for the kitchen door of Luchow's, where he calmly appeared before the startled chef.

One of the stranger displays at Huber's was "Abbot Parker's Picture of the Crucifixion," which opened in August 1904. It was billed the "world's twentieth-century wonder" and it played Huber's for eight solid weeks, an unusually lengthy run for an exhibit of this nature. The picture of Christ's crucifixion engraved on Abbot Parker's bare back was said to have been created when he was struck by lightning one afternoon on his farm in Morristown, New Jersey. Though lightning strikes sometimes do leave tattoo-like marks on victims' skins, Parker's version was likely an ordinary tattoo done at Charlie Wagner's studio. Still, some "medical authorities" of the day examined Parker and pronounced the picture not a tattoo. Parker wasn't the only attraction at Huber's that summer; he shared the bill with Juline the Snake Charmer, Eusabio Santos the Glass Eater, and the renowned pugilist "Emergency" Kelly.

Other museums declined in quality as one made one's way down the Bowery. A short stroll down from Huber's was the next major museum, Bunnel's. The place started out in modest circumstances at 103–105 Bowery in 1876, with Bunnel introducing the then-novel policy of reducing museum admission to five cents, but with an extra five cent charge to visit the theater. Three years later, the profits were enough for Bunnel to sell out, and the property became the home of the Windsor Palace and Owney Geoghegan's dive. Bunnel then set up in larger quarters up at 298 Bowery, and named it the Great American Museum. A bit of a country lad at heart, Bunnel celebrated the opening of the new place by hosting a grand poultry show, an odd choice even for the Bowery. He added, however, a tattooed man and a double-brained child, and the new place was a success. Later on, Bunnel installed a wax museum of particular interest to New Yorkers—the centerpiece was a depiction of Dante's Inferno, with several contemporary figures writhing in the flames, among them "Boss" Tweed, Jay Gould, Henry Ward Beecher, and Victoria Woodhull. After a few successful years, Bunnel sold the place to George Middleton, who renamed it the Globe Museum. One of the Globe Museum's performers in the spring of 1894 was the young magician Harry Houdini, sharing the bill with Emma the Ossified Girl.

Alexander's Museum at 317 Bowery created a new Bowery star when it featured Steve Brodie after he made his supposed jump off the Brooklyn Bridge. The New York Museum at 210 Bowery made a name for itself by featuring the brothers Bob and Charlie Ford, telling the story of how they shot Jesse James. Jesse James was seen along the Bowery, too, or at least pieces of him were; at one time, at least three trigger fingers of the famous outlaw were being displayed in various museums. The New York's proprietor, John Burke, had interests ranging beyond western outlaws, and he became a specialist in displaying tattooed people, for whom he frequently advertised in the papers.

Worth's Museum at 99 Bowery was a fun place for anyone interested in natural history. Worth himself had a great fascination for snakes, which he had no trouble obtaining, as there was a local menagerie supplier whose ad headed "Snakes! Snakes! Snakes!" ran regularly in the entertainment newspaper the *New York Clipper*. Worth had no problem in feeding his snakes either—he let it be known that any boy coming to the museum with a live mouse got in for free. There was no lack of rodents in the nearby tenements, and for a boy it was a doubly good deal—you not only got in for free, but you got to see the snake eat the mouse. Worth played with his snakes once too often, however, and he lost a thumb to a rattlesnake bite. With a true showman's aplomb, he pickled the severed thumb in a jar of alcohol and put that on exhibit as proof that his snakes were fearsome creatures indeed. Snakes weren't the only reptiles, so to speak, that could be seen in Worth's. George Williams the flipper-limbed "Turtle Boy" was a featured attraction there, and in 1899 Worth's hosted a special evening in which Williams was presented with a silver-mounted banjo in honor of his musical achievements.

The London Zoo and Temple of Mystery at 141 Bowery had all sorts of animals on display, conveniently procured from Louis Ruke down at 98 Chatham Street, who handled an exotic animal import trade. In one advertisement in 1875, he announced that he had "on hand at present here," among other creatures, an Indian elephant and a rhinoceros, and he was expecting delivery of a polar bear. There was always a demand for animals along the Bowery in those years; in addition to the Luchow's-lunching lion at Huber's, there was a regular lion-taming act at the Gaiety Museé at 138 Bowery.

The Grand Museum at 132 Bowery was generally considered the worst of the dime museums. Owner "Broken-Nose" Burke was noted for his bad taste, obscenity, and vulgarity, even on a street that wallowed in such. His place was especially popular with newspaper boys. Broken-Nose thrived on diseases; he specialized in fake monstrosities and lithographs illustrating the symptoms of venereal afflictions. He also had a unique wax museum, with graphic life-size figures of people suffering from horrible and exotic diseases. It was enough to give anyone hypochondria and to wonder just what that cold sore was about to turn into. Ever eager to assuage the fears of the public, Burke kept a genuine quack on hand for consultation at all times. Luckily, the quack always seemed to have an appropriate patent medicine available no matter what it was that he diagnosed, and profits from the sales of the patent medicines lined Burke's pockets.

More scientific-minded museumgoers could visit Kahn's Museum of Anatomy at 252 Bowery, which opened in 1892. Exactly what anatomy he had in mind is open to conjecture. By 1899, it had become Doctor Kahn's Museum of Science, Anatomy, and Art, located up the street at 294 Bowery. Art could mean a lot of things to different people, but the young male crowd that haunted the Bowery museums in those years read the word "art" with the hope of seeing more graphic nude female figures than those that graced the paintings in the saloons.

Healey's Museum earned the historic distinction of being personally smashed up by the anti-vice crusader Anthony Comstock, who gleefully went to work on the collection of nude plaster "medical figurines" displayed there. Aghast at this early demonstration of "Comstockery," proprietor John Healey protested that the figures had been made in Paris and cost him $2,000. They represented the legitimate medical interest of the place, he said—after all, the museum was also the home of Healey's Kickapoo Indian Medicine, which was sold there as well as by some fifty touring medicine shows across the country.

Morris and Hickman's East Side Museum insisted on bucking the trend of catering to the most salacious tastes and let it be known that they ran their place on Chatham Square strictly as a "clean house" without any lewdness. Apart from Huber's, the East Side was about the only museum on the Bowery considered fit for mixed audiences, and for some time its biggest draw was a phrenologist who read the bumps on the heads of members of the audience and was able to deduce amazing things about their lives and characters. As things turned out, the phrenologist was a questionable character himself; he was really an expert pickpocket who robbed his subjects and deduced their personal details from the contents of their pockets.

There were still other museums on the Bowery that lived out their lives without becoming either very famous or notorious. The Muller Museum at 101 Bowery was situated right next to the infamous Windsor Palace dive, and the ballyman there could do very well for himself by snagging drunks as they stumbled out of the Windsor, or out of Geoghegan's next door, and shortchanging them as they went in. The National Museum at 104 Bowery was directly across the street for anyone who managed to make it that far. And there was the A. B. Sprague Museum at 171 Bowery.

"Paul Prowler" of the *Police Gazette* left a description of a night on the Bowery as it approached its height of glory in 1879. "Starting from Chatham Square," he wrote, "it almost seems as though every other building is occupied by a saloon or a cheap beer dive, or a free-and-easy [an even more casual establishment]":

> Some room has been given over to the several theaters and the few respectable business concerns, but otherwise it is a place of cheap lodging houses, oyster saloons, dime museums, pawn-shops, cheap clothing stores, lottery shops, shooting galleries, and the like. The way to most of these places, even the lowest of the dens, is lighted by various colored devices in the form of transparencies. The museums have a frontage that is made up of gaudily-painted figures on canvas which are supposed to represent the attractions within.
>
> Let us invest a dime and peer inside one of these museums. They are nearly all the same. Giants, dwarfs, fat ladies, living skeletons, tattooed men. The midget is always "the smallest man in the world, weighs only ten pounds," and so on. There is the "expansionist" who can inflate his chest until he breaks a strap which has been bound about him; the Turtle Boy, who has nothing much in the way of legs; the Champion Egg-eater and the Dog-faced Boy, whose bark has a Celtic ring. Snake-charmers, glass and fire eaters, sword swallowers. The Transparent Man, who looks as if his wife might have no trouble seeing through him; the Human Pin-Cushion, who allows you to stick needles and pins into him; the Human Anvil, who permits large stones to be broken on his chest; and the Claw-Hammer Man, who

drives tacks with his thumb and would be a handy person to have around the house.

"Freaks," sometimes animal, but usually human, were a mainstay of the Bowery dime museums as well as of the many circus sideshows that toured the country. In recent years public opinion has turned against the display of deformed people for entertainment, but back then people were quite unabashed in their fascination. There were various reasons the "freak shows" were so popular. One was simply to witness the often horrible deformities, but there was also the fascination of seeing some people, such as the armless and legless wonders, managing to live and perform common tasks under conditions most normal people would consider unlivable. And then there were the tattooed people; apart from the artistry, for most boys (of any age), going to see the tattooed lady was really a means of beholding a nearly nude female body.

The freak shows took off in the 1870s, and as time went on the freaks came to outnumber the variety performers in many museums and sideshows. They were certainly the bigger draw, and being not as easily replaceable as were the "artists," they could command more money. The economics of their situation left many freaks philosophical about what many people would consider a degrading way of life. "What," asked one famous exhibit when asked if he had ever considered surgery to correct his condition, "I'm gonna take a meal ticket and punch it full of holes?"

The employment market for museum and sideshow exhibits was a lively one. Typical advertisements in the papers read: "Wanted: Living Curiosities, with paintings, and a good sleight of hand performer. John C. Myers, 414 Bowery." "Wanted: Curiosities for the fair. Fat Lady, Little Lady, Small Man. Address Aaron McIntyre, 36 Forsyth Street."

"Living Curiosities" that weren't displayed on the Bowery often made their way to the Bowery to have their pictures taken. Photographs were an important part of the business, not only to attach to your resume, but in postcard-sized reproductions they sold briskly, and were an important part of the exhibit's income.

The Bowery's leading theatrical photographer was Charles Eisenmann. His third-floor studio at 229 Bowery, later part of the Bowery Mission, was the mecca for living curiosities on their way up in the business. Born in Germany, Eisenmann came to New York during the Civil War, and started out in a shop on 6th Street, where he first started photographing circus freaks. In 1879, he set himself up at 229 Bowery, placing his studio on the top floor where he could best catch the daylight, while living with his wife and daughter on the floor below. His wife Dora had more than a casual part in the business, having herself listed as a photographer in the 1880 census, one of the first women to do so.

Eisenmann advertised in the *New York Clipper*, "If you want any photographs in large quantities to sell for souvenirs—Eisenmann, theatrical photo artist, 229 Bowery, is your man every time." An innovator as well as an artist, Eisenmann introduced the first gummed photographic stamps: "You can make your face go much further by using stamp photos, with name $1 per hundred," he advertised. He inaugurated a rush service in 1890, and also ran a production photo lab where negatives could be sent to be made into multiple prints.

Eisenmann was an artist, but one whose artistry went to illustrate an underside of American culture. Nearly every significant living curiosity in those years made their way to Eisenmann's studio, where he continued his work even after his success enabled him to move his home up to 190th Street. John Hanson Craig, the "heaviest man alive" at 907 pounds, somehow made it up the three flights of stairs to the studio in 1887. Distributing your photograph in one of Eisenmann's trademark pink cardboard frames was a mark of distinction. Some customers, such as the giant circus strongman Colonel Ruth Goshen, sent in negatives shot by other photographers to be run off by Eisenmann and slipped into those pink frames.

The names of some of the people in authenticated Eisenmann photos are unknown, but the names that are known virtually make up a who's who of the living curiosities of the late nineteenth century. Apart from the various fat people, and tattooed men and women, a partial list of Eisenmann's known customers includes the legless acrobat Eli Bowen,

the midgets Admiral Dot and General Willis Carver, the Sacred Hairy
Family of Burma, the Texas Giant Brothers, the hydrocephalic "Aztecs
of Ancient Mexico" Maximo and Bartola, the four-legged woman Myr-
tle Corbin, the banjo-playing Turtle Boy George Williams, the Wild Men
of Borneo, the living skeleton J. D. Avery, the Frog Boy Avery Childs,
the elastic-skin man Felix Wehrle, the lobster boy Fred Wilson, and the
Ohio Big Foot Girl Fanny Mills. Apart from the often-reproduced photo
of Jo-Jo the Russian Dog-faced Boy, Eisenmann's most famous customer
was Zip the Pinhead, whose memory lives on today as the comic strip
character "Zippy the Pinhead."

12 The Mayor of the Bowery

SOME OF THE MOST INTERESTING characters along the Bowery weren't seen in either the museums or the freak shows. Steve Brodie had his own saloon at 114 Bowery where he himself was the prime attraction. Brodie's fame dated from July 23, 1886, when he claimed to have jumped off the Brooklyn Bridge. There was good reason to doubt that he actually did the feat—his buddies were said to have dropped a weighted burlap sack from the bridge, while Brodie, who was already in the water out of sight under a pier, bobbed up a couple of seconds after the splash. Whatever the truth of the matter, Brodie dined out on this story for the rest of his life, though he never tried to do it again.

A newly made Bowery celebrity, Brodie did a stint at Alexander's Museum. He found that he liked show business, and moved on to star in a three-act play entitled *On the Bowery*. The play opened on October 22, 1894, and it featured an exact mock-up of Brodie's saloon in the second act. The play climaxed with a recreation of Brodie's jump off the Brooklyn Bridge, with him diving through a trapdoor in the stage while stagehands threw in the air handfuls of rock salt to simulate the splash. The best part of all was to hear Brodie singing "My Poil is a Bowery Goil."

Offstage, Brodie held court in his saloon, which had a back room where he could have a quiet drink with selected admirers, a billiard room on the second floor, and a huge mural over the bar depicting his famous leap. Anyone expressing doubt about the veracity of the feat would be shown the mural as proof that the event really happened. When R. E.

Odlum died after trying to duplicate Brodie's feat, it only increased Brodie's aura. So durable was Steve Brodie that long after his death tourists wandering into his saloon would be introduced to a Steve Brodie imposter quietly sitting by the bar and always ready to recount his wondrous feat. Brodie's fame even got him into the dictionary. "To do a brodie" became vaudeville slang for taking a big chance with something, though by 1915 it meant to flop or fall down. Among police reporters, "to do a brodie" meant to take a suicide leap off a bridge.

While Steve Brodie held court at his place below Grand Street, the spectre of revolution haunted the northern end of the Bowery. Kleinedeutschland had produced its share of revolutionary activity what with the Eight Hour Day parade and the various radical and socialist *vereins*, but after the turn of the century a new generation of revolutionaries arrived in the neighborhood. The feminist and anarchist Emma Goldman lived on 13th Street, in an apartment that coincidentally became the production headquarters for the film *Ragtime* in the 1970s. (In spite of this, the character of Emma Goldman was left out of the film version of E. L. Doctrow's novel.)

At 60 Cooper Square, the Irish labor leader James Connolly worked for the radical Industrial Workers of the World, and setting out to share speaking platforms throughout the city with such IWW luminaries as Big Bill Heywood and Elizabeth Gurley Flynn. Connolly often joined Flynn as they commuted to the Astor Place station from their homes in the south Bronx. James Connolly eventually returned to Ireland where he helped organize the Easter Uprising of 1916, for which he was executed by a firing squad. The year after Connolly died, the Astor place station was used by another Bronx commuter, the Communist Lev Bronstein coming down from his Bronx home on Vyse Avenue, on his way to edit his newspaper *Novy Mir* on St. Mark's place, or to play a game of chess at one of the cafes on Second Avenue. Shortly into the year 1917, Lev Bronstein returned to Russia where, as Leon Trotsky, he played a key role in the Bolshevik revolution. The feisty Elizabeth Gurley Flynn stayed home to help organize the Communist Party USA.

Other figures strolling down the Bowery in those years may have included Jack the Ripper. The flamboyant medical quack Francis J.

Tumblety had enjoyed a colorful career before he arrived on the Bowery in the early 1880s where he set up an herbalist shop on the corner of 10th Street and sold an all-natural pimple medication. An outspokenly misogynistic "doctor," Tumblety had been, among other things, an Indian herbalist, a suspect in the Lincoln assassination conspiracy, and a self-proclaimed Irish revolutionary. It was these Fenian pretensions, often advertised in the meetings he organized on East Broadway, which brought Tumblety to the attention of Scotland Yard's Special (Irish) Branch when he traveled to London in 1888. While the Special Branch kept its eye on him, the London Metropolitan Police suspected him of being the Whitechapel killer, whose murderous spree began shortly after Tumblety's arrival in London. His lodging house was only a few minutes' walk from Jack the Ripper's killing sites, and his landlady's suspicions led, two days before the last slaying credited to the Ripper, to Tumblety's arrest on four counts of acts of "gross indecency" with men. The record from this point isn't clear, but it appears that Tumblety was in custody during the slaying of Mary Jane Kelly on November 9. Held on misdemeanor charges, Tumblety was granted bail on November 16.

Tumblety jumped bail and fled the country. Despite being in jail when Mary Jane Kelly died, Tumblety was still suspected of at least three of the Ripper murders, and an English detective was detailed to follow him to New York. The detective was joined by two New York detectives keeping an occasional watch on Tumblety's lodging house at 79 East 10th Street, but as he was not yet charged with an extraditable offense, there was little they could do but keep an eye on him. The investigation was hardly a secret; if Tumblety didn't know he was being trailed as a Jack the Ripper suspect he could have read it in the newspapers.

The English detective on the case got into the habit of nipping off to a saloon a few steps away on the corner of the Bowery, and one day, while he was entertaining the barman with his tale of how he was bird-dogging Jack the Ripper, Tumblety escaped his surveillance by the simple maneuver of walking out his front door and hopping an uptown streetcar. After issuing an indignant pamphlet in which he attacked the press for its "slanders," Tumblety eventually surfaced in St. Louis, where he died in 1904.

Tumblety was never formally charged with being Jack the Ripper, but, as revealed in a recently discovered letter, his Special Branch case officer John Littlechild thought that he was a "very likely" suspect, and a number of modern researchers have come to suspect that he committed some of the Ripper murders.

If Steve Brodie was hard to believe and Dr. Tumblety hard to find, the best Bowery character of all was in Barney Flynn's Old Tree House Saloon on the corner of Pell and Bowery, where Chuck Connors made his headquarters. The place was steeped in Bowery history. It was originally the same building where Charlotte Temple lived, and where Frank Chanfrau was born, and was later converted into the Old Tree House Saloon. When the old frame building at last wore out, the saloon was relocated on the second floor of a larger, modern building, but it retained the old name. It was a popular meeting place for local racketeers, and the third floor was reputed to have a "panel room," where the preoccupied customers of prostitutes had their clothing rifled and valuables lifted by a man poking his arm into the room through a sliding panel.

Variously known as "the Mayor of the Bowery," "the Mayor of Chinatown," "the Sage of Doyers Street," or "the Bowery Philosopher," George Washington "Chuck" Connors was the ultimate Bowery character. Born in Connecticut, he had drifted to New York as a boy, where he got the nickname "Chuck" for his habit of buying chuck steaks and cooking them on a stick over a fire built in the gutter of the street. He was, and had been, all sorts of things: sailor, prizefighter, Tammany ward heeler, and streetcar driver. On one occasion, he had been shanghaied as a sailor on a voyage to London, where he was so impressed by the traditional garb of the pushcart peddlers, or costermongers, that he adopted their garb as his own. To the end of his life, Connors was known by his unique uniform: blue flannel shirt, white neckcloth, and double-breasted blue pea jacket, topped off by a bowler hat a tad too small for his large head.

He was a popular character among local reporters because, like his contemporary George Washington Plunkett of Tammany Hall, he was always around and always good for an amusing observation and a quotable quote. The publisher of the *Police Gazette* was a particular patron of his, and, for reasons that are not clear to this day, set him up for many years rent-free in a building at 6 Dover Street.

Connors's real calling in life was "King of the *Lobbygows*," as tour guides were known in Chinatown. Although not from the original Irish contingent that in those years still existed within the growing Chinese neighborhood, Connors had made himself many friends among the Chinese community, and had even gone to the length of learning some basic Cantonese, something no other white man was known to do. As a *lobbygow,* Connors had the important task of touring visiting *lo faan* through the district. The Chinese community leaders trusted him with this task because they knew that he could be relied upon to give the "barbarians" the sort of sensational sights they expected to see while safely steering them away from seeing anything that might have caused a problem. Connors would show his tourists a fake opium den, and point out random European women as drug-enslaved prostitutes; they would not see the real opium dens, brothels, or gambling halls that were often only a few feet away from the simulated sights that Connors pointed out. At the end of the tour, the satisfied *lo faan* would go home to Kansas or wherever, and nobody, Chinese or European, would have gotten into trouble. It was a sensible arrangement all around.

In his heyday in the 1890s, Connors could usually be found at the bar of the Old Tree House on almost any afternoon (or morning or evening for that matter), holding forth on whatever subject came to mind or else sharing a schooner of "Barney's Best"—an extra-large glass of beer—with his beloved "Slats" or one of his many other girlfriends. The smart thing to do, to get on his right side, would be to buy a ticket to the annual ball of the "Chuck Connors Association." Chuck Connors invented the "racket"—the ball was the annual fund-raiser for the Chuck Connors Association, and the sole stated purpose of the Chuck Connors Association was the support and upkeep of Chuck Connors. Still, it was one of the best events you could go to; as a loyal friend of the local political luminary Tim Sullivan, Connors held his event in Tammany Hall itself. You might even get to become an honorary member of the Chuck Connors Association—the roster included not only Tim Sullivan, but such distinguished visitors as the tea magnate Sir Thomas Lipton and the noted Manx novelist Hall Caine.

Carry Nation, however, was one celebrity who would not become a member of the Chuck Connors Association, even though she did attend, uninvited, the annual Tammany Hall racket on December 18, 1903. After that enchanted evening, Connors always said that he would like to erect a statue to the temperance militant on the Bowery—draped in black.

The 1903 ball of the Chuck Connors Association was well underway when the hatchet-wielding Midwesterner suddenly barged her way into Tammany Hall. In classic form, Carry Nation slapped cigarettes from people's lips, swept bottles and glasses from tables, and mounted the stage, where she began to read a purported letter from a distraught mother whose daughter had been led to ruin by attending just such promiscuous dances as was going on that evening. Connors, normally a tolerant and easygoing man, avoided directly confronting Carry, but a redhead known as "Pickles" seemed to take the sermon personally and shouted at Carry in true Bowery fashion, "you get out of here, or in a minute I'll push your nose through the back of your neck!"

Never one to let herself be upstaged, an enraged Carry yanked her trusty hatchet from her belt and began chasing Pickles around the dance floor, running into people right and left. The confusion started to dissolve into a general donnybrook when Connors, his patience at last at an end, signaled his bouncers to eject Carry and the rest of her troublesome crew. Pickles was proclaimed Queen of the Ball, and Connors resumed dancing. He had his own vigorous style of dancing, which he habitually did with a lit cigar in his mouth. "Any bundle wot takes a whirl with me knows she's been on the floor," he'd say, "for I turn 'em to a knockout."

If Chuck Connors was the mayor of the Bowery, "Big Tim" Sullivan was its boss. The Bowery was his bailiwick, and his headquarters was the Timothy D. Sullivan Association at 207 Bowery. A longtime Tammany operator, Sullivan kept close connections with Tammany Boss Richard Croker, for whom he distinguished himself by managing election repeaters, and, when necessary, election violence and intimidation. Monk Eastman, whose gang controlled the east side of the Bowery, was in Sullivan's pocket, and could be relied upon to handle that sort of thing. In addition, Eastman's gang provided ten to fifteen repeaters each election, good for up to four votes apiece. When it came to providing repeaters, Eastman's rival Paul Kelly was said to be the greatest. He was said to have managed as many as one thousand repeaters, dispatched from his saloon on Great Jones Street, where an enormous portrait of Big Tim Sullivan smiled down from over the bar.

Kelly and Eastman reported directly to Sullivan, and Big Tim ran a tight ship; even after he was elected state senator, he still came down from Albany at the beginning of November and personally oversaw the electioneering in his district. His control was nearly perfect. In the 1892 presidential election, Benjamin Harrison got a total of four votes from Big Tim's district. "Harrison got one more vote than I expected," Sullivan told Croker, "but I'll find that fellow."

But Sullivan was more famous for being the Bowery's Lord Bountiful. The big annual event at the clubhouse was the chowder party. Political "chowders" were at first little more than expanded free lunches, but Sullivan's chowders were the stuff of legend. Money was raised by sales of five-dollar tickets exacted from the local merchants and pushcart peddlers, who knew that buying a ticket was the best way to avoid a sudden city ordinance crackdown. Of course, not everyone who bought a ticket was really supposed to attend—Sullivan's example inspired Chuck Connors in the art of organizing a "racket"—but as many as six thousand would fill excursion steamers for a full day's outing at College Point, Long Island. At College Point the beer, champagne, and whiskey flowed freely, with an abundance of clams, oysters, and chowder. Under the trees every kind of gambling game went on—Chuck Connors would bring his Chinese friends, who would set up a daylong game of *fan-tan*. Sullivan preferred card games to the roulette-like *fan-tan*. He kept a suite of rooms in the Occidental Hotel on the onetime site of the Bulls Head Tavern on the corner of Bowery and Bleecker Street, and up there, legend has it, Sullivan and his cronies kept a poker game going nonstop for over five years straight.

The financial surplus generated by the chowder ticket sales made for some equally grand acts of charity dispensed from the clubhouse at

207 Bowery. The annual Christmas dinner was the main event, and it was a serious meal, too. It reached its greatest heights as Sullivan's career drew to a close, feeding some five thousand homeless men at the 1909 dinner, with vouchers given out to everyone for a free handout of shoes a month later.

Although famous as a consummate corruptionist, Tim Sullivan was responsible for one major piece of reform legislation, the 1911 Sullivan Act, which bans the carrying of any kind of unlicensed weapon by private citizens in New York. It was said, however, that Sullivan's motives were less than reformist, since the act would enable the police to put away any street gangsters not loyal to Sullivan's machine. The sting of the new law was soon felt on the streets of New York—some prominent gangsters had their coat pockets sewn shut to prevent the police from planting revolvers on them, while they had their girlfriends carry a gun hidden in their hairdos.

Sullivan left his mark on the Bowery in other ways as well. The new Williamsburg Bridge was opened in 1903 without any serious thought having been given to its approaches on the Manhattan side. The bridge lined up with Delancey Street, which ran to the Bowery, where it would have abruptly dumped the traffic in the middle of a block. To prevent the flow of traffic getting jammed up under the El pillars of the Bowery, the city carved out a new street to extend west of the Bowery from the end of Delancey Street to disperse the traffic. Sullivan saw to it that the new street was named Kenmare in honor of his birthplace in Ireland, and at the junction of Kenmare and the Bowery he put up a modest monument (since destroyed) to commemorate the fact.

But monuments, charity, and chowders could not shelter Sullivan from the forces of reform as they gathered strength after the turn of the century. By the autumn of 1909, Big Tim was being hemmed in by charges of corruption from all quarters, and he chose the evening of Halloween to rent out Miner's Theater and explain himself to the public.

"The trouble with reformers," he told a packed house, "is that they don't know our traditions down here." He was indeed a millionaire, he told them, but he had become one through the profits of his theatrical management agency. He did in fact own many of the theaters along the old Rialto on 14th Street, and he said he was able to save the profits by leading an abstentious life. That last part was true enough; though he may have been the only such person on the Bowery, Big Tim didn't drink or smoke. Charges that he had a financial interest in local prostitution were countered by a flat denial that he had any knowledge of the business.

From there, in the best tradition of Bowery melodrama, Big Tim played to the galleries, telling of his poverty-stricken upbringing and harping on the theme of the local immigrant boy who made good, but who had always remained the local boy at heart: "I've never professed to be more than the average man. I don't want you to think I'm very good, for I've done a lot of wrong things. I'm just an average man. . . . There isn't much to it to be a leader. It's just plenty of work, keep your temper or throw it away, be on the level, and don't put on any airs, because God and the people hate a chesty man."

Dementia saved Sullivan from prosecution. Declared legally insane, he died in August 1913, hit by a train while wandering near his brother's country home in the Bronx. His funeral was held at the Bowery clubhouse, and when the coffin was carried over to the nearby Old St. Patrick's Cathedral, over seventy-five thousand people lined the Bowery to mourn his passing. Paddy Sullivan tried to keep things going in the style of Big Tim, opening his own clubhouse at 259 Bowery in 1913, but the magic was gone. They just didn't make Tammany operators like Big Tim any more.

13 Nickel Kickers

THROUGHOUT ITS CRAZY DAYS BETWEEN the Civil War and World War I, the Bowery remained an entertainment center. Middle-class people went to the Broadway theaters or to the Rialto, and the upper classes to the Academy of Music on 14th Street or the new Metropolitan Opera House on 39th, but for the poor man the Bowery was still the place to find affordable entertainment.

The dime museums represented the lowest form of entertainment on the Bowery. Next were the concert saloons where, if the singers were not the celebrities who performed at the Academy of Music, they might just be up-and-coming stars in their own right. When the entertainment impresario Mike Saulter converted the old Chinese Opera House at 12 Pell Street into a dance hall in 1904, one of his first performers was a singing waiter named Izzy Balin. After a brief, Izzy, renamed Irving Berlin, would in a few years build himself into a song-writing giant.

A career as a child singer, or "nickel kicker," was the first step on the ladder of Bowery stardom. A freelance child singer sang on the barroom floor, earning the odd coins tossed at his feet by tipsy or sentimental patrons. These coins he would deftly kick into a well-guarded pile by the piano while he continued singing. A young kid named Isidore Itzkowitz from Eldridge Street started his career on the Bowery as just such a nickel kicker in the early 1900s, before going on to become Eddie Cantor, star of the Ziegfeld Follies and later the silver screen.

Jimmy Durante started out as a child piano player working various dives on the Bowery and around Chinatown. Durante's career eventually took him to Broadway and the best nightclubs in the West 40s, and from there to movies, records, and even television. But he was never ashamed of his Bowery origins, and years later he would fondly remember those times in his autobiography:

> What a street it was! . . . Lined on both sides with saloons, music halls, night clubs, exhibitions of freaks, cootch dancers, Japanese Ping Pong stands, a thousand and one different kinds of catch-penny and shakedown places. It had the Coney Island smell ten times as strong as Surf Avenue. It was so noisy with the yelling of barkers, the harmony of singing waiters, the blare of bands, and the shouting of drunken men and women you couldn't hear yourself think.

A step above the concert saloons and the dime museums was the still-thriving theatrical district along the Bowery. The Old Volks Garten at 45 Bowery had been converted into the New Stadt Theater in 1864, and was shortly joined by the New Volks Garden at 293 Bowery, The London Theater at 235 Bowery, and in 1880 by the National Theater, later called the Oriental, offering a mix of comedy, melodrama, and vaudeville.

An infrastructure of support businesses grew up around the Bowery to support the theaters. R. B. Kent's Theatrical Hosiery at 202 Bowery blossomed into a major business once the rise of burlesque increased the demand for stockings and tights. There was also Gardner's at 344 Bowery, and the leading business, Bloom's Theatrical Supply at 338–340 Bowery. Actors and dancers were shod at N. Nestrock, Theatrical Boot and Shoemaker at 270, later 272, Bowery. Van Derlip & Taylor sold theatrical costumes at 96 Bowery before it joined the rising "Tenderloin" by moving up to Broadway and 26th Street in 1875. Calcium lights could be had around the corner from the Bowery at Hamar and Connor on 3 Bleecker Street, or a bit further down at the New York Calcium Light Company at 414 Bleecker. Before electricity became widely available, calcium light was in great demand in the theater industry, as it shed a brighter light than could be obtained by gaslight, and the "limelight" became a byword for the theatrical life.

One of the greatest of the Bowery Theaters in those days was Harry Miner's Theater at 165–167 Bowery. Ex-cop Harry C. Miner started up the place on the crest of the burlesque craze in 1878, and eventually expanded to gain himself a chain of theaters and a seat in Congress. Miner's developed the classic two-part format nostalgically associated with the gaslight age, in which specialty acts were followed by a short melodrama or a burlesque (more often the burlesque as time went on). By 1883, Miner acquired his second theater, Miner's People's Theater at 199–201 Bowery.

Miner's was a safe and orderly place—he had security guards patrolling the upper tiers armed with a club or rattan cane, which they didn't hesitate to use in keeping order. The amateur nights there were legendary, and sometimes gave rise to real talent. Eddie Cantor started there when he was done with nickel kicking on barroom floors. So did George M. Cohan, who soon left to become a Broadway star and composer of the song "I'm a Yankee Doodle Dandy." Though he would go on to write "Give My Regards to Broadway," Cohan never gave his regards to the Bowery. But for lesser talents, there was the hook. Often thought of as a cartoon cliché, the stage manager at Miner's really did use a long-handled shepherd's crook to coax the untalented from the stage after they had worn out their welcome with the audience.

Burlesque, however, made Miner's, and breathed new life into a fading Bowery theatrical scene when it exploded into prominence just after the Civil War. Burlesque had its origins in the mainstream theater, but it developed on the Bowery into the sort of entertainment later generations would associate with the terms "burlesque" or "girlie show."

The precursor to burlesque, as well as the ancestor of the American musical, was the legendary production, *The Black Crook*, which opened at Niblo's Garden Theater on September 12, 1866. The producers (or rather improvisers) of *The Black Crook* hadn't set out to make theatrical history. The Academy of Music on 14th Street had just burned down, and a newly out-of-work ballet troupe was making the rounds in search of an engagement. The ballet dancers, along with their props, were blended in to bolster a rather weak melodrama, and the result was a spectacle that went through numerous revivals, revisions, and outright piracies, but whose main feature was invariably a lot of dancing women in tights. In the hoop-skirted 1860s, that in itself was a sensation, and enough to ensure a packed house.

The sensation drew a predictable response. An editorial in the *New York Herald* condemned the show, but that only amounted to additional free advertising, and tickets sold like mad. In November 1866, the Reverend Charles Smyth rented out the Great Hall of Cooper Union to denounce *The Black Crook* as an immoral display, much as Madame Hutin's ballet at the Bowery Theater was denounced back in 1827. But even as he spoke, producers and concert saloon owners down the Bowery from Cooper Union were busily preparing to cash in on the craze by producing leggy epics of their own.

In 1868, the actress and producer Lydia Thompson arrived in New York from England with her troupe of "British Blondes," and after a successful run on Broadway, they went on tour to introduce burlesque to the rest of the country. Thompson's troupe wore tights, too, but her conception of burlesque was more than displays of un-bustled hips and dancing legs. The British Blondes performed comic pieces, and often lampooned the male-female relations of the day with barbed and liberated humor.

But burlesque as Lydia Thompson knew it was not to last. As burlesque was picked up along the Bowery, the subtle wit and understated feminism of Thompson's productions wouldn't go over in the local saloon culture, and the emphasis quickly shifted to the display of female figures with no attempt at plot or wit beyond the most bumptious low comedy. And low comedy meant that the women acted in stereotypical and sexually subservient roles. By the 1890s, Lydia Thompson complained that burlesque had become something so completely different from what she had pioneered in 1868 that it was unrecognizable. With some disgust, she wrote a poem about what burlesque had turned into:

And way down in front by the footlights' glow,
The bald-headed men sat in the front row.

They had big glasses to see all the sights,
Including the blondes, who danced in silk tights.

The bald-headed men Thompson saw were the beginning of the traditional mainstay of burlesque houses for generations—the squad of "regulars" who showed up nearly every day, and who took in the show with ritualistic devotion, becoming upset at the slightest misstep or deviation from the routine. The rise of pornographic movies eventually killed off the burlesque houses, but one of the last burlesque houses in New York would continue on the Bowery before folding at last in the mid-1990s.

Vaudeville developed on the Bowery largely in reaction against an increasingly sleazy burlesque. Tony Pastor, seeking more of a family trade at his newly purchased Opera House at 201 Bowery, presented a cleaned-up version of *The Black Crook*, entitled *The White Crook*, in June 1867. *The White Crook* would, in its way, be nearly as important to theatrical history as *The Black Crook*, as it helped settle Tony Pastor on a course away from the lowering common denominators of the Bowery. As the 1870s dawned he began to shift the emphasis of his place away from drinking and toward entertainment. He sought to build a more middle-class audience by enticing women into his theater, using such devices as matinees, free Ladies' Nights, and door prizes. The door prizes were things of practical value to local housewives on tight budgets: dress patterns, or sacks of coal or flour. The Opera House at 201 Bowery became a different place from its neighbors. Pastor restricted drinking to the intermissions, and placed an outright ban on performances of vulgar songs and obscene skits. He would soon move off the Bowery altogether, setting up next door to Tammany Hall on the 14th Street Rialto.

The format for vaudeville—a cycle of short skits, magic tricks, and musical pieces—owed a lot to the concert saloons, and included a lot of coarse humor. "Refined vaudeville," as it came to be known, cut out the raunchy stuff, and offered instead "nice, refined, pleasing theatrical entertainment," as B. F. Keith proudly advertised. Keith's theaters and their cleaner brand of stage show became known as the "Sunday School Circuit" among performers, but the coarser forms of vaudeville continued merrily on in the Bowery theaters, and by the 1880s had begun to replace melodramas as the keystone of the local business.

"Cheap variety," one critic complained in 1899, "is now about the only staple of the American Bowery theater. Time was, and not so very far back, when the spectacular melodrama, lurid, coarse-grained, and silly at times, but always essentially sound in its ethical teachings, was popular. But it appears to have had its day. Now it is the 'smart' thing that goes."

The Bowery was becoming more and more a place to start out on, and then to quickly leave without a glance backwards. Comedians Joe Weber and Lew Fields started out making the rounds of the Bowery dime museums in 1884, and soon graduated to Miner's Theater doing a German dialect skit called a "Dutch Knockabout." Curiously, such performances on the Bowery did not prompt an ethnic riot from Kleinedeutschland, but then the Germans had their own theatrical district down on the lower end of the Bowery where they could go and hear performances in real German. Weber and Fields went on performing their German dialect act up until 1896, when their success enabled them to buy the old Imperial Music Hall at Broadway and 29th Street. They renamed it the Weber & Fields Music Hall and left the Bowery for good.

A number of noted magicians began their careers on the Bowery. As noted, Harry Kellar risked the wrath of Short Change Charlie in McGurk's by beating him at his own game. Another famous magician ended his career on the Bowery. Chaubert the Fire King made a name for himself in Europe and in America with an act in which he entered a blazing hot oven carrying a raw steak and then emerged unharmed with the steak fully cooked. A number of imitators sprang up with fireproof acts of their own, but none could exactly duplicate Chaubert's performance. Chaubert then made another career for himself with an act in which he seemed to swallow all sorts of poisons and corrosive substances without harm. When he grew too old for that sort of thing, he made yet another career change for his retirement—appropriately enough, he opened up a drugstore on Grand Street, around the corner from the Bowery, in 1833. For many years The Fire King's Drugstore was a neighborhood fixture where Chaubert sold his own cures for cholera and tuberculosis before he himself died of TB in 1859.

The riddle of Chaubert the Fire King intrigued many later magicians, including Harry Houdini, who tried without success to break the secret of his oven act. Whereas Chaubert ended his career on the Bowery, Houdini began his there. The young Eric Weiss developed a fascination for magic after reading the memoirs of the French magician Jean Robert-Houdin, and in the 1890s he quit his job as a necktie cutter on lower Broadway to embark on a career of magic. There was only one place other than the sidewalk where a greenhorn magician could get a start, so Eric, renamed Harry Houdini, headed for the Bowery with his older brother Theo in tow.

Together Harry and Theo worked the concert halls and dime museums along the Bowery, including the Globe at 298 Bowery. It was during their Bowery period that they developed the famous Metamorphosis act, in which one of the brothers would instantly change places with the other, despite the fact that the latter had been shackled and locked in a trunk. This act was so difficult and seemingly impossible that it remained almost unique to the brothers Weiss; only recently has the act been revived and performed by such teams as the Pendragons.

For Harry and Theo, Metamorphosis was the ticket to get them out of the Bowery and on to the next rung up the ladder: Coney Island. On the Coney Island, Harry met and married Bea Rahner, who took over as his partner in the Metamorphosis act. The years after Coney Island were frequently rocky ones for Harry Houdini, but they led upward until he had become an international sensation, and like many other people he never looked back at the Bowery. In his later years, Houdini would frequently reminisce about his early days, but he usually started his autobiographical tales with Coney Island, not the Bowery.

Little-remembered today is yet another great magician who worked the Bowery at about the same time that Harry Houdini did. Max Malini, "The Last of the Montebanks," was an odd parallel to Houdini. He was born within a few months of Harry Houdini, and like Harry Houdini he came from the Jewish community in Austria-Hungary. While Houdini was born Eric Weiss in Budapest, Max Malini was born Max Katz in Ostrov in Poland.

A not yet white-haired Buffalo Bill Cody had his 1870 theatrical premier on the Bowery. *Library of Congress*

The arrival of the Third Avenue elevated train in 1878, shown here chugging past the Bowery Savings Bank on the extreme left, redefined the character of the Bowery. *Library of Congress*

In the heyday of Tammany Hall, Big Tim Sullivan was the undisputed political boss of the Bowery. *Library of Congress*

"Repeaters" who voted the right way would be rewarded by Big Tim Sullivan—in this case, with vouchers for new shoes. *Library of Congress*

Upscale New Yorkers would head to the Bowery for an evening of "slumming," here satirized in a burlesque production. *Library of Congress*

Whether or not he actually jumped off the Brooklyn Bridge, Steve Brodie was a popular character who held court in his Bowery saloon. *Library of Congress*

The sharp bend of Doyers Street in Chinatown was the scene of multiple assassinations by tong "hatchet men," earning it the nickname of "the Bloody Angle." *Library of Congress*

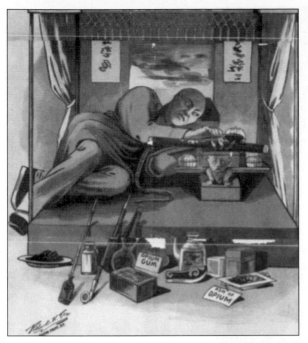

In the 1890s, opium smoking added new words to the language, and drew the attention of reformers and a young reporter named Stephen Crane. *Library of Congress*

No dime museum was complete without a tattooed lady, and Chatham Square became a center for tattooing for both sailors and "human curiosities." *Library of Congress*

Eddie Cantor began his career as "nickel kicker," joining Irving Berlin, Jimmy Durante, Harry Houdini, and many others who rose to stardom after a Bowery beginning. *Library of Congress*

By 1910, the Bowery was in deep decline, and had become a locale for charities and rescue missions serving an increasingly transient population. *Library of Congress*

Opened without fanfare in 1910, the Manhattan Bridge, with its ornate "Court of Honor" in the foreground, brought interborough traffic to the Bowery. *Library of Congress*

An icon of the Depression, breadlines were a common sight on the Bowery a generation earlier. *Library of Congress*

The Depression brought the Bowery to its nadir as the "Boulevard of the Forgotten," where it would remain until the 1980s. *Library of Congress*

Surviving a disastrous fire in 1978, the church of Old St. Mark's In-the-Bouwerie endures as a link to the Bowery's past, and flourishes today as a center of progressive culture. *Library of Congress*

Malini embarked on his Bowery career a few years before Houdini arrived there. He was apprenticed at the age of twelve to one Professor Seiden who worked the dime museums with various magical acts. The career of Malini's mentor had its ups and downs, and Malini often found himself busking on the sidewalks alongside Seiden when Seiden found himself "between engagements." So uncertain was Seiden's work that he had his handbills printed up with blank spaces provided where he could write in by hand the exact time and place of his next performance, a task presumably left to his young apprentice.

But Max Malini grew up and developed his own career after leaving the Bowery. Unlike the ambitious and driven Houdini, Malini had a laid-back style of career management. Whereas Houdini worked the vaudeville stage, Malini preferred to avoid vaudeville engagements and specialized in small, private performances before wealthy patrons, sometimes royal or even presidential patrons, such as President Theodore Roosevelt. When Malini appeared at the White House, Roosevelt recalled seeing him busking on the Bowery sidewalk when Roosevelt prowled the place as New York police commissioner.

In this respect, Malini harked back to the days of eighteenth-century court magicians rather than toward the age of the mass media star as Houdini did. This earned him the name of "last of the montebanks," as Malini specialized in small-scale parlor magic, mainly sleight-of-hand tricks. Relying on skill rather than stagecraft, he made things disappear and reappear in the most unlikely places, as when he would make a marked dollar bill disappear and then be found inside an uncut lemon. Or, in what would be an apt comment on legislative genius even today, making a brick suddenly appear inside a congressman's hat. He quietly flourished for many years under the slogan, "You'll wonder when I'm coming, and you'll wonder more when I'm gone!"

As the Bowery of dime museums, nickel kickers, and burlesque dancers reached its height, an entirely new entertainment medium appeared: motion pictures. Often accused of the crime of having killed vaudeville, the movies actually started out as a novelty item in vaudeville programs. Soon after the invention of the motion picture in the 1880s, short films showing the arrival of a train in a station or the crowds promenading the Boardwalk in Atlantic City would be screened on the vaudeville stage between feature acts.

The popularity of moving pictures made them an item in the penny arcades once the mutoscope and the kinetoscope were invented. Both these devices were coin-operated machines that showed a short moving picture using a flip-card device, and were viewed through goggles. The mutoscope and kinetoscope took their places in the arcades and theater lobbies alongside the slot machines, perfume machines, and fortune-telling machines.

With these "penny vaudeville" machines proving so popular, the next step for Bowery arcade and museum operators was to curtain off a space in the back of the hall and set up a projector that would show longer features for a five-cent admission. By 1905, storefront five-cent theaters, or "nickelodeons," were springing up along the Bowery, aided by a quirk in the local licensing laws. A nickelodeon operator needed only a "common show" license, which could be had for just twenty-five dollars, far cheaper than the licenses needed to operate a theater or a concert hall, and there were fewer requirements, such as theater fire codes, to be met. By 1910, apart from the arcades, there were eight full-time moving picture shows set up along the Bowery, mostly in the lower-rent district toward Chatham Square where the old German theaters were starting to go out of business.

"Movies" on the Bowery had a ready audience at hand, mainly local women who were otherwise excluded or frozen out of the saloons or the increasingly raunchy concert halls. Movies were cheap and free of the male-dominated atmosphere that reigned elsewhere along the Bowery. The popularity of the movies among women wasn't dampened even by the rumor that sprang up about a prowler that supposedly haunted the darkened Bowery movie places. While the audience was enrapt by the film, the prowler supposedly pricked women with a drugged needle and spirited them away into white slavery, presumably in Chinatown on the other side of Chatham Square. This tale, eerily similar to a famous rumor that rocked Orleans, France, in the early 1960s, gained such wide currency that the civic watchdog Committee of Fourteen took time out to investigate it, but could find no basis for this story.

In spite of such stories, the women kept coming to the Bowery movies. Even though the "nickel dumps" were not as highly regarded as regular theaters, they were convenient for busy women to take time out from their working or household tasks, and were considered places that were acceptable for women to go to alone. Even the strictest traditional households in neighboring Little Italy would permit their girls to go to the movies unchaperoned.

As New York's first motion picture center, the Bowery was an early exhibition place for foreign films, especially those from France. The American movie industry was slow to get started, and for many years the rooster of France's Pathé studios dominated the market. As long as the films were still silent, international distribution was a snap, with only a few title cards needing to be changed to bridge the language gap. Nor had foreign films yet acquired the deadly reputation of being "intellectual." Quite the opposite; the industry journal *Views and Film Index* noted in 1907 that "thousands of dwellers along the Bowery are learning to roar at French buffoonery, and the Gendarme is growing as familiar to them as the copper on the beat."

Still, not all films were made for the family trade, and the privacy afforded by the mutoscope permitted some pioneering peep shows. Between 1896 and 1902, the American Mutoscope and Biograph Company produced mainstream films alongside such arcade classics as *Poor Girls—It Was a Hot Night and the Mosquitoes were Thick.* Customers at certain arcades might treat themselves to such inspirational numbers as *A Busy Day at the Corset Models,* or *The Boarding House Bathroom.* Pajamas were a hot-button item in those days—*Pajama Girl, Pajama Statue Girl,* and *A Dance in Pajamas* drew a lot of nickels down the slot. Another enduring item of those early years, *The Trapeze Disrobing Act* is still mentioned today as a pioneer work of trick photography. Such mutoscope wonders could still be found in old amusement parks well into the 1970s.

History would of course continue to repeat itself along the Bowery, and it wouldn't be long before the voice of censorious morality would be heard once again. The popularity of the nickelodeons prompted calls to enforce the Sunday "blue laws" by compelling all such amusement places to close on Sundays. Various moralistic crackdowns, such as that by the National Board of Review in 1909, spurred the movement of the movies away from the Bowery storefront theaters and into venues more acceptable to middle-class audiences, in much the same way that vaudeville moved out of the Bowery concert saloons and into large theaters. The trend was confirmed after 1909 when the Unique Theater was built on 14th Street. With 1,200 seats and lush decorations, it was the first purpose-built movie theater (and not, as some claim, the Regent Theater on 116th Street, which was built in 1913).

Scarcely ten years after movies arrived on the Bowery, they were being shown throughout the city to audiences reluctant to venture to the Bowery. As the new wave in popular entertainment, movies might have extended the Bowery's career as an amusement destination; instead, their failure to establish themselves there only marked the beginnings of the Bowery's decline.

14 I'll Never Go There Anymore

THE BOWERY'S DOOM WAS SEALED on the evening of November 9, 1891, at the Madison Square Theater when Harry Conor stepped onto the stage and sang for the first time the song "The Bowery." It was part of the premiere of *A Trip to Chinatown* written by the Boston newspaperman Charles P. Hoyt, who wrote the words to the song that musical director Percy Gaunt set to music. "The Bowery" was intended to be an incidental song in a play that actually was supposed to be describing a trip to San Francisco's Chinatown. But the song was an instant hit by itself, and its popularity led people to believe that the play was about the New York Chinatown. Ever happy to please the public, Hoyt made a few changes in the script and the scene was shifted from San Francisco to New York.

Thanks to a Bostonian, the Bowery thus acquired its own national anthem, so to speak, and before long the song was being sung everywhere. The only problem was that the words of the song and its catchy chorus made it the worst possible advertisement for the Bowery. Reflecting the attitude many New Yorkers had toward the Bowery, the song described the misadventures of an out-of-towner on the Bowery:

Oh, the night that I struck New York
I went out for a quiet walk.
Folks who are on to the city say,
Better by far that I took Broadway.
But I was out to enjoy the sights,

There was the Bowery, ablaze with lights—
I had one of the Devil's own nights!
I'll never go there any more.

Chorus:
The Bowery! The Bowery!
They say such things and they do strange things
On the Bowery! The Bowery!
I'll never go there any more!

I went into a concert hall.
I didn't have a good time at all.
Just the minute that I sat down,
Girls started singing "new coon in town."
I got up mad and spoke out free,
"Somebody put that man out," said she.
A man called a bouncer attended to me—
I'll never go there any more!

I struck a place they called a dive,
I was in luck to get out alive.
When the policeman heard my woes,
Saw my black eyes and battered nose,
"You've been held up," said the copper, "fly!"
"No, Sir, but I've been knocked down," said I.
Then he laughed, though I couldn't see why—
I'll never go there any more!

The song was taken up along the street and in the saloons, and in vain did many point out that singing such a refrain as "I'll never go there any more" was unlikely to encourage business. The song illustrated the reputation the Bowery had acquired; it was a place that existed outside the bounds of civilized society, an anarchic realm where society's laws did not rule, and where society's representative, the policeman, didn't function in his job.

Those who preferred to avoid the increasingly infamous Bowery could find other Bowerys elsewhere. By this time, Coney Island had developed as a colony of the Bowery, and much of Coney Island's endangered tawdry charm is a direct outgrowth of its being spawned by the Bowery.

Before the great amusement parks rose at the Brooklyn seashore, there was "the Bowery," a lane of amusement concessions laid out by George Tilyou in the 1890s. Tilyou, a leading entrepreneur of cheap amusements for the growing working-class market, took his inspiration straight from the original Bowery. "Life is strenuous on the Bowery," a guidebook to Coney Island warned the visitor in 1904, "It is no place for the weak-hearted or the languid." Indeed, the Bowery on Coney Island was a remarkably accurate recreation of the Bowery on Manhattan, full of freak shows, dime museums, dance halls, variety houses, and single-viewer kinetoscope movies, plus penny slot machines, shooting galleries, and amusement arcades. The freak show/dime museum became a Coney Island tradition, outlasting all sorts of clean-up campaigns and surviving on Coney Island long after they had died out on the original Bowery, and may still be seen there today.

There was also "the Bowery of the West Side" on Eighth Avenue between 14th and 23nd Streets, which flourished for several years after 1905. In addition to the sideshows that survived on Coney Island, both Coney Island and the West Side Bowery offered the last tattoo parlors in New York City until they were outlawed in 1961, long after the New York tattooing industry had left its Chatham Square birthplace.

There was even a Bowery Beach on Long Island's Bowery Bay beneath the runways of present-day La Guardia Airport, but it was named for a different Bowery, a Dutch Bouwerie that was set up in the 1660s to support the poor of New Amsterdam. Whatever the origin of its name, Bowery Beach had been a popular destination for East Side excursion boats in the 1890s.

As the Bowery's infamy grew, it became a nickname for locations considered gritty or disreputable. There is to this day a "Bowery District" along Michigan Street in far-off Duluth, Minnesota, and "The Bowery" was the unofficial name for the temporary village of mostly Italian laborers and stonemasons working on Westchester's Kensico Dam in 1915.

But society hadn't entirely written off the Bowery, and the rising tide of corruption and cynicism along the Bowery and in the rest of the city provoked an organized backlash even while the chorus of "The Bowery" echoed along that street.

The Fassett Committee was organized in 1890, a year before "The Bowery" premiered. Under the leadership of State Senator J. Sloat Fassett, the committee took the first steps in investigating police corruption in New York, the corruption that allowed places such as the Bowery to flourish. The Fassett Committee was a prelude to a great wave of urban reform efforts known as the "Progressive Era." If anyone thought Fassett was a passing thing, they were wrong.

A far more serious wave of reform began on Valentine's Day 1892 when the Reverend Charles H. Parkhurst stepped to the pulpit of the Madison Square Presbyterian Church to deliver a blistering sermon on urban corruption. Performances of *A Trip to Chinatown* and its song "The Bowery" were still going on in the nearby Madison Square Theater, but the reverend had more serious matters on his mind that day. A vigorous proponent of the religious-oriented reform movement known as the "social gospel," Parkhurst pulled no punches that day in attacking the police department and city officials for corruption.

Despite Parkhurst's standing as head of the Society for the Prevention of Crime, he was widely criticized for going too far in his indictment, and for besmirching the name of the city, exaggerating the scale of vice to be found there. His veracity called into question, Parkhurst set out on his own fact-finding tour. Accompanied by a private detective hired to by a fellow member of the society to protect the reverend, a disguised Parkhurst undertook a Dante-esque journey into the lowest pits of vice and degradation. He found plenty of material.

Parkhurst started off easy, visiting a Bowery "tight house," so called because all the waitresses wore tights. Parkhurst asked one of the girls why she ran around wearing nothing but tights. "In case of fire," he was blandly told, "There are no fire escapes on the house and it won't take me long to dress." Puzzled perhaps by that explanation, Parkhurst dropped in on a Forsyth Street building that proved to be a brothel. The madam there presented to the gentlemen five young women of about equal age, explaining that they were all nevertheless her own daughters, and that they included two sets of twins. Having little or no experience of such places, Parkhurst wondered why the girls were so scantily clad, and the madam explained with a straight face that the high overhead costs of the place left little money for a clothing allowance.

After this and other forays, Parkhurst was able to present to a grand jury no less than 284 notarized affidavits attesting to police protection of brothels, gambling halls, opium dens, etc. all over the city. Parkhurst's activities drew the attention of the Republican-dominated New York State Legislature, which was interested in finding ways of driving a wedge into the control of New York City by the Democratic Tammany Hall machine and its flamboyant "Boss" Richard J. Croker.

Reverend Parkhurst was not the only explorer of the decaying Bowery in those years. Another was a young freelance reporter named Stephen Crane. In 1892, twenty-one-year-old Crane began making forays into the East Side slums while living in his brother Edmund's house in Paterson, New Jersey. He was gathering material for (and possibly had even begun writing) his "Bowery novel," *Maggie, A Girl of the Streets.* But commuting to the story wasn't good enough for Crane, and in October 1892 he moved into a rooming house on Avenue A to get closer to his sources and finish *Maggie.* It was difficult for Crane to make ends meet, and he sometimes got deeper into the story's background than he may have planned. His brother Edmund later recalled when a shabby-looking Crane would show up at his Beekman Street office to borrow a nickel. But Crane's in-depth research paid off— *Maggie,* published under a pseudonym, drew favorable comment for its unflinchingly realistic portrayal of life in the slum neighborhoods along the Bowery.

Crane had used a pen name for fear of being charged with obscenity or of pandering to prostitution, but times had changed. The Progressive Era was dawning, and the success of *Maggie* showed that the reading public was ready to take a hard look at urban realities without the veils of sentiment that had obscured earlier reform efforts.

In the spring of 1894, Crane got an assignment from the Bacheller and Johnson syndicate to report on the "bum lodging houses" on the lower Bowery. Going his *Maggie* research one better, Crane and his friend W. W. Carroll set out from their lodgings in the old Art Students' League building in early March disguised as tramps and set off down the Bowery. Carroll recalled how they got a meal from a famous Bowery personage: "The saloon men were good to us, especially at Steve Brodie's. We saw Steve himself, acting as his own bouncer, handling 'repeaters' in his daily bread and soup line." Outside Brodie's, the two picked up a native guide when a real tramp, "a big raw-boned Howard Pyle type of pirate," saw through their disguises and offered to steer them around for a while.

Crane and Carroll, and their piratical friend, made the rounds of the Bowery. "In Chatham Square," Crane wrote, "there were aimless men strewn in front of saloons and lodging houses, standing sadly, patiently, reminding one vaguely of the attitudes of chickens in a storm."

The Third Avenue El prompted Crane to new heights of descriptive writing: "Overhead elevated trains with a shrill grinding of the wheels stopped at the station [Chatham Square], which, upon its leg-like pillars seemed to resemble some monstrous kind of crab squatting over the street. The quick fat puffings of the engine could be heard."

From Chatham Square Crane and Carroll spent a night in a verminous flophouse, from which they emerged the next morning and went looking for a Bowery breakfast. "No mystery about our hash" said the sign at one basement restaurant, and on the strength of that pledge they went in. In the 1890s, hash on the Bowery was already being called "mystery," and for good reason. There, Crane found a classic Bowery hash house. "There was a long counter, dimly lighted from hidden sources. Two or three men in soiled white aprons rushed here and there."

The youth [Crane] bought a bowl of coffee for two cents and a roll for one cent. . . . The bowls were webbed with brown seams, and the tin spoons wore an air of having emerged from the first pyramid. Upon them were black, moss-like encrustations of age, and they were bent and scarred from the attacks of long forgotten teeth. But over their repast the wanderers waxed warm and mellow.

Crane's article "An Experiment in Misery" was published in the April 22, 1894, edition of the *New York Press*. He followed this up with another Bowery piece in October 1894, "The Men in the Storm," describing Crane's experiences on the Bowery in the blizzard of February 1891. Crane was exhilarated with his adventures and his journalistic success, and went to his parents' home in Port Jervis that summer perhaps a little bit full of himself. He arrived home with a black eye and told everyone how he had gotten it "in a grand fight on the Bowery." His sister remembered him shocking relatives by interrupting the dinner conversation to ask if anyone had ever seen "a Chinaman murdered on Mott Street."

While Stephen Crane prowled the Bowery, the Lexow Committee began its investigations. Under the chairmanship of a junior senator from Rockland County, Clarence Lexow, the committee sat from March 9 to December 29, 1894, deposing 678 witnesses and accumulating over ten thousand pages of sworn testimony. The testimony painted a depressing picture of life along the Bowery and the rest of the city as well. Prostitution was virtually a licensed activity, with the inmates of each brothel being counted and classified, and an assessment of the place's moneymaking potential being made by representatives of the local precinct captain. A monthly assessment of $25 to $50 was collected from each such house, with a special fee of $500 collected for its opening, as well as another special assessment customarily made to welcome a new precinct captain. In all, the Lexow Committee estimated that the police department was hauling in something like $7 million annually—an impressive figure, considering that the department's annual operating budget was only some $5 million.

Apart from contributions collected from saloons that enabled the police to overlook such inconveniences as Sunday closing laws, a wide range of illegal and semi-legal businesses were also part of the system. "Policy shops," dealing in the gambling game that was the forerunner of the "numbers," paid $15 per month. A poolroom could be hit up for as much as $300 per month. Abortinists, bootleggers, and stolen-goods dealers also paid regular fees to avoid official interest in their activities.

The committee even collected testimony that some policemen were taking part in street scams. One example was the "green goods" scam that was especially popular along the Bowery, where it took over from the similar "ring trick" and "dropped purse" scams. A con artist would lure a sucker into purchasing what purported to be a box of greenbacks. The greenbacks were not counterfeit, he was assured, but were an "unauthorized printing" by the Treasury Department that the seller was anxious to get out of his possession before the treasury agents caught up with him. The mark would be shown a box filled with real treasury notes and a rendezvous would be set up to close the deal. After handing over enough cash to buy the "unauthorized" bills at a 10-to-1 discount (the minimum was usually $300 for $3,000), he would be handed a carefully wrapped box, and the seller would disappear. When he came in off the street to unwrap his treasure trove, the mark would discover he had been handed a box weighted down with blank paper. If he were dumb enough to complain to a policeman, he would be warned to get out of town for partaking in an illegal transaction. The policeman usually knew the local swindler, and would collect one half the take for deflecting official inquiry.

The Lexow Committee's widely publicized activities created the kind of trouble that wouldn't go away, as public demands rose for "cleaning up" New York. The direct result of the Lexow Committee was the appointment of Theodore Roosevelt as New York police commissioner, and that spelled problems for the Bowery saloons. Closely identified with the reform element in New York politics, Roosevelt had failed to be elected mayor, and instead had spent the previous six years on the Civil Service Commission. The new mayor, William L. Strong, knew the energetic Roosevelt could be relied upon to shake things up in the police department.

On May 6, 1895, Roosevelt took over as president of the Board of Police Commissioners at the headquarters at 303 Mulberry Street. Across the street, the police beat reporters made their own headquarters, and among them was the young Norwegian named Jacob Riis. Riis already displayed the deep interest in social conditions that in a few years would result in his lanmark book, *How the Other Half Lives.* There were few people alive who knew the slums and back alleys of New York better than Jacob Riis (not even the Reverend Parkhurst), and Riis soon got in well with Roosevelt as a sort of unofficial advisor. On Friday, June 7, 1895, Riis took Roosevelt on an all-night patrol around Manhattan, including the Bowery. Roosevelt had the pleasure of surprising a number of officers sleeping or goofing off on the beat, and ended up with a surprise inspection of the Eldridge Street station house.

Having undoubtedly already heard of the pair's exploits earlier that night, the Eldridge Street station house was in good order when Roosevelt swept in shortly before dawn. But on the following Monday, June 10, Roosevelt revealed the results of his researches in announcing the crackdown policies of his administration. And heading the list was the strict enforcement of the Sunday saloon closing law.

The product of upstate sentiment, the Sunday closing law hadn't been taken very seriously in New York, and was not regarded at all along the Bowery. But now, directed by Roosevelt, the police started coming around and forcing the saloons to close. Consternation was widespread along the Bowery, and several places had to send out for locksmiths and padlocks. They hadn't been closed for even an hour since the day they opened, and their front doors no longer had working locks or even locks at all. Demonstrations marched and petitions flew, and some thirsty inhabitants of Kleinedeutschland were even spotted heading across the Brooklyn Bridge with empty beer "growlers," seeking refills in the neighboring city where Roosevelt's authority didn't run.

The public outcry over the enforcement of the Sunday closing laws forced the state legislature to consider revising the law, but rising prohibitionist and anti-saloon opinion meant that they couldn't simply repeal the Sunday saloon law. Instead, they compromised, resulting in one of the most abused and creatively evaded enactments of the waning years of the Bowery's heyday: the Raines Law.

Officially titled the Raines Liquor Tax Bill, the new law took effect on May 23, 1896. The Raines Law sought to placate competing public demands by permitting saloons to sell liquor on Sundays—if they were part of a hotel, and the liquor was served as part of a meal. Otherwise, a saloon would have to be closed all day Sunday right up to 5:00 a.m. Monday morning, and would also have to close on weekdays between 1:00 a.m. and 5:00 a.m.

As Sunday was traditionally the day on which a saloon made its profit (the Monday-through-Saturday trade paid for the rent and overhead), interest in the precise provisions of the law was intense to say the least. The solons of the state legislature were no fools, and made it clear what they defined as a hotel for purposes of the law: a hotel had to have at least ten rooms of eighty square feet each above the basement level, each enclosed with a full partition, and each furnished with a bed, and opening onto a hallway, and with an eight-square-foot window opening onto the street or an air shaft. The establishment also needed to have a dining area entirely separate from the bar with at least three hundred square feet and twenty tables, and a kitchen capable of preparing meals.

It was a boom time for carpenters along the Bowery as the saloons raced to convert themselves into Raines Law hotels. Those that needed to relocated into three-story buildings whose upper floors could be made to meet the requirements of the law, and the upper floors were quickly partitioned off with sheets of plywood into something resembling rooms. There was a brisk trade in secondhand bed frames, and when the supply of these gave out, beds were knocked together from two-by-fours. The law didn't say anything about mattresses, sheets, or blankets. One Raines Law "hotel" posted a sign in the saloon: "Sleeping in this hotel positively prohibited."

The food provisions of the law came in for some discussion, as the provision about selling meals might mean that the free lunch didn't count as a meal, and might even in itself be illegal under the new law. The City Corporation Counsel studied the matter, and at last weighed in with an opinion that the Raines Law meant the banning of the free lunch.

It was the sad end of a venerable Bowery institution, however diminished it may have become in recent years. A *New York Times* reporter described the "consternation" among the "weary willies" along the Bowery, who set out to load up on the last of the free lunches in the hours before the law took effect: "The frowsy gentry alighted in a body on the pickled herring, the potato salad and liver pudding, and devoured it in a jiffy. It was as though a horde of locusts had swarmed through the Bowery in search of wild honey."

To meet the requirements of the law, some places began selling sandwiches for a penny (with the purchase of a five-cent beer). There was also talk in some places of selling meals at regular rates and giving the beer away for free, but that idea wasn't acted upon. Like the mattress-less bed frames, the food served in most Raines Law hotels was strictly for show. The law only specified that the liquor be served as part of a meal—it didn't say that the meal had to be eaten, or even that it had to be edible. The brick sandwich became a Bowery classic—a common building brick placed between two slices of stale bread satisfied the letter of the law as long as it was placed on the table when the drinks were served. Other places would concoct dishes made of mainly inedible ingredients such as sawdust that would be served intact to the next drinker. Woe betide the occasional rube who in his ignorance actually bit into one of these "meals."

It was only a matter of time before proprietors found new and profitable uses for the unused interior spaces that the law stuck them with. The result was a large number of "houses of accommodation." A euphemism for a lodging house that catered to prostitution, such places served as convenient berths for streetwalkers or their pimps. The demand was increased as Progressive Era reforms made it more difficult to operate a regular brothel. John McGurk owned one of the more lucrative Raines Law hotels; the floors above his Suicide Hall at 295 Bowery were divided into cubicles, and were rented out by street pimps as places to lodge their streetwalkers.

The effect of the Raines Law was to bring prostitution to the Bowery in a big way; whereas the street previously had almost no brothels before the Raines Law, afterwards it was chock-full of "houses of accommodation." The situation was investigated by a body of concerned citizens known as the Committee of Fifteen. Looking into "flagrant offenses against public morality and common decency" in the fall of 1900, they had to admit that the Raines Law had only worsened the "social evil," increasing the number and range of streetwalkers in New York by ensuring that a convenient supply of trysting rooms were distributed all around town.

With accommodation rooms located right upstairs, the saloons themselves were now, thanks to the Raines Law, places where prostitutes would solicit business. "Persons who would hesitate to enter a brothel," they wrote in their report, "or notorious rendezvous are easily 'victimized' in the Raines Law hotel with summer garden or roof garden or other facilities for public entertainment. The uncompromising moralist will probably say that it is a matter of small importance what befalls such moral imbeciles. He might, however, change his opinion if he knew how many of them there are."

There was one more way around the law. If you didn't want to open up a "hotel" you could organize a "club." The Corporation Counsel determined that "clubs" were exempt from the requirements of the Raines Law. No doubt the Corporation Counsel had such places as the posh Union League Club in mind, but the effect along the Bowery was somewhat different. Various "clubs" sprang up around the Bowery, usually located in tenement basements on side streets. Sometimes, having evaded the Raines Law, they decided to go all the way and dispense with licenses altogether, keeping their activities behind locked doors and requiring passwords to admit the initiated. The *New York Times* on May 11, 1896, recorded the first use of the term "speakeasy" to describe such a place over on Avenue A.

In 1899, the Mazet Committee followed hard on the heels of the Fassett and Lexow Committees. The revelations of the Mazet Committee came as something of a surprise to those who thought things were improving, but the fight against police corruption had stalled. Theodore Roosevelt had long departed the scene, and corruption was quickly returning to its pre-1895 levels. Roosevelt had succeeded in shaking things up, introducing some reforms, and removing some bad actors from the police department, but bureaucratic inertia and a divided chain of command (Roosevelt was only one of four police commissioners who shared equal power) severely limited his ability to accomplish major change. At loggerheads with his fellow commissioners and, increasingly, with Mayor Strong, in 1897 Roosevelt resigned as commissioner to become secretary of the navy under President William McKinley.

Among other things, the Mazet Committee revealed the system of payoffs involved in running a Bowery saloon. One Simon Buttner testified that "I started a business on the Bowery between Houston and Bleecker Streets in 1890 . . . . A certain politician . . . told me I have got to see the police if I wanted to do business on the Bowery." Buttner soon learned what was expected of him. He was to pay one hundred dollars a month to Captain James K. Price, plus one-third to one-half of the proceeds of any "tricks turned" (meaning robberies) taking place in his saloon. As robberies were reported to the precinct house, Price would come around the next day to collect his share, whether or not Buttner had had a hand in them at all. Price also demanded twenty-five to fifty cents each for settling complaints made to the police about the noise coming from Buttner's establishment.

Apart from tales of police corruption, and the testimony it got from a rare survivor of McGurk's Suicide Hall, the Mazet Committee shone a light on the activities of the Bowery's gay scene, especially around Paresis Hall. These revelations in particular prompted much official denial. Tammany Mayor Robert A. Van Wyck was called to the stand to testify to what he knew of the matter, only to insist that he knew nothing of male prostitution in New York. "They didn't indulge in that when I was a boy," he told the committee.

If it was unknown to the mayor, it was obvious to a lot of other people. The area around the Washington Statue was known as the "slave market" for the unemployed actors who gathered there to offer themselves for short gigs or walk-on parts, but some of the strollers in the park pursued another kind of business. James Gibbons Huneker later recalled his friend Stephen Crane's encounter with a male child prostitute one evening in the spring of 1894 in Union Square: "A kid came up and begged from us . . . . I saw he was really soliciting. Crane was damned innocent about everything but women and didn't see what the boy's game was. We got to the Everett House and we could see the kid was painted. He was very handsome—looked like a Rossetti angel—big violet eyes—probably full of belladonna—Crane was disgusted. Thought he'd vomit." The kind-hearted Crane wound up borrowing fifty dollars to have the child treated for venereal disease, and interviewed him over supper, thinking to write a novel about a boy prostitute.

If legislative investigations and citizen watchdog committees didn't seem to know what to do about the social problems besetting New York, others knew how to take a more direct approach. On the 28th of August 1901, Carry A. Nation blew into town.

Carry had made a name for herself out in Kansas and other places as a violent opponent of drinking and saloon culture in general. Armed with short carpenter's hatchets, Carry and her associates would boldly enter saloons and proceed to smash up everything they could find within arm's reach. Carry's fame preceded her to New York, and there had been sporadic incidents of violence by Carry wannabes. The attacks had been far-flung: Edward O'Brien's Bar on Third Avenue had its front window smashed, and McMahon's Bar on East 138th and Jacob Wehle's on Hudson Street were also visited by hatchet-wielding prohibitionists. But so far none of them had the nerve to take on the Bowery.

Nor did Carry, at first. She arrived to a mixed reception, with local prohibitionist organizations issuing only lukewarm statements in her support, while sending no representatives to greet her arrival. Many bars hung out signs saying, "all nations welcome but Carry," while the elegant Hoffman House hired security guards to keep her from wrecking its famous "Nymphs and Satyrs" painting. Other bars openly invited her to come, trusting that the free publicity would bring in additional business that would compensate for whatever they lost to her hatchet. Still others concocted blindingly strong "Carry Nation" cocktails.

Police Commissioner Michael C. Murphy, advised Carry to go home, telling her in no uncertain terms that, "if you violate the law here I'll have you locked up." For the most part, a subdued Carry confined herself to symbolic exploits, such as smashing two water-filled beer bottles an obliging barman set out for her at Mulberry and Houston, after which she marched up to Tammany Hall to demand that they hold Sunday school classes there. Her temper eventually did get the better of her, and she chased a waitress down Sixth Avenue after the girl told Carry to go to hell for criticizing her low-cut bodice. Carry finally got herself arrested on Coney Island for smashing a cigar case with her satchel. It was only on a later visit to the city that December when she summoned the courage to invade Chuck Connors's Tammany Hall racket and confront the redoubtable Pickles.

Carry Nation or no, the Bowery had been fading all through the 1890s, and by the turn of the century it was generally understood that its sparkle was gone for good. Part of the problem was that street gang violence was rising to new heights. The Dead Rabbits and the Bowery B'hoys were long gone, but they were quaint and old-fashioned compared with their successors.

By the 1900s, the Bowery was again the dividing line between two major contending gangs, the Five Pointers and the Monk Eastmans. With his battered face and cauliflowered ears, Monk Eastman was everyone's image of a street thug. He was also one of the most effective street gang leaders the Bowery would ever see. He began his career as a bouncer at the New Irving Dance Hall, where he made a reputation for his skill with a club and brass knuckles. He made a point, however, of never hitting women with a club or knucks—the chivalrous Eastman only hit them with bare fists, "enough to put a shanty on her glimmer," as he would put it.

By 1900, Eastman had gathered a personal following, and set out to establish himself as a major gang leader. He claimed the area east of the Bowery as his turf, and began contending with rival gangster Paul Kelly of the Five Pointers for a piece of Pell Street. He was smart enough to first line up political protection, offering his services to Big Tim Sullivan as a provider of election "repeaters" and strong-arm squads.

The violence between the Monk Eastmans and the Five Pointers soon began to spin out of control, thanks partly to the availability of snubnosed pocket revolvers, something previous gangsters never had. Eastman himself was nearly killed in 1901 when he was ambushed on the Bowery near Chatham Square. Taking two revolver bullets in the gut, he held

the wound closed with his fingers and made his own way to the hospital. The gang war culminated in August 1903 with a grand shoot-out in
which nearly one hundred gangsters blazed away beneath the pillars of the
Second Avenue El at Rivington and Allen Streets. A peace was patched
together soon afterwards, but Eastman was drawing too much attention,
making him a liability to his political patrons, and his downfall would
soon follow.

Another noted gang leader of this period was a hunchbacked Ulsterman named Humpty Jackson. Jackson was an intellectual sort of gangster who had taught himself to read Latin and Greek, and was usually
to be seen with a volume of the classics in his coat pocket. Living in the
shadow of the Monk Eastmans, the Jacksons carried on their business in
the time-honored way, through robberies, shakedowns, and contract beat-
ings. Jackson himself may have been something of an egghead, but he was
not a man to be trifled with. He was an irascible sort with a hair-trigger
temper who would draw and shoot at the slightest provocation. He always
carried a three-gun arsenal—besides a revolver in his coat pocket, he had
a special holster to carry one under his hump, and another fitted into the
crown of his derby hat. The erudite Jackson also had a feel for historic
Bowery terrain; he held most of his gang meetings in the isolated stub of
the old St. Mark's In-the-Bouwerie Churchyard that was long ago severed from the church by Second Avenue. Now surrounded by tenements,
the remnant graveyard was both a convenient and a fitting place for the
reflective leader to hold his gang meetings.

The old neighborhoods lining the Bowery were also changing, and
new ethnic groups no longer supported the sort of saloon culture that had
made the Bowery what it was. Part of Kleinedeutschland died on June 15,
1904, when the excursion steamer *General Slocum* caught fire. Most of the
1,031 people who died were women and children on an excursion from
St. Mark's Lutheran Church on 6th Street. In the years that followed the
mass grief from the *General Slocum* disaster, Kleinedeutschland emptied
out as broken families migrated to other neighborhoods in the city. As
the Germans left, the *vereins* and *lokales* closed up. Meanwhile, arriving
Italians were establishing Little Italy on the west side of the Bowery. The

residents there had little use for Bowery saloons, gravitating instead to restaurants and wine cellars along Thompson and Sullivan Streets.

The old-time players were also leaving the Bowery. The notorious John McGurk closed up the Suicide Hall and headed out to retirement in California. Billy McGlory closed his infamous Armory Hall, and late in 1899 opened up a new place at 313–315 West 59th Street, handy to the burgeoning new theater district of "the Great White Way." But like John McGurk, he found he could not elude his reputation. The powerful Paulist Fathers at the nearby church of St. Paul the Apostle led the community opposition to his establishment, and McGlory found himself under continuous police harassment. It was completely unlike the compliant atmosphere he had once known on the Bowery. When someone abruptly shut off his gaslight supply in his place just before a grand ball was to begin, McGlory conceded the game to the Paulist Fathers, rented the building for nondenominational religious meetings, and opened a new place in Morrisania in the Bronx.

Street gangsters, too, were leaving the Bowery in search of better pastures. Monk Eastman was far off his home turf when he met his Waterloo. In the small hours of the morning of February 2, 1904, Eastman and an associate went uptown to carry out a blackjacking at the request of one of his clients. At Sixth Avenue and 42nd Street, they stopped to rob a drunk. The drunk, however, was the son of a wealthy family who had hired a Pinkerton detective to shadow him. The detective opened fire on Eastman, who fled down 42nd Street only to collide with a policeman at the corner of Broadway. Arrested with his weapon in his hand, Eastman expected his patron Big Tim Sullivan to pull the usual strings and get him out of his jam. But the battle of Rivington Street a few months before had made Eastman a serious liability to Sullivan, who left him to take the fall. Monk Eastman soon found himself on his way to Sing Sing for a ten-year stretch. A penny-ante impulse crime produced a rather sordid end for the man who had once counted himself the virtual king of the Bowery.

With Monk Eastman and Humpty Jackson removed from the scene, gang activity along the Bowery revolved around the rivalry between the gang of "Big Jack" Zelig and the gangs of Chick Tricker and Jack

Sirocco. This rivalry brewed up into a full-scale gang war in December 1911 when Tricker and Sirocco failed to come to Zelig's aid in beating a rap involving the robbery of a brothel. Recriminations led to an exchange of death threats and an attempted assassination of Zelig at one of his social functions at the Stuyvesant Casino, opposite Old St. Mark's on Second Avenue.

In return, Zelig mounted raids on Tricker's and Sirocco's dives, including a spectacular shoot-up of a bar on the Bloody Angle of Doyers Street. Although nobody was killed in this raid, Zelig was arrested the next day, only to be boldly shot down on the sidewalk in front of the Tombs, from which he had just emerged after making bail. Zelig was critically wounded, shot behind the ear, but several of his men mounted their own revenge. The result was the first drive-by shooting. Eight Zelig men piled into two taxicabs and blasted away as they drove past Tricker's saloon, the Fleabag, at 241 Bowery. Submachine guns, the weapon of choice in later gangster classics, hadn't been invented yet, so they made do as best they could with revolvers. The results were more spectacular than lethal—though only one man inside was wounded, every piece of glass in the place was shattered into smithereens.

Even the dead were leaving the Bowery. The old Bowery Common cemetery down by Houston Street had been home to several denominational cemeteries, but after the city banned new burials in lower Manhattan, most of these denominational cemeteries were relocated outside Manhattan, freeing up room to build such things as McGurk's Suicide Hall. By the end of the century only the Quaker burial ground remained. The notoriety of the next-door Suicide Hall no doubt had a hand in convincing the Society of Friends that the time had come to relocate their burials to more restful surroundings. A careful inventory of the burials was made in 1904, and after that the graves were moved to other Friends cemeteries in Brooklyn and Long Island.

An era was ending along the Bowery, and it seemed that things were just going from bad to worse. On June 18, 1909, the body of the missing nineteen-year-old Elsie Siegel was found stuffed in a trunk hidden above an Eighth Avenue Chinese restaurant. Elsie had been living on Doyers

Street while working as a Christian missionary to the Chinese community. Suspicion immediately fixed on the Chinese community, and the murder (which was never solved) became a focusing point for growing anti-Chinese attitudes in the city. There was already a clean-up campaign being carried out in Chinatown, following a scandalous report that there were no less than 195 white women married to Chinese males, a violation of the racial norms of the day. That campaign now intensified, and enforcement of tenement sanitary codes was used to harass interracial couples. Far from regarding Chinatown as a colorful ethnic neighborhood, a police captain noted that he would prefer to "pile all of it on a barge and sink it in the East River."

The once merry Chuck Connors was seeing his world crumble about him, with his publisher patron losing interest in him, his political patron under reformist fire, and his beloved Chinatown under official assault. He had already written off much of the Bowery by this point, telling people that he seldom ventured above Canal Street anymore, except for his annual racket at Tammany Hall. In the midst of the Elsie Siegel scandal, one newspaper reporter spotted him making his way up the Bowery with his shoulders hunched and his eyes downcast. Connors, who normally would have spotted and buttonholed a reporter a block away, simply brushed past him. Time was drawing short for the Bowery philosopher. Chuck Connors died, alone and nearly forgotten, in a hospital on Hudson Street in 1913.

The Bowery by then was also under assault by a rising volume of vehicular traffic. The star-crossed Manhattan Bridge was finally completed in 1909, without much thought having been given to its Manhattan approaches. The bridge knifed its way inland at an odd angle and deposited its traffic just above Chatham Square at the junction of the Bowery and Canal Street, in the process demolishing the historic Bowery Theater. Neither street was well set up to accommodate a significant addition of vehicular traffic, and, anticipating Robert Moses some fifty years later, plans were put forth to carve bridge approaches clear across the island to link up with widened avenues running up the West Side. After an impassioned debate (and a timorous look at the costs), nothing was done in the end, apart from erecting a colonnaded "court of honor" to grace the Manhattan entrance of the bridge and preside over the vehicular chaos below. The Manhattan Bridge was the unloved orphan of New York's bridges, and it appropriately linked up with the Bowery, the unloved orphan of Manhattan's boulevards.

But as much as things were now changing along the Bowery, in one place the old days were literally being nailed down. A few steps east of the Bowery, McSorley's saloon at 15 East 7th Street had been opened by "Old John" McSorley back in 1854. He originally named it the Old House at Home after a pub he had known in Ireland, and, under Old John's posted injunction of "be good or be gone," it had continued on in its quiet way through the Civil War and the years that followed.

Noted for his sometimes surly disposition, Old John refused to let women in the door of his establishment, claiming that their presence spoiled the atmosphere in which a man could drink in peace. The sign in the door made it clear: "Notice. No Back Room Here for Ladies." He did make one exception to that, though. A woman known as Mother Fresh Roasted worked the street selling roasted peanuts held in her apron. Learning that she was the widow of a Spanish-American War veteran, Old John would let her in once a week to sell a few peanuts and down a mug of McSorley's ale. Perhaps the weekly peanuts relieved Old John from having to add any variety to his free lunch counter, which consisted invariably of crackers, onions, and cheese. Old John, it seemed, was a great onion enthusiast, otherwise the free lunch would have been crackers and cheese alone.

Old John liked to keep a regular trade in the place, and apart from Mother Fresh Roasted, one of his most regular customers was the aged philanthropist Peter Cooper, who in his last years liked to hang out in McSorley's back room, almost in the shadow of Cooper Union, the institution he had founded in the 1850s. After Peter Cooper died on April 4, 1883, Old John ordered that Cooper's favorite chair be draped in black each year on the anniversary of his death.

The last substantial change to take place at McSorley's was when the pub sign blew down in a gale in 1908. Needing to replace the banged-up sign, Old John decided to officially name the place what it had been unofficially called for many years: McSorley's.

Old John collected variegated memorabilia that he hung all about the walls and ceiling. When Old John died in 1910, his son Young Bill McSorley came down one Sunday morning with a hammer and nails and affixed all the decorations in place, intending to preserve the saloon exactly as it appeared on the day his dad died. And other than a few minor changes (such as allowing women in), the saloon remains that way to this day.

While Bill McSorley nailed down the past, a few blocks down the Bowery a little-known piece of old New York remained frozen in time. Built in 1835, Seabury Treadwell's townhouse still stood around the corner of the Bowery at 29 East 4th Street, a relic of the days when 4th Street and Bond Street were among New York's more fashionable addresses. Inside the house, however, Seabury's last surviving daughter, Gertrude, still lived amid furnishings that hadn't changed since the 1850s, an unseen Pompeii of antebellum New York. Gertrude would live on until 1933, and after her death her relative George Chapman purchased the still unchanged house and converted it into a museum. The Old Merchant's House remains a museum to this day, complete with a mysterious secret passageway and a resident ghost, thought by many to be Gertrude.

Meanwhile, the rest of the Bowery was fading away. "I ain't getting mournful, old pal," Chuck Connors had commented in 1905, "but when I look up the old Bowery, what do I see? . . . Bum clothes joints, a bunch of booze warehouses where they're afraid to tap a key for fear the noise'll put a cop on. And only one free and easy, and that's got crepe on the door. The Bowery? They ought to get together and call it the Weeping Willer, because it ain't got nothin' now, except the Reservation, and that's where I am. Some day, I suppose, the street cleaning department'll find out where we are and they'll come down with a bunch of them Ginney white wings, with brooms, and wipe us off the map. We're the last of the old times, and there ain't no other place for us to go."

But not everyone was brokenhearted at seeing the Bowery change. "A new day is shedding a dull light on the Bowery," local historian Edward Ringwood Hewitt wrote in 1897:

Still the gardens and saloons and the occasional pistol shot at night; still the museums and cheap amusements; more and more frequent the three golden balls, and the shops offering the cheapest clothing in the world; and the 25 cent and the 10 cent lodging houses, with all they mean of homeless men ever increasing. But from it all the zest is vanishing, and the Bowery, first the home of simple, serious, contented dignity and prosperity, then the great processional road and home of plenty; next the scene of vigorous, lusty youth in its frolic and madness, then the haunt of low-browed crime, is seeming to slumber before awakening to a new phase.

By the beginning of the 1900s, the Bowery was clearly in decay, but the last of its bright lights was a flourishing Yiddish-language theater scene, Springing from a rich and lively theatrical tradition of the Yiddish-speaking ghettos of eastern Europe, Yiddish theater arrived in America with the new wave of Jewish immigrants at the end of the 1800s. It began modestly, with immigrant troupes performing in improvised costumes in borrowed lofts.

The first regular Yiddish theater in New York was established on August 12, 1882, at the Turnhalle, just off the Bowery at 66 East 4th Street. There, the Hebrew Opera and Dramatic Company staged a five-act opera in Yiddish, *The Witch*.

In June 1886, the Jewish Operetta Company arrived from Romania. After a run at Lexington and 58th Street, their backers leased the National Theater (the old Bowery Garden at 104–106 Bowery), and in January 1887 they renamed it the Roumania Opera House. The newly named opera house failed a fire inspection, however, and had to close the following spring. The Order of David's Harp, a Jewish benevolent society, stepped in to save the Romanian troupe, and they leased John Poole's theater on 8th Street and Fourth Avenue, where they opened in August 1887. To celebrate the occasion, a parade was formed up, stepping off from Schreiber's Cafe on Canal Street and heading up the Bowery to the new theater.

Reflecting the theatrical traditions of the Bowery, the Yiddish theater in those early days kept a light touch, usually doing only light operettas, and rarely producing a full opera on a Jewish theme such as the revolt of Bar Kochba. That was about to change.

In later years, people would say the ground shook when the great Jacob Adler strolled the sidewalks of the Bowery and Grand Street, but his arrival in New York was anything but auspicious. The audience hissed him off the stage of the National Theater at his first New York appearance in *The Beggar of Odessa*, which he had successfully performed in London. Adler suffered a second failure in *Under the Protection of Sir Moses Montefiore*, but he finally scored a success when he appeared in *The Russian Soldier, or Moishele Soldat*.

By the 1890s, Jewish immigrants were making the southern and eastern stretches of Kleinedeutschland into what is now known as the Jewish Lower East Side. With the influx came a rising demand for Yiddish-language entertainment. Back in the ghettos of eastern Europe, the Yiddish theater had been a means by which people could relax, reaffirm their identity, laugh, and maybe blow off a little steam with satirical portrayals of the manners and attitudes of their enemies (or, for that matter, themselves). The richly expressive Yiddish language was especially suited to this lively theatrical tradition.

Friday and Saturday nights were the peak times for Yiddish theater. The economic demands of life in the new world made Sabbath observance problematic for many people who had little choice of when their brief leisure time fell. For many, going to the theater was a compromise—it wasn't proper Sabbath observance, true, but if you went to the Yiddish theater and saw a production on a Jewish theme, especially a religious or historical theme, then maybe it wasn't such a bad thing after all. Others, forced to work Saturdays by gentile employers, would recover their identity as best they could by going to such a production on Saturday night.

The New York Yiddish theater scene that Adler encountered in 1890 was curiously like the old days of blood-and-thunder Bowery melodramas. Contending rival actors and troupes would try to impress their audiences with exciting and animated performances. Baruch Thomashefsky recalled the rivalries of those days: "If they had thunder, I had lightning. If Kessler sang the Evening Prayer, I sang the Prayer for the Dead. If they shot arrows, I stabbed with daggers. If they killed six of the enemy, I killed all of them with one blow. If they came in on horses, I came in with three horses and a golden chariot. And believe me, next to me they looked like plain foot soldiers."

Adler wanted to move Yiddish theater in New York beyond simplistic formulaic plots and into serious drama. When Poole's Theater reopened as the Union Theater, Adler got his opportunity to do such pieces as *Samson the Great, Quo Vadis?,* and *La Juive,* pieces that won the approval of the Jewish intelligentsia, and of the audiences as well. Adler's productions were what they were waiting for—something entertaining but with a serious core. Adler's next step, working with Jacob Michailovitch Gordon, was to develop original dramatic works in Yiddish. Gordon's first play, *Siberia,* was indifferently received at its Union Theater premiers, but the ice had been broken.

In the fall of 1892, living on St. Marks Place, Adler felt confident enough to issue his own manifesto: "The Union Theater, under the sole artistic direction of Jacob P. Adler, has been reorganized with the aim of driving from the Yiddish stage all that is crude, unclean, immoral, and with the purpose of lifting the Yiddish Theater to a higher level. The Independent Yiddish Artists Company will present to the public only beautiful musical operas and dramas giving truthful and serious portrayals of life."

Gordon persisted with his efforts, and the result was the Yiddish *King Lear.* In this play, Shakespeare's Lear story was adapted into the tale of a Jewish merchant reduced to beggary by his two wicked daughters. The audience was stunned when Adler appeared on stage crying "*Shenkt a neduue der Yiddisher Kenig Lear!*" (Alms for the Yiddish King Lear!) It was acclaimed as a landmark performance. Adler's *Lear,* and his later portrayal of *The Wild Man* marked for many the coming of age of the Yiddish theater in America.

In the fall of 1899, Harry Miner gave up on the failing Miner's People's Theater at 201 Bowery. Thomaschesfky signed a lease and the place became the People's Theater, a leading venue for Yiddish drama. Four years later the Grand Theater was built at Grand and Chrystie Streets.

The Grand was the first place specifically built as a Yiddish theater, but tragedy and bad luck seemed to dog it at first. There were disputes about ownership, and ugly tensions between Jacob Adler and investor Moishe Finkel. Eventually, the matter was settled in the State Supreme Court with Jacob Adler retaining possession. The loss of the Grand Theater may have unhinged Moishe Finkel. A few months later, he came up to his estranged wife Emma as she was walking along the Bowery with another man. Finkel pulled a gun and shot the two of them before turning the gun on himself. Emma survived, but her rising theatrical career was ruined, as she was confined to a wheelchair for the rest of her life.

Meanwhile, the People's Theater hosted the legendary production of *The Merchant of Venice* in 1901. Adler played Shylock in what many people considered his greatest, and nerviest, role. The sheer audacity of the production—playing Shylock in Yiddish before a Jewish audience—drew the attention of mainstream theater critics, and the production eventually played in Proctor's 58th Street theater and the American Theater on 42nd Street. Adler's *Merchant of Venice* proved to be a truly historic production; for the first time the attention of the mainstream American theatrical world was drawn to the Yiddish theater, and they learned that what they had previously dismissed as parochial ethnic entertainment had in fact developed a considerable pool of recruitable talent. The Yiddish theater would become a seedbed of much of America's popular culture.

With new waves of immigrants arriving and seeking light entertainment, popular melodrama in Yiddish made a comeback after 1906. Adler found himself forced to produce a melodrama called *The Living Orphans* to balance the books at the Grand, but he didn't do it gladly. He brought the author onto the stage on the play's opening night. Expecting congratulations, both author and audience were shocked to instead hear Adler roar, "you and this man are ruining the theater!"

By then, the Yiddish theater was about to depart from the Bowery. Kessler's Second Avenue Theater was built in 1912, and in a short time there were no less than six new Yiddish theaters along a short stretch of

Second Avenue between 4th and 12th Streets. Ironically this new Yiddish theater district ran through Peter Stuyvesant's old bouwerie and right past his burial vault. The old governor-general who had once tried to harry the Sephardic Jews out of New Amsterdam now had Yiddish theaters flourishing on what had been his doorstep.

By the time the great Jacob Adler died in 1926, the last of the Yiddish theater had long left the Bowery where it had started. But its memory was not entirely forgotten. After funeral services for Adler were held in Kessler's Second Avenue Theater, hundreds of vehicles formed up to follow the funeral procession down the Bowery to Delancey Street before crossing the Williamsburg Bridge and on to Mount Carmel Cemetery in Brooklyn. It was perhaps as much a funeral for the old Bowery as much as it was a funeral for Jacob Adler. As the last cars swung off the Bowery, they left behind in the gathering spring twilight a street from which it seemed that the lights had departed for good.

15 Boulevard of the Forgotten

THE LAST NAIL IN THE Bowery's coffin was driven in at 12:01 on the morning of January 16, 1920. At that moment, the Eighteenth Amendment and its accompanying federal statute, the Volstead Act, took effect, banning the manufacture, sale, and transportation of alcohol in the United States.

The Bowery had survived over a hundred years of blue laws and moral cleanups. It had survived Reverend Parkhurst, Carry Nation, the Lexow Committee, the Mazet Committee, and the Raines Law. It had even survived Theodore Roosevelt. But Prohibition was something bigger—more than just another moralistic enactment concocted by upstate apple-knockers, it enjoyed a broad if shallow national consensus, and had the force of the federal government behind it. Whatever the Bowery had survived before, it would not survive Prohibition.

The new law struck a Bowery that was already on its last legs. The place had decayed rapidly following the 1911 Zelig-Tricker shoot-out, and the departure of the Yiddish theaters took away the Bowery's cultural vibrancy. New uptown movie palaces took the business away from the nickelodeons, and mainstream theater had long since decamped for the newer theatrical district along the Great White Way. The old Bowery Theater staggered on, in its last years devoted entirely to German, Yiddish, or other foreign-language productions. Since 1826 it had burned and been rebuilt four times, but in 1929 it suffered its fifth and final fire, and was torn down.

Most of the old saloon culture that had defined the Bowery had long since departed as well. The Irish neighborhoods had followed the El and moved uptown, where an echo of the old Bowery saloons would eventually establish themselves along Second and Third Avenues. The Germans had abandoned their *lokale* and dispersed even further afield, following the Third Avenue El to Yorkville in the East 80s, and later to the Bronx and Queens.

Prohibition thus struck a Bowery that already was little more than a hollow echo of its former self. It was not as if people had abruptly stopped drinking. Indeed, Prohibition made boozing chic, but by driving drinkers into speakeasies, it shifted business uptown, where high front stoops rising over doors to basement apartments provided every brownstone block with twenty or more locations custom-made for speakeasies. In many ways, it became easier to get liquor—of a sort—after Prohibition was enacted than it was before, as speakeasies sprouted up on streets that never before had even had a corner bar. New Yorkers "in the know" now were seldom more than a block or two away from a convenient source of bad liquor and a low-down place to drink it in.

While the remaining Bowery saloons closed up, one place remained in business. Young Bill McSorley, having nailed the place down the way it looked on the day his father died in 1910, saw no reason that Prohibition should make him change anything. By now, McSorley's was almost a speakeasy itself, with its business drawn from a reliable corps of "regulars." Many of these men could be depended upon to show up at a particular time of day, leaving Young Bill with a predictable flow of business that allowed him ample time in which to relax and read the newspaper. Among the regulars was a gentlemanly young journalist from North Carolina named Joseph Mitchell, who would preserve McSorley's in his own way by writing about it in his book, *McSorley's Wonderful Saloon*.

McSorley's survived because the Volstead Act had a loophole in it that permitted the sale of "near beer," or beer with an alcoholic content of .5 percent or less. It was hardly an acceptable substitute, for as the saying went, "whoever called it near beer was a poor judge of distance." Nevertheless, Young Bill would insist that near beer was all that McSorley's sold, and his demeanor didn't encourage anyone to pursue the argument. At any rate, the contented regulars sitting in their accustomed spots weren't about to offer a contradictory opinion. Strangers wandering in off the streets would get a mug of precisely that—near beer. Trusted regulars, though, would be served the real thing—Bill had hired a retired brewer named Barney Kelly, who would come down from his home in The Bronx three times a week to brew ale in McSorley's basement, using a variety of barrels and washtubs.

With the cooperation of his regulars and the benign patronage of Tammany Hall, McSorley's came through Prohibition intact, even though it was only a few blocks away from the apartment of the famous Prohibition agent Izzy Einstein over on Ridge Street. Izzy and his neighborhood pal Moe Smith closed down speakeasies from Van Cortlandt Park to Far Rockaway, but not McSorley's. About the worst thing that happened at McSorley's during the Prohibition years was that afternoon in the winter of 1924 when a woman entered disguised as a man, drank her mug of near beer, and then triumphantly swept off her cap, letting her long hair tumble down to her shoulders. Young Bill was thunderstruck at this stealthy violation of his dad's sacrosanct men-only policy. Despite such an audacious breach of tradition, the building remained standing, and so did the no-women rule, which continued in force until 1970.

While life continued in the old way at McSorley's, elsewhere the Bowery was sliding into a new incarnation as New York's skid row. The homeless problem had been growing for some time along the Bowery, even in its heyday in the 1880s and 1890s. Tradition has it that the Bowery became a place for the homeless in 1873 when the YMCA opened a branch there, but a transient population had been a fixture of the scene long before that. Cheap lodging houses and flophouses had been clustering along the stretch north of Chatham Square since about the time of the Civil War. The first missions appeared in the area about that time. By the end of the Civil War the problem had grown so acute that the City of New York rented out a building in the area to serve as its first homeless shelter in 1866, and in 1909 it built the Municipal Lodging House, or the "Muni."

The Salvation Army established itself in the area in the 1880s, first setting up shop in the building that later became the home of Arnold's Cider Mill. Within a few years, the Salvation Army—the "Sallys," or the "Starvation Army" as it was variously known—moved across the street to a larger building. The Salvation Army home—or "workingman's hotel," as it was officially termed—was hardly a place of ease and leisure. A bed and a meal cost eleven cents, or two hours of work. The guests were expected to be actively looking for employment, and were discharged from the building early in the morning. A large bell was mounted on the cornice that was rung in the evening to announce to the groups of men gathered on the sidewalk that the evening meal was on and the building was open again. As the 1890s wore on, the Salvation Army would build a total of four such hotels along the Bowery.

Between the Salvation Army, the Muni, the YMCA, and the cluster of cheap hotels and flophouses, as well as Tom Noonan's Chinatown Rescue Society, the Bowery Mission, and John Callaghan's Hadley Mission, the Bowery was already serving a large transient population by the time Prohibition turned out the saloon lights for good. But not all these transient men and women were the derelicts Stephen Crane encountered at Steve Brodie's free lunch, nor were they all the "bums" that many established citizens assumed they were.

From the 1870s on, the Bowery was a major stopping point for hobos, and a hobo subculture would exist on the Bowery into the 1960s. To many people the distinction between hobos and derelicts was a matter of splitting hairs, but the hobos themselves thought otherwise. Ben Reitman, the Chicago-based doctor, author, and acknowledged "King of the Hobos" outlined the social order succinctly in the 1920s: "The hobo works and wanders, the tramp dreams and wanders, and the bum drinks and wanders."

The word "hobo" was in fact derived from "hoe-boys," describing transient agricultural workers. The hobo was a man (or woman) who wandered about from one temporary seasonal job to the next, and enjoyed (or endured) a long winter off-season. The Bowery became a popular locale for these winter stopovers. New York City, being the terminus of several freight lines, was a place hobos headed to at the end of the season. For a hobo, it was not an entirely disagreeable place to winter in, and in the spring the wanderers would again hop the rails and depart, leaving behind the "home guard."

It was most likely the hobos who introduced the term "skid row" to the Bowery. Throughout the 1920s and 1930s the local term for the Bowery was "the Main Stem," after a common slang term for the main street of a town or village, though some old-timers still referred to the Bowery as "the Lane." The word "skid row" began in the Pacific Northwest as "skid road," the lumber camp trail down which logs were skidded to the sawmills. Skid Road became the stretch along which bunkhouses, flophouses, saloons, brothels, and gambling dens would cluster to service the lumbermen.

Exactly how many derelicts, homeless, and transients were left behind on the Bowery when the saloons closed down is anyone's guess, though the numbers certainly grew as the Great Depression followed hard on the heels of Prohibition in 1929. The numbers were difficult to estimate (and, in truth, few in authority cared) because "mission stiffs" rotated around from one mission to another, claiming conversions and drifting off again when the missionaries saw through the charade or began to put the heat on them to undergo real transformations. One indication of the extent of the homeless population is the fact that Jerry McAuley's Water Street Mission gave out a total of 79,115 meals during 1932, or over two hundred meals a day.

In the late 1930s, social worker Eugene Bertram Willard recorded his impressions of his twenty-five-year career on what he termed "this strange street . . . America's premier highway of human wreckage." The fact that his observations were printed as a serial in his hometown paper—the Everett, Massachusetts, *Gazette*—indicated the Bowery's nationwide notoriety and the fascination Americans had for tales of the social degradation found there.

Willard claimed that about twenty-five thousand were to be found every night in missions and lodging houses. Although he noted that the Bowery of 1937 was a somewhat better place than when he first found it in 1910, he still had plenty of material to work with.

Willard's picaresque tales of Bowery life fed America's fascination with the Bowery, and also helped perpetuate some enduring myths about the place. Despite his claimed twenty-five-year career as a social worker, Willard seemed willing to take many of the life stories he heard at face value. This helped launch the enduring myth that many of the Bowery's derelicts were originally men of high position in life, ruined by drink. Willard met men on the Bowery who, by their own account, were former actors, clergymen, physicians, and bankers, plus a former judge, a former mayor of a New Jersey town, and even a onetime member of the London Stock Exchange. The myth of the highborn derelict wasn't new in the 1930s, either; a generation earlier, Chuck Connors claimed to have rescued a girl of an unmentionably prominent New York family from opium addiction and white slavery on Doyers Street.

The myth continued in the 1980's urban legend of the homeless "bag lady" with thousands of dollars in a bank account (or an old sock). The fact that such cases do occasionally crop up from time to time helps keep the myth alive. It's also fed by the self-aggrandizing recollections of the downfallen themselves. By convincing themselves that they "could have been a contender," many manage to ease their disappointments in life, or at least provide a compelling story to a sympathetic listener. In this way, a former bank teller would retroactively promote himself to branch manager or even bank president; a lawyer would become a judge; a Wall Street messenger would become a member of the exchange.

One notable exception to this was Professor Edwin Peck. Professor Peck didn't like to "blow his bazooka" or seek the sympathy of strangers, and thus he managed to elude Willard's roll of the once-mighty. But he had earned a PhD from Oxford University, and had taught English literature uptown at Hunter College. He'd made a scholarly name for himself by discovering two previously unknown poems by Percy Bysshe Shelley, and had gone on to write the definitive biography of the poet. But shortly after this triumph, in 1929, what was coyly referred to as a "romantic scandal" forced his resignation from Hunter College, and the professor found himself on the street just in time for the Great Depression. He landed on the Bowery not long after that, and remained there for the rest of his life.

Distinguished by a professorial mane of long gray hair, Peck gathered a circle of men who spent hours in Mike's Bar near Broome Street discussing mathematics, physics, art, poetry, and, of course, English literature. In later years, Professor Peck wrote for and sold the *Bowery News* before his death on January 15, 1954.

Another prominent Bowery intellectual in those years was the colorful Joe Gould, better known as "Professor Seagull." The good professor had an affinity for seagulls, and claimed to be able to speak to them in their own language. Like the seagulls, he got by on a catch-as-catch-can basis. Unlike many of the anonymous men wandering the Bowery, Gould had friends in mainstream society, such as the artist Alice Neal, who painted his portrait in 1933; the poet E. E. Cummings; and Joseph Mitchell, whose book *Joe Gould's Secret* was made into a movie in 2000. Gould told Mitchell that he lived on "air, self-esteem, cigarette butts, cowboy coffee, fried egg sandwiches, and ketchup." Especially ketchup—for dinner he would eat a sandwich in a Bowery hash factory, then dump the contents of the counter ketchup bottle on the plate and proceed to eat that with a spoon. "It's the only grub I know that's free of charge," he told Mitchell. Professor Seagull had a wide-ranging and original mind, claiming, for instance, that he had uncovered a link between eating tomatoes and train wrecks. (Ketchup apparently didn't count.)

Professor Seagull's magnum opus was supposed to be a carefully guarded historical project that he kept up in his room at the Hotel Defender at 300 Bowery. Entitled *An Oral History of Our Time*, the manuscript became a Bowery legend, running by some accounts to thousands of pages, though only a very few people ever claimed to have seen it. But when the professor died, no trace of this manuscript could be found among his effects. By then many, including Mitchell, no longer believed it ever existed, but sporadic attempts to track it down continued for years.

While Joe Gould kept Joseph Mitchell tantalized with his mysterious *History*, down at the Venice Movie House, just below Chatham Square, the redoubtable Mazie P. Gordon kept house and observed the passing Bowery scene. The poet Edgar Guest, haunting the Bowery in those years, would sometimes drop by and say hello, but otherwise Mazie remained unimpressed by the grandiose life stories she heard along the street. "To hear them tell it," she told Joseph Mitchell, "all the bums on the Bowery were knocking off millions down in Wall Street when they were young, else they were senators, else they were general managers of something real big, but, poor fellows, the most of them they wasn't ever nothing but drunks."

All by herself, the short, plump, bleach-blonde Mazie P. Gordon was a one-woman Bowery institution in the 1930s and '40s. She saw to it that her Venice Movie House, with its ten-cent double feature, stayed a clean place, and she acted as her own bouncer, ejecting at least one customer every day. Her weapon was a rolled-up copy of *True Romances* secured with rubber bands. She felt the daily example was necessary to keep her customers in line. Otherwise, she sat in her ticket window, a green eyeshade on her head and a bottle of Canadian whisky handy in the cash drawer. She herself never saw the movies being played in the theater. "They make me sick," she said.

Though she suffered no fools gladly, Mazie was by no means a callous or uncaring individual. After the theater closed up, she would make her own midnight rounds up and down the Bowery. A matronly version of John D. Rockefeller, she was generous in dispensing dimes to the bums and the destitute she encountered. Missionary types would sometimes reproach her for this, saying that she was only facilitating their alcoholism by handing out dimes that way, but Mazie had no patience for their objections. She'd just tell the missionaries to go have a beer. Like Joe Gould, Mazie Gordon attained her own literary afterlife with Jami Attenberg's 2015 novel *Saint Mazie*.

The depression tidal wave of respectable men fallen into the ranks of the unemployed did not lend any respectability to those who had already been there, and as the 1930s wore on, the Bowery became a place even more exclusively for the homeless and the truly down-and-out. Although in the depths of the Depression new homeless camps rose throughout the city, such as the "Valley of Forgotten Men" in Central Park, social distinctions were maintained and strictly enforced in these "Hoovervilles." The unemployed men in such places were anxious not to be associated with those they saw as habitual bums, and would forcibly eject them from their camps, leaving them with few places to go but the Bowery.

Along the Bowery, they existed in a shadow world of their own. Prohibition or no, alcohol wasn't too difficult for them to get a hold of there. "Bowery Smoke," an impure and often toxic bootleg brew, was commonly available, offering quick and sometimes permanent oblivion for a few cents. A paint shop on Hester Street worked on the edge of the Volstead Act by offering jugs of supposedly grain alcohol—"paint thinner"—for fifty cents a gallon. Before the repeal of Prohibition made more standardized rotgut available, an unknown number would be maimed, killed, or blinded by drinking toxic wood alcohol.

For those not interested in submitting themselves to missions, the Bowery YMCA offered a nickel cafeteria, where one could eat one's fill for five cents. The Bowery missions weren't always good places to go to. Eugene Bartram Willard found many of them somewhat lacking in Christian charity, sometimes staffed by recently recovered drunks who were inclined to be harsh with their clientele, whom they saw as lacking in character.

The onset of the Depression brought about a new interest in social problems in the city, and in 1934 reformist Mayor La Guardia tried to provide a new escape hatch by which some of the down-and-out could reshape their lives in a place far removed from the streets of New York. Camp La Guardia was established in a former women's prison near the town of Chester in rural Orange County, New York. Before it was closed in the 1990s, the place had grown to accommodate as many as 1,150 residents. Another escape was up in the "Holy Mountains" of the Hudson Highlands at Graymoor Manor in Garrison, New York. There the Franciscan Friars had established a short-term residence in 1909 in a former chicken coop. Graymoor Manor, however, was difficult to get into, hosting only ninety-four residents at a time.

Adding to the sense of degradation were the "rubberneck" tour buses driving down from Times Square, giving out-of-towners a glimpse of the notorious Bowery that they could write home about. The term "rubberneck" was inspired by the sight of live poultry wagons making their way through city streets with the long-necked geese poking their heads through the slats to take in the passing scene, and lives on today in the traffic news phrase "rubbernecking delays."

Tourists had their choice of buses: Grey Lines' #8 and Times Square Sightseeing Lines' #7 and #8 all made stops on the Bowery. Streetwise New Yorkers never, of course, described themselves as rubberneckers. Instead, they went "slumming," a custom dating from the 1890s, in which they went down to the Bowery or other places to—in a term borrowed from the Civil War—"see the elephant."

But by the late 1940s it wasn't necessary to hop a rubberneck bus or venture south of Cooper Square. A safer form of Bowery slumming was available in movie theaters nationwide. Nostalgia for the gaslight Gay Nineties brought the Bowery to the silver screen in 1933 in a movie titled *The Bowery*. A fictionalized account of the Bowery in its heyday, the film starred Wallace Beery as Chuck Connors, and George Raft as Steve Brodie. Taking liberties with history, it depicted Connors and Brodie as friends and rival saloon keepers. Though filmed in Hollywood, the spirit of the old Bowery somehow found its way onto the set as friction grew between the film's two stars. The usually affable Beery grew increasingly annoyed by the extras that Raft recruited from his underworld acquaintances, and eventually a fight scene between Connors and Brodie over the love of a woman erupted into the real thing, with Beery swinging at Raft and the extras joining in on both sides in a classic Bowery brouhaha. The gaslight Bowery would be shortly followed by a more up-to-date but equally fanciful version.

The saga of the Bowery Boys followed the classic Bowery trajectory from drama to melodrama to comedy to farce. The movie series originated from a popular Broadway "social realism" drama, *Dead End*, by Sidney Kingsley. In 1937, the cast members, now collectively known as the Dead End Kids, were brought to Hollywood to make the film version of the play, with a script by Lillian Hellman. Teamed up with Humphrey Bogart, the Dead End Kids—Gabriel Dell, Huntz Hall, Billy Halop, Bernard Punsly, Bobby Jordan, and Leo Gorcey—looked and acted the part of Lower East Side slum kids, even though Gorcey was from Washington Heights, and the Dead End referred to in the play was actually the (then down-market) Sutton Place. Nevertheless, they lived up to the stereotype. They were pale, skinny, and sallow chested, and they drove the sound technicians batty with their high-pitched "dese, dem, an' dose" accents. The movie was nominated for several Oscars, but offscreen the boys seemed to remain permanently in character. After a studio rampage ended with the boys ramming a truck into a soundstage, Samuel Goldwyn sold their two-year contract to Warner Brothers.

Warner Brothers used the team to make a series of hard-boiled crime dramas: *Crime School* (with Humphrey Bogart), *Angels with Dirty Faces* (with Humphrey Bogart and Jimmy Cagney), *They Made Me A Criminal* (with Claude Rains), *Hell's Kitchen* (with Ronald Reagan), *Angels Wash Their Faces* (Ronald Reagan again), and *On Dress Parade*. Universal then picked them up, renamed the maturing Dead End Kids as "the Little Tough Guys," and made a number of poorly regarded pictures, as well as such cliff-hanger serials as *Junior G-Men* and *Sea Raiders*.

Early in 1940, they were redubbed "the East Side Kids" and made a number of movies for such studios as Four-Bell and Banner, including *Pride of the Bowery* and *Bowery Blitzkrieg* (1941). Their work had been leaning toward "B" movie comedies for some time, and Leo Gorcey developed the character of Ethelbert Aloysius "Muggs" McGinnis for such movies as *Mr. Muggs Steps Out* (1943) and *Bowery Champs* (1944) and added what became his trademark crushed fedora with the front brim squashed back. His sidekick, Huntz Hall, sported his own headgear of a baseball cap worn askew.

In 1946, the gang became the Bowery Boys and took another stab at making crime melodramas. In the public eye, though, they had established themselves as a "B" movie comedy troupe. Typecast, they were soon locked into making an average of two movies a year for Monogram. With the movies all filmed on a soundstage in Hollywood, the Bowery itself was far away in space, and, increasingly, in time as well, and the street-smart verisimilitude they had brought to Hollywood as the Dead End Kids faded into stock buffoonery. The Bowery Boys were a hit with American moviegoers, even if such real Bowery types as Mazie P. Gordon refused to set eye on their productions.

Although they were supposed to be based on the Bowery, the Bowery was hardly ever mentioned. Louie's Sweet Shop, where their far-ranging adventures usually began over banana splits, was described as being located on the nonexistent intersection of Third and Canal Street. Leo Gorcey, as Terence Aloysius "Slip" Mahoney, and Huntz Hall as Horace Debussy "Sach" Jones, were the central characters in escapades that ranged into ever more improbable situations, bringing the Bowery Boys to such places as London, Paris, and Bagdad [sic] and even prospecting for uranium out west, all the while spouting colorful malaprops and such cryptic slang as "da moolah's in da p'tollah."

Leo Gorcey dropped out in 1956 after filming *Crashing Las Vegas* wherein, according to the ads, "the Bowery Boys are busting out all over with a blonde, a bankroll, and a blue-chip brawl." Leo's departure was occasioned not so much by grief at the downfall of the Third Avenue El as by the death of his father and intractable personal problems. The Bowery Boys effectively ended there, though Huntz Hall would carry the memory through a few more films.

While the Bowery Boys created a fake Bowery in Hollywood, another man was going about documenting the real thing. An Austrian immigrant to the Lower East Side named Arthur Fellig learned his trade with the Acme News Service before going freelance in 1935. By 1940, the rumpled, cigar-chomping Weegee (as he now preferred to be known) was the very archetype of the hard-boiled news photographer, and he made the nighttime streets of New York his domain.

The only press photographer in those days permitted to have a police-band radio in his car, Weegee roamed around in his '38 Chevy, whose trunk he had fitted out into a mobile office and darkroom. His path often crossed that of the roving columnist Walter Winchell cruising in his own specially fitted "radio car." Winchell occasionally steered his way up the Bowery, gathering improbable tales of secret tunnels linking the old buildings for criminal enterprises.

Weegee, however, was only interested in what he could take pictures of, and some of his best work was done on the Bowery at Sammy's Bowery Follies saloon between 1943 and 1945. The photos he took there remain classics today, and were among those chosen for the International Center of Photography's inaugural exhibit in its new Bowery location in 2016. At Sammy's, a dwarf in a diaper personifies the new year of 1943, as he stands with one bare foot on the rail of a bar that reaches above his head and coolly notes the viewer's gaze while sipping a beer. A smiling blonde in a satin dress sits at a side table. Two hefty women dance together, one sporting a fresh black eye. Weegee also photographed the aging vaudevillians performing at Sammy's, including Norma, the house's plump star attraction.

Though his police-band radio was a valuable asset to his work, Weegee relied more on a sort of sixth sense that enabled him to steer toward the action. Indeed, Weegee's seeming predictive powers earned him his nickname, as to rival reporters he seemed to perform like a Ouija board. Although his work appeared in such upscale magazines as *Vogue*, his fame rested on his news photographs. Collected and published in 1945 as *The Naked City*, Weegee's photos depicted the hard-edged, working-class world of the tenement neighborhoods along the Bowery.

In that year of 1943, the New York of Weegee's photographs was just emerging from the poverty of the Depression, boosted by the industry and the high wages brought by World War II. For many people on the East Side, the children and grandchildren of the poverty-stricken immigrants of Jacob Riis's day, it looked like things were at last about to get better. But among the partygoers at Sammy's that New Year's Eve of 1943, few perhaps had any inkling of the rapid changes that were about to engulf the Bowery.

16 Sneaky Pete

THE BOWERY EMERGED FROM THE Depression greatly the worse for wear. But the old days remained the same at McSorley's, despite some changes of ownership. When the childless Bill McSorley felt the heavy hand of age settling on him, he sold the place in March 1936 to a retired policeman named Daniel O'Connell. Bill McSorley died on September 21, 1938, and Dan O'Connell followed him in December 1939. Dan willed the saloon to his daughter Dorothy O'Connell Kirwan, who found herself inheriting a saloon that, as a woman, she had never been allowed to enter. After some reflection on the matter, Dorothy decided to continue John McSorley's venerable no-women tradition. She allowed herself no exception to this rule, setting foot in the place only when it was closed on Sunday mornings to tally up the week's receipts.

While the old days were maintained at McSorley's, they were re-created at Sammy's Bowery Follies. Shortly after the repeal of Prohibition in 1934, Sammy Fuchs took over an old saloon space once owned by John McGurk of Suicide Hall fame. With an eye on the prowling rubberneck buses as well as on the growing nostalgia for the Gay Nineties, Fuchs recreated an authentic 1890s Bowery concert saloon—minus the psychotic bouncers, chloral hydrate, bad liquor, pickpockets, peter players, and prostitutes. The music was for real, though, and Fuchs hired retired vaudeville veterans to perform the hit songs of the gaslight era, and Sammy's became a hangout where nostalgic ex-vaudevillians sang and socialized.

Sammy's was a center for hobos as well. Interested in preserving the remnants of the old hobo culture that still persisted along the Bowery, Fuchs convened a "Bowery Chamber of Commerce" that met monthly in a back room of the saloon. Unfortunately, the complete minutes of this remarkable body seem not to have been preserved, but some records have come down to us. The meeting of August 1946 was a notable one, during which they discussed a proposal for setting up a "Bowery College" to pass on such fading hobo arts as "dinging" (begging), "stemming" (panhandling), "boiling up" (cooking a hobo meal), and "jungling up" (camping out hobo style).

The past and the future came together at that August 1946 meeting. The noted hobo author "Boxcar Betty" nominated Harry Baronian, editor of the *Bowery News,* as president, and the young Linda Folkard of Toronto, Canada, who claimed to have hitchhiked some fifteen thousand miles, was elected "Miss Hitchhiker 1946." It was a symbolic moment in hobo history, as the old-school railroad hobos such as Boxcar Betty greeted a new breed of hitchhiking wanderers.

Dave Gould, the executive secretary of the Bowery Chamber of Commerce, described the social scene as he found it along the Bowery in those years:

> Among them are scissorbills—small town characters who came to the big city and can't make the grade; ex-newspapermen and writers who permanently lost their weekends; doctors who wrote one prescription too many; brilliant eccentrics who find themselves unable to adjust to society's rules; and congenital jungle buzzards who are satisfied to live with and off their fellow misfits. Here and there are also found occasional philosophic types who are sincerely concerned with lifting the level of those who call the Bowery home.

One of those philosophic types was Harry Baronian. From the late 1940s into the 1960s, Baronian edited the *Bowery News,* a monthly newspaper that chronicled the life along the street and once a year assembled the choicest items into a *Bowery Social Register*. With a jocular style that concealed a deep concern with the denizens of the Bowery, Baronian pulled no punches in pointing out some of the less savory characters working the street. In the *Bowery Social Register* for 1960, for example, he pilloried "Queen Bee Sally—for steering live wires . . . into darkened hallways on the pretext she'll be cozy and cuddlesome with them. Her victims are lucky to be left on the floor in the hallways unconscious with their underwears on after Sally's strongarm boys go to work on them."

One would think that the pathetic derelicts shuffling along the Bowery would have little on them worth stealing, but Queen Bee Sally wasn't the only character preying on them. "Tipoff Wally" worked as point man for a gang of "jackrollers" working skid row, beating and robbing incapacitated alcoholics.

And then there was "Sneaky Pete Mary." By the 1950s, "Sneaky Pete" had replaced "Bowery Smoke" as a sidewalk swill. Selling for about forty cents a pint, it consisted of cheap muscatel, port, or sherry, heavily diluted with water and brought back up to proof with the addition of raw grain alcohol. The name came from the way its effects snuck up on its drinkers, especially those who commonly drank it on an empty or a nearly empty stomach. Sneaky Pete Mary's trade came from New York State's blue laws, which mandated the closing of bars on Sunday mornings and forbade the selling of bottled wine or liquor for the entire day. The improvident often found themselves waking up on Sunday morning dry, but far from high, and were happy to buy pints of Sneaky Pete that Mary and others vended from their coat pockets.

In publicizing Sneaky Pete Mary, Harry Baronian at least had the gallantry to print her side of the story: "All right," she told the *Bowery News*, "I'm no angel but at least I gave the lushes what they want—not colored water in pint bottles, which is what some guys sell to grab a fast buck on a Sunday, then they run like hell."

Walking the street alongside the exploiters were still those who sought to ameliorate or call society's attention to the human degradation along the Bowery. One mysterious figure, known only as "the Sky Apostle," pioneered his own city harvest program, daily gathering up the leftovers discarded by the Chinese restaurants and redistributing the food along the Bowery.

Caring souls on the Bowery sometimes came from far afield. In the autumn of 1952, a Mennonite bishop from Gap, Pennsylvania, came to New York for a meeting at the United Nations, and took time out for a visit to the Bowery Mission. He returned home to organize what became an annual food drive among his community on behalf of the Bowery Mission. Eventually, the Mennonites of Gap dedicated an entire field to growing crops for donation to the Bowery Mission, and after the harvest was in they'd dispatch a truckload of food from Gap to the Bowery.

In 1962, Elmer Bendiner examined the life along the Bowery for the *New York Times Magazine* and drew a sympathetic portrait of the men he found there:

> The Bowery man's drinking style is less formidable than that of the respectable working alcoholic. The Bowery man rarely drinks alone with the single-minded objective of a quick knockout. He is a social drinker, and not only does he pass the bottle, but he must combine with his fellows to raise the price of one.
>
> He drinks to achieve a pleasant plateau from which he can survey the world and his fellows with some equanimity. He craves an illusion of friendship without the responsibilities that friends impose. His alcoholic haze fragments the harsh light of the world and diffuses it so that edges are blurred and the world is soft.

Other social workers were driven to the brink of despair by the men they sought to minister to, finding that many of them didn't want to be salvaged or reformed, but simply left alone. "They only drink to keep on dying," noted Ammon Hennacy of *The Catholic Worker*.

Julian Raeder drew a portrait of the Bowery man in a poem published in the *Bowery Social Register*:

> As he hunches his shoulders
> Against winter's sting

He harbors a memory
Of a greener spring . . .
Draped in the robes of discontent
He wanders about the city,
An unemployed soul, lost
In a complex society.
Alone without family,
A soul who once felt free;
Heavy lies his heart
Weary is his step
Devoid of all pep;
Shorn of all confidence,
Robbed of all respect.
Alone, dejected and forlorn,
An endless question
In his mind has formed:
Was it for this
That man was born?

There were various means for those seeking to get "mokus" (drunk). Apart from the aptly named rotgut dispensed in the various bars, or Sneaky Pete, other options were further down the scale. Street drugs appeared along the Bowery in the 1950s in the form of "goofballs," or sleeping pills, that the daring or careless sometimes mixed with Sneaky Pete. That was no problem if the Sneaky Pete was one of those bottles of colored water, but mixed with real alcohol it could land the drinker in the city morgue or on the "flight deck" at Bellevue Hospital. The more desperate would make ends meet by drinking "bayzo," or bay rum aftershave lotion. A small minority risked central nerve damage with "pink lady," or canned heat squeezed through a handkerchief to separate the alcohol from the jelly, giving pink lady its more common western name of "squeeze." At the very bottom were the "rubby-dubs," men who drank rubbing alcohol and who sometimes woke up blind.

Hustling up enough money to get by was a daily concern. A dol-lar or two would make the difference between sleeping in a flophouse or "carrying the banner" (sleeping out on the street). "Plingers," or panhandlers, would "hit the stem" or "go on the stem." But pickings were slim along the Bowery, and those venturing out into other parts of the city to "bum a card" would quickly run afoul of the police, or "stew feet," who would tell them in no uncertain terms to get back to the Bowery.

More enterprising sorts would try to peddle scavenged or stolen goods "on the curb," the continuation of the old "thieves' market" that grew up on the Bowery sidewalks in the 1930s. "Sharks," or employment agents, could sign up men in the "slave markets," or informal street corner employment markets, for summer jobs in "the mountains" (i.e., Catskill resorts). Closer at hand were "hasher jobs" in one of the various Bowery restaurants, otherwise known as "slop joints," "horse markets," or "hash foundries," where the hash was always, and with good reason, known as "mystery," and fried eggs were termed "two shipwrecked." A man might get a temporary job as a short-order cook or counterman, but more often the job was "pearl diving," or dishwashing.

The "squeegee men" who drove New York motorists to distraction in the 1980s had their origin on the Bowery in the 1950s, working the traffic spilling off the Manhattan and Williamsburg Bridges, which, with no place else to go, sat waiting for the lights to turn so they could swing up the Bowery and exit lower Manhattan as quickly as possible. But the hustlers at the Bowery intersections in the '50s hadn't worked their way up to such advanced technology as squeegees. The *Bowery News* commented on this phenomenon in 1960, singling out "Grease Rag Sam" as the type of fellow who was already bringing this emerging industry into disrepute.

With food and lodging secured, one could obtain secondhand clothes in one of the "cheap johns" still clustered above Chatham Square, around which the barber colleges offered haircuts—at your own risk—for fifteen cents.

There were many terms with which the characters of the Bowery described each other. The old-time hobos still held themselves somewhat apart from the derelicts, but postwar times were rapidly catching up with them in the 1960s. The classic hobo "boxcar riders" distinguished themselves from the newer breed of "rubber-bums," or hitchhikers. "Steeple

bums" still wandered from mission to mission, preached at by the "sky
pilots." A variety of terms, none complimentary, were directed at the
minority of female derelicts along the Bowery. Apart from the "B-girls,"
or barroom prostitutes, female Bowery denizens were described as "glue-
necks," "blisters," or "hag bags," but most often simply as "bags."

While social workers labored in frustration, Colonel S. H. Bingham,
executive director of the New York City Transit Authority, had his own
proposal for bringing a ray of sunshine to the Bowery. "The Third Avenue
Elevated Line," he flatly reported to the transit authority on May 4, 1954,
"has outlived its usefulness."

The ill-starred Third Avenue El had somehow managed to outlive the
other three elevated lines in Manhattan, but an engineer's inspection had
led Colonel Bingham to what was perhaps a foregone conclusion, with the
report bluntly subtitled, "Demolition of the Third Avenue Elevated Line
South of 149th Street." The El had grown and evolved since its opening in
1878. After the line was electrified in 1902, it was extended to Bronx Park
in 1902, and in 1920 extended once again to White Plains Road, allowing trains from the Bowery to go all the way to the northern border of the
city. A third track was added for express service in 1916.

But by the 1950s, decay and deferred maintenance were taking their
toll, and like a dying tree the El had been shedding its branches for years.
The 42nd Street branch to Grand Central Terminal had ended in 1923,
and the 34th Street branch to the East River was shut down in 1930. The
stretch south of Chatham Square to South Ferry was terminated in 1950,
followed by the branch line from Chatham Square to City Hall in 1953.

What remained of the truncated El was in increasingly poor shape.
Since March 1952, the El ran only weekday rush-hour and midday service. Three months later, the Board of Transportation Maintenance Engineers reported that the life expectancy of the structure was only about
five or six years more, unless an estimated $80 million reconstruction was
carried out.

The engineers described the El as a "mongrel" structure, with sec-
tions of varying ages and types of construction. This wasn't a new revelation, either; as far back as 1924, inspecting engineers had reported that

the stresses borne by some spans were above what were currently allowed by industry standards.

But with money lacking even to clean the windows of the cars, nothing could be done other than limiting the loads as much as possible, forcing the El to rely on long-obsolete wooden-bodied cars, some dating back to 1904. Even with these efforts the weight of the cars was still too high once they were jammed full of people, so rush-hour cars were run on the center track to distribute the weight, then returned empty down the local tracks. This practice made rush-hour service uncertain and frustrating for people waiting on platforms and seeing full cars go past them on the express track. Passenger numbers abruptly declined, falling from some eight-six million in 1946 to thirty-five million in 1953, a loss of over half its passengers in only seven years.

To make things worse, the local tracks still didn't have automatic signals, a safety feature that had been standard on other lines for many years. Dogged by delays, the automatic signaling conversion project was supposed to have been completed by 1936, but automatic signals, like a lot of other things on the line, fell off the scale of priorities when the IRT went into receivership in 1932.

On May 12, 1955, the Third Avenue El south of 149th Street came to its end. "The Third Avenue El is dead at 87," proclaimed the *Daily News*. It "couldn't have picked a nicer day or a more graceful way to die." While Transport Workers Union chief Mike Quill sought a court injunction to stop the closing, the old El spent its final day carrying crowds of passengers for a last sentimental ride. With photographers on every car, the passengers waved to people lining the tenement windows and the conductors called out farewells to the familiar stations. The last train pulled out of the Chatham Square station exactly at 6:00 p.m. with veteran motorman William W. Foy at the controls. Eight hundred people filled the five-car train and stripped the cars of any souvenirs that could be detached, destination signs being an especially sought-after prize. Kids had fun pulling the whistle cord as the train moved up the express track and crowds packing the bypassed stations cheered and threw paper streamers.

"We doubt whether we ventured to ride on the dusty, dying 'L' more than three or four times in the past ten years," the *New Yorker* opined. "Perhaps in another ten years we will begin to miss it sorely. Twenty more years and a brand-new 'L,' the 'L' of recollection, will go darting among the rooftops, at a speed the old 'L' never reached, through a city fairer than any of us has ever seen."

Silence of a sort now fell again over the Bowery, but the old El seemed reluctant to disappear. For the next two months, the city dithered over bids for the El's demolition before accepting Morris E. Lipsett's offer to pay the city $330,775 for the privilege of tearing down the El. Lipsett had previously demolished the Second Avenue El, as well as the Fulton Street El in Brooklyn, and he figured that the sale of the forty thousand tons of scrap steel would fetch him a tidy profit. With an almost audible sigh of relief, the city fathers gave Lipsett the go-ahead.

Throughout 1955, demolition crews worked their way up the Bowery, turning the once innovative Third Avenue El into scrap. Though the tracks quickly disappeared from Third Avenue, the stumps of the upright girders were left standing for months along either side of the Bowery street like rows of denuded iron trees before the city got around to the troublesome task of uprooting them.

17 Operation Bowery

THE DEMOLITION OF THE THIRD Avenue El let sunshine into parts of the Bowery that had seen little of it for nearly ninety years, in the process drawing attention to a street the city had tried to forget.

The Bowery's status as New York City's skid row was an embarrassment to many, but as the 1960s dawned some social commentators were predicting the demise of skid rows in general. On the Bowery this seemed at first to be true, as its population was declining. Such social statistics are dubious at best, for they sought to tabulate a group of people who largely didn't want to be counted. Still, it was clear that the Bowery was, as usual, not what it used to be. The skid row population had declined by some ten thousand over a twenty-year period, falling to an official figure of 5,406 by 1966.

To some observers, the situation along the Bowery seemed to be getting worse. Cooper Union was spending an additional $25,000 a year on security guards to shoo derelicts away from the building. Over at Old St. Mark's In-the-Bowery, the Reverend Michael Allen carried a small bottle of ammonia with which to gently wake up the people he found sleeping in the church pews, though he stopped this when the police told him this could be dangerous for someone with a heart condition.

Once again, calls for a cleanup of the Bowery were being heard. In 1961, Mayor Wagner charged Assistant for Housing Hortense W. Gabel with the task of devising a housing program for the Bowery. Gable dutifully set out to make a personal reconnaissance of the Bowery, examining its flophouses and hotels.

As a result of Gable's efforts and other proposals, Wagner, in 1962, unveiled the ambitious "Operation Bowery" designed to rehabilitate the Bowery and adjoining areas of the Lower East Side. The Bowery's remaining population had been described as an "immovable obstacle" to rehabilitation efforts, and the plan called for a referral agency to connect with the street people and assign them to psychologists, hospitals, Alcoholics Anonymous, or vocational guidance experts to help them get on their feet again. Spokesmen for Operation Bowery described their approach as "chipping away the problem" rather than tearing it down.

Not everyone concerned with the Bowery was happy with the proposals. Milton Levenstein, director of the Lower East Side Neighborhood Association, wanted a "halfway house" added to the program with professionals on duty who could "bolster the egos" of those who had "withdrawn from society." Their egos duly bolstered, they would be rehoused in dormitories or low-income units projected to be built as part of the middle-income and commercial buildings that would replace the decaying nineteenth-century buildings lining the Bowery.

W. H. Auden, the neighborhood's poet emeritus living at 77 St. Marks Place, was aghast at all these proposals. "One sees bums around," he told the *New York Times,* "but they don't annoy us. I'm terrified. All this tearing down of old neighborhoods. Leave the Bowery as it is!"

But the Bowery, it seemed, wasn't going to be left as it was, for gentrification was already nipping at its fringes. A pioneer redevelopment targeted the Renwick Triangle in the mid-1960s. The block of town houses occupying the triangle of land on Stuyvesant Street opposite Old St. Mark's was originally built in 1859, supposedly designed by the noted architect James Renwick Jr. Converted into cheap rooming houses before the turn of the twentieth century, the Renwick houses were decayed but still intact when the Triangle became one of the first places in New York to win a designation as an historic district in 1966. At that time, an entire townhouse could be bought for as little as $10,500. Shortly after becoming an historic district, the block was bought up by developers and renovated into upmarket properties.

The Bowery had been the birthplace of vaudeville, and on September 27, 1970, vaudeville died on the Bowery. The latest plan to rehabilitate the Bowery, the Cooper Square Urban Renewal Project, called for six parcels of land lying along the Bowery between Stanton and East 5th Streets to be demolished and redeveloped into one thousand low- and middle-income apartments. One of these parcels was 267 Bowery, the home of Sammy's Bowery Follies.

Sammy Fuchs had died on April 3, 1969, but the place had carried on, sustained by a loyal clientele of nostalgic ex-vaudevillians. The last night at Sammy's was certain to be a major event. "The Bowery Follies Folds In Last Vaudevillian Fling," the *New York Times* reported, and a closing-night crowd of over seven hundred people packed the place. The last vaudevillians, many of them by now aging grandmothers, sang old gaslight era showstoppers for the enthusiastic crowd. But the greatest applause was saved for the very end of the evening, when the popular bartender, the young Jeanne Jordan, stood up on the bar to take a last graceful bow.

Though Sammy's was forced out of business, the projected redevelopment would wait for more than thirty years, leaving the building with its upper floors abandoned and bricked up, and a pizza oven dealer occupying the old saloon space. Sammy's Bowery Follies long forgotten, number 267 eventually fell to a new redevelopment initiative at the beginning of the twenty-first century.

While rehabilitation projects stalled, the Bowery scene began to shift as the 1970s dawned. One important fact was that the skid row population was no longer as confined to the Bowery as it once had been. A Supreme Court decision in 1968 ruled that the homeless could not be denied the use of public spaces such as parks, streets, and sidewalks. With this decision handed down, the Bowery's panhandlers found themselves able to seek prospects in parts of the city once denied to them. "The best thing about the Bowery was that no cop ever told you to move on," Richard Kopperdahl was told years later. "If you were a bum, it was your place.

In fact, if you were an obvious bum anywhere else in town, the cops would tell you 'get down to the Bowery where you belong.'"

For many, leaving the Bowery was less a matter of choice than of necessity. The cheap hotels and flophouses began to fade away from the Bowery in the 1970s, but nobody could say for certain just how many otherwise homeless people were still trying to live on or about the Bowery. A New York State Senate report in 1976 claimed that the Bowery homeless population was down to about five thousand, though the nearby municipal shelter was serving about eleven thousand a year.

Along the Bowery the decline was rapid. Nathaniel P. Lyons had established his chain of cheap Lyons houses around the turn of the century, and had made a fortune doing so. When he died he left twenty of these inexpensive hotels. By 1978, his estate executors had sold off or converted all but four of them.

In all, only twelve flophouses were remaining on the Bowery by 1978, and their owners were complaining that declining business and rising costs were making it difficult for them to remain in business. The price of a two-bit bed had long ago risen to $2, and now the $2 bed was becoming a thing of the past, rising by the mid-1970s to $2.25, which with taxes that came out to $2.68. The Municipal Lodging House continued to send the homeless over with room vouchers, but each of those vouchers brought the hotel management only $2.05.

A few hotels remained open: the Comet, the Fulton, the Sunshine, and the Pioneer in the old Occidental Hotel. But the Alabama Hotel was converted into artists' studios in 1975, and the Clover, the Majestic, the Uncle Sam, the Houston, and the Lincoln all closed down as well. By 1986, the Fulton was gone too, renamed the Fu Shin to keep expensive changes of the signage down to only three letters, and serving as lodging for new arrivals to an expanding Chinatown.

By 1982, weekly rates at the remaining Bowery "bug houses" or "scratch houses" went from twenty dollars to forty dollars per week for what were at best rudimentary accommodations. Once past the steep entry staircases (said to have been designed to prevent the too inebriated from getting in), the lodging houses were divided into four-foot-by-seven-foot cubicles each containing a bed, a locker and a night table. The partitions only reached partway to the ceiling, and were covered by chicken wire to foil the "lush divers." There was usually a floor set aside for the more long-term residents with a simple television room, as opposed to the plain cots that were given to the overnight visitors sent from the "Muni." In 1986 the *New York Times* estimated that there were no more than three thousand cheap beds left along the Bowery.

Even the cheapest lodgings, though, were often beyond the means of those unfortunates "on the stick" (living in the streets). While the old hobo term "carrying the banner" was still heard, living on the street was more often referred to for some unknown reason as "sleeping in Bush Thirteen." Those with a few dollars might have the opportunity to "cat in the flick," or to escape the cold or the heat and nap in a movie theater.

It was becoming more difficult to raise money in the old, time-honored ways. Photographer Michael Zettler interviewed one of the squeegee men standing on the corner of Houston Street. Once upon a time, he told Zettler, he could make four or five dollars a day doing windshields, but with air-conditioning in cars, people kept their windows rolled up all summer, and thus felt no need to tip him for his services. And just about every street-smart New Yorker rolling off the Manhattan or Williamsburg Bridges knew to keep his air-conditioning on with the windows up and the doors locked for the ride up the Bowery.

In spite of the rising crime rate, some of those still on the Bowery in the mid-1970s affected an unconcerned attitude. One assured Michael Zettler that they had no trouble from the young people of the area, "and it ain't just because we ain't got nothing. . . . They respect us. They know we seen it all. . . . What good is it anyway, we ain't got nothing, we ain't nobody . . . just bums."

But the street population was changing as well. The backwash from the late 1960s and its East Village "scene" brought an influx of younger, addicted, drug-impaired, or outright psychotic street people to the Bowery in the early 1970s. By the early 1980s, the word on the street was that the Bowery was deteriorating, even as a skid row, due to the rising incidence of violent and irrational crime. Old-timers had begun calling it Little Vietnam and began migrating to less hazardous parts of the city.

The migration wasn't confined to individuals. In the 1970s, the Manhattan Bowery Management Corporation grew out of a detox program that cleaned up parks as a community service. In 1981, it launched a venture called Project Renewal, and, gathering together some of its more successful clients from the Bowery, set about renovating an apartment house—in Brooklyn. Some said it was the old pattern again—a successful venture beginning on the Bowery, only to move away from the Bowery at the first chance.

In June 1981, the convict author Jack Henry Abbott, author of *In the Belly of the Beast*, arrived on the Bowery to find himself in the belly of another kind of beast. Staying at the Salvation Army, he recorded his impressions in an essay, "On the Bowery" published in the literary journal, the *Portable East Side*. Abbott found a Bowery engulfed by the first waves of mental hospital closings. With a new generation of medications coming onto the market, thousands of mental hospital inmates were suddenly deemed capable of looking after themselves, and found themselves abruptly discharged onto the streets with little more than a prayer and a pill prescription. Many found their way to the Bowery and adjoining areas, bringing their problems along with them. The Bowery, Abbott discovered, was not only a place where heroin could easily be bought, it was also a place where parked cars were firebombed, aging transvestites roamed the sidewalks, and a character called the Slasher had been at work.

By the 1960s, the lower end of the Bowery was being absorbed into Chinatown, a place once considered an appendage of the Bowery. Now, with immigration restrictions loosened, Chinatown was bursting out of its traditional three-block area and spreading east of the Bowery and north into a fading Little Italy, epitomized by the erection of the Confucius Plaza housing complex in 1976. Situated on the east side of the Bowery north of Chatham Square, Confucius Plaza's construction demolished some of the most historic turf on the Bowery, including Stephen Foster's last abode, Paddy Martin's Saloon and opium den, and the once-notorious World Poolroom, home of the peter players. Hardly a voice was raised in protest as these crumbling buildings came down, as they represented the sort of history most New Yorkers would as just soon forget.

Although Chinatown now extended across the Bowery, the street still played its old role as a dividing line between communities—in this case between two divisions of the Chinese community. Controversy erupted in 1976 when a statue of Confucius was erected on the corner of Confucius Plaza overlooking Chatham Square. A gift of the Chinese Consolidated Benevolent Association, the statue was well received by the pro-Taiwan government population in the traditional Chinatown west of the Bowery. But strong protests were heard from east of the Bowery, where newer, and often pro-mainland government, immigrants had settled. The Fukien American Association, headquartered on Division Street, was a focal point for the pro-mainland Chinese, who protested that the statue of Confucius represented an unwanted relic of the imperial past that was being wiped out in the new China. The protests were to no avail, and Confucius remained, gazing serenely at the traffic chaos of Chatham Square.

The "new" Chinatown got its own statue a few years later with a larger-than-life sculpture depicting Lin Zexu, the Fukien official instrumental in igniting the Opium Wars against the drug-importing British in the 1840s. Billed as an antidrug message, the statue, situated just a couple blocks down the Bowery, faced the Fukien main stem of East Broadway with its back turned to Confucius and the old Chinatown.

Other changes were afoot on the lower end of the Bowery, as stories circulated of new and vicious street gangs battling for control of gambling, protection rackets, and a revived heroin trade. "Chasing the dragon" meant smoking opium in Chuck Connors's day. Now the term referred to smoking heroin.

The 1960s had been a decade of false starts and disappointments for the Bowery. But even as the street reached its nadir, signs, or rather sounds, of a possible revival were being heard.

18 A New Bowery?

IT SEEMED MUSIC HAD DEPARTED the Bowery forever when Sammy's closed, but in the 1970s Bowery looked poised to once again become an entertainment center. As loft prices in SoHo began to shoot up, artists in search of cheap rents prompted talk of the Bowery becoming the next SoHo. Indeed, some well-established artists had moved into the area. Joining the poet W. H. Auden at 77 St. Mark's Place, was the painter Jay Maisel, who bought the old Germania Bank building at 190 Bowery, and Jasper Johns, who bought the Provident Loan Society building on the corner of Houston and Essex Streets. Preparing for a lucrative upswing, the executors of the Lyons estate started converting some of the old hotels into artists' studios.

The Bowery, though, fell short of becoming a second SoHo. The chief problem was the lack of loft space. The old industrial lofts of SoHo were ideal artist studios, but the brick and stone buildings of the Bowery, built before the cast-iron boom of the 1860s, lacked SoHo's high ceilings, large windows, and industrial elevators, which modern painters and "installation" artists needed to manage their huge creations.

While the plastic arts bypassed the Bowery, music trickled back. The pioneer was the Amato Opera House at 319 Bowery, where for years excellent full-length operas were performed for as little as four dollars a ticket. Curiously, the Amato Opera for a time found itself next door to one of New York's last burlesque houses.

The Amato was joined in 1963 by the Bouwerie Lane Theater, which took over the old Bond Street Bank building at 330, using one of the Bowery's few cast-iron buildings to host the Jean Cocteau Repertory Company. Across the street, Phebe's Restaurant ("open 364½ days a year") became a dining and socializing center for the off-off-Broadway crowd.

Phebe's and the Bouwerie Lane at Bowery and Bond Street became the anchor around which other entertainment venues could cluster. The next wave was jazz clubs, some of which set up in Bowery lofts in the mid-1970s. Leading examples of this jazz scene were the Tin Palace at 325 Bowery and Ladies' Fort around the corner at 2 Bond Street.

On the heels of the jazz lofts came CBGB's. Its full title, CBGB & OMFUG, proclaimed its origins: Country Blue Grass Blues and Other Music for Uplifting Gourmandisers. CBGB's opened in 1973 as a jazz and country music bar, but its owner Hilly Kristal began to sense the possibilities in the newer sounds of avant-garde rockers who came to the Bowery in the 1970s fleeing both high rents and progressive rock. Kristal decided to take a chance on some of these experimental bands playing in nearby basements and lofts. As Kristal later recalled, "Although it was raw, it was distinctive. . . . Eventually I began stimulating things by insisting on original material and creativity."

Described as "a long, dark esophagus," under Kristal's direction CBGB's became the showcase for what became known as punk rock. The esophagus at 315 Bowery became the launching pad for such bands as the Ramones, the Talking Heads, and Patti Smith. It was a long way from the days of nickel kickers and player pianos, but in its own way punk rock was a continuation of a Bowery tradition of edgy entertainment.

But once again, a nascent Bowery revival proved stillborn. CBGB's remained an important platform for innovative rock and roll, but the bands whose careers were launched there were soon successful enough to move on to major record deals and play gigs in mainstream places throughout New York and the nation. Punk rock was born on the Bowery, but it didn't stay around long enough to build an industry in the area.

A few weeks after hailing a Bowery revival, the *New York Times* changed its tune. "The Bowery Would Be Chic They Said—Ha!" it reported on May 29, 1977. The expected Bowery revival not only hadn't happened, it looked as if it was never going to. "The Bowery never took off," real estate broker Jack H. Klein was quoted. "It did a little twinge and then it stopped."

By the early 1990s the Bowery had seemed on the brink of a revival for nearly thirty years, with little to show for it. But this time it looked as if it was really going to happen at last. Gentrification, a process that had begun at the Renwick Triangle back in the 1960s, was reshaping neighborhoods throughout Manhattan as a new generation of young urban professionals left their parents' suburban homes for the conveniences and excitement of the city. By the end of the 1980s, developers were looking into previously unthinkable areas of Manhattan, such as the once infamous Bowery.

Cooper Square and Astor Place set the tone. With such institutions as the Cooper Union, the Public Theater, and New York University's School of Information Management serving as anchors, new shops and restaurants set up in the surrounding blocks. Around the nearly extinct Astor Place secondhand book district, a new generation of retail bookstores arrived, including Esoterica, East-West, St. Mark's Bookshop, and the Astor Place Bookshop. While retail revived, a tenant advocacy group, the Cooper Square Committee, was reported to be assembling a $33 million construction project designed to bring 600 new housing units into the area while rehabilitating an additional 450 existing apartments.

East of Astor Place, an important part of the Bowery's past was nearly lost. In 1978, as if to mark the two-hundredth anniversary of the burning of Peter Stuyvesant's mansion, and the three-hundredth anniversary of the death of Peter Stuyvesant, the venerable church of Old St. Mark's In-the-Bowery caught fire. The interior was completely gutted, and the historic pews, including the pew reserved for visiting representatives of the Dutch government, were lost. When the building was slowly restored in the 1980s, the church decided not to replace the traditional pews, and opted for an open seating arrangement instead. The loss of the historic pew did not in the end deter the Dutch government when in 1982 Queen Beatrix of the Netherlands came to St. Mark's to mark its reopening.

Another link with the past was severed in 1985 when the venerable Bowery Savings Bank followed the Third Avenue El into memory. Despite the optimism that attended the bank's 150th anniversary, the early 1980s brought hard times as the winds of deregulation buffeted the banking industry. The Bowery found that the income from its traditional portfolio of low-paying fixed-rate home mortgages was inadequate to finance its high-rate deposits. By 1985, it was on the brink of collapse when a group of investors saved it with a combination of $100 million of their own money and $300 million of federal aid and support. The investors soon sold the bank to H. F. Ahmanson & Co. for $200 million.

Baseball legend Joe DiMaggio had for years been almost a local institution by himself, advertising the Bowery Savings Bank on radio and TV with a jingle loosely adapted from the old song "The Bowery." (*The Bowery, the Bowery, the Bowery saves a lot . . .*) Ahmanson & Co. decided to return DiMaggioto ads in 1989, and the Bowery Savings Bank held on to its name until 1992. In April 1992, it was decided to retire Joe for good and absorb the Bowery Savings Bank into Home Savings of America. Joe DiMaggio went on the air for a last farewell. "In 1949," he recalled for his listeners, "a new name went up on the Yankees manager's door, and fans wondered what would happen to the team. Well, during Casey Stengel's tenure, we won ten pennants and seven World Series. I tell you this story because today there's a new name on the Bowery's door." Within a few years the bank would be sold again, this time becoming part of Greenpoint Savings Bank. But the name of the Bowery remained chiseled in stone on the bank's two landmark buildings. Following further mergers, early in the twenty-first century, the magnificent Stanford White Bowery Savings Bank building at Bowery and Grand Street was turned into the upscale restaurant Capitale. (Its opulently appointed sister location on East 42nd Street became a Cipriani restaurant.)

Meanwhile, the old skid row continued fading away. The One Mile House liquor store closed, leaving only a rusting metal sign swinging in the wind above a store selling secondhand cash registers. Al's Bar, the last of the Bowery gin mills, closed down in December 1993, and a few months later the Salvation Army announced that it was closing its Booth House shelter at 225 Bowery, citing financial pressures.

It wasn't as if one couldn't get a drink anymore on the Bowery, it was just that drinking there had gone upmarket. In 1994, the Bowery Bar opened on the unlikely site of an old filling station—it had been at first intended to be called the Garage, but gentrification and a renewed awareness of the city's past made a name such as the Bowery Bar, which at one time would have been a kiss of death, into a trendy signpost. It soon became an "in" nightspot, complete with visiting celebrities having photogenic run-ins with pesky paparazzi on the sidewalk.

Hotel space, too, enjoyed a tentative revival on the Bowery, even as the last of the old flophouses closed or were converted into lodging houses for Asian immigrants. A renovated century-old lodging house, the Bowery Whitehouse Hotel, opened at 340 Bowery at the end of the 1990s. Catering to the student/budget traveler crowd, it offered rooms beginning at twenty-five dollars per night. It was a far cry from the twenty-five-cents-a-night hotels of Stephen Foster's day, but by New York standards it was a bargain indeed.

As the 1990s drew to a close, the Bowery was once again under the threat of redevelopment projects that gave little regard to historic preservation. A case in point was 295 Bowery, the building that once housed McGurk's Suicide Hall. Long since taken over by the city as derelict, 295 Bowery was leased out in 1973 to a number of hardy artists and writers, including the noted feminist author Kate Millet. In the late 1990s, the city announced that it was reviving the old Cooper Square Urban Renewal Plan, which called for the demolition of the building and several adjoining properties, including the Bowery-Houston Garden, the city's oldest community garden, founded in 1973 on the site of the old Bowery Commons Cemetery. While the residents organized a "Save 295 Bowery" campaign, in the summer of 2001, the city chose a developer for the site and began an Urban Land Use Review Process. Despite the efforts of author Luc Sante, whose 1991 book, *Low Life*, put McGurk's Suicide Hall back in New York's memory, the review process found no compelling reason to save 295 Bowery, and the building was demolished shortly after, though the Bowery-Houston Garden was allowed to remain.

A new era began on the Bowery in 2007 when the New Museum for Contemporary Art opened its flagship building at 235 Bowery. The ultra-modern fifty-eight-thousand-square-foot building quickly became a major cultural destination, and young, fashionably dressed people now thronged the Bowery, a scene unimaginable even a few years before. Though devoted to contemporary art, the New Museum didn't break entirely from the Bowery's past—a 2012 exhibition, *Come Closer: Art Around the Bowery, 1969–1989,* chronicled the Bowery's beginnings as an artistic neighborhood, with such artifacts as the door from the late Keith Haring's studio at nearby 325 Broome Street. In the spring of 2016, the New Museum would be joined by another major arts destination when the International Center for Photography opened its new gallery space across the street at 250 Bowery.

Music still had a home on the Bowery, though on a more affluent scale than the edgy days of the 1970s. The Bowery Ballroom at 6 Delancey Street became a crucial stop for up-and-coming new musical groups, and the ancient Webster Hall up on 11th Street now hosted some of New York's most trendy parties and musical events, complete with velvet ropes and T-shirted security at the gate. On the other hand, CBGB and the Amato Opera closed, victims of rising property values and the aging of their founders.

Just up the street from the New Museum, the five-star boutique Bowery Hotel offered rooms beginning at $400 a night, and nearby, one of the last remaining Lyons Hotels hosted a young, multilingual clientele of visitors at prices that would have shocked Bowery old-timers. The glass boxes that replaced such sites as McGurk's testified to the power of redevelopment along a once-neglected street suddenly turned fashionable—in 2012, for example, a new condo building at 250 Bowery quickly sold out its apartments at prices of nearly a million dollars apiece. Nor would the Bowery Hotel remain unique, as in late 2015 the Salvation Army sold off its old Bowery location to the multi-star Ace Hotel.

Redevelopment can sometimes serve the cause of history, as with a current project at 50 Bowery, where demolition in 2013 for a projected twenty-two-story luxury hotel revealed the original roofing beams of the Atlantic Garden that once reverberated to oom-pah bands and full-throated renditions of German songs. Farther down were what may have been the timbers of the Bull's Head Tavern. Though not legally obligated to, as the existing building was not landmarked, the owners agreed to an archaeological survey, which by early 2016 turned up over seven hundred artifacts, the remnants of the site's long and colorful history.

The Bowery, a street that once seemed pickled in time, had at last encountered the dynamism of a city that legendarily reinvents itself every thirty years or so. Much of the Bowery's history was the kind that many New Yorkers preferred not to remember, but the growing gulf of time turned repulsive memories into a colorful gaslit past. The Bowery's rapid redevelopment has begun to prompt concern about preserving some of its raucous history amid the glass-and-steel sterility of its new streetscape. In 2011, local preservationists succeeded in placing the Bowery on the New York State Register of Historic Places, and in 2013 on the National Register of Historic Places. In 2013, the Bowery Alliance of Neighbors proposed an "East Bowery Preservation Plan," which would put an eight-story limit to new development on the east side of Bowery between Bleecker and Canal Streets. The plan also called for the preservation of at least eight nineteenth-century buildings, including the old Germania Bank building at 190 Bowery. The plan won the support of Martin Scorsese, who grew up on nearby Elizabeth Street and who directed such quintessential New York movies as *Mean Streets* and *Gangs of New York*. Citing the influence of his childhood neighborhood on his artistic vision, Scorsese urged the City Planning Commission to "insure that the Bowery remains preserved and intact so its history continued to influence and inspire the upcoming artists of tomorrow."

The state and national historical designations, though, gave no legal protection to individual buildings or blocks. Despite historic designations and preservationist plans, by 2016, only a handful of buildings on the Bowery (Bouwerie Lane Theater, Bowery Savings Bank, Cooper Union, Germania Bank, and the Young Men's Institute) had attained the New York City Landmark designation that would have afforded such protection, and with a flood tide of development money rushing into a revitalized New York, the city government showed little interest in historic preservation.

"You're shooting it all wrong," an old man had told Michael Zettler in 1974 as he was photographed in a Bowery gin mill, "All you got in the picture is a drunk. . . . You should get the entire place in. Show the happiness and the gaiety; some of the pictures on the wall, the jukebox and the pool table. . . then you show the drunk along with them."

The gin mills are gone, but the memory of the Bowery's onetime gaiety lingers in the air and draws a new generation of walkers and urban history explorers. It remained to *Daily News* reporter Richard Kopperdahl to write the Bowery's epitaph, one of many over the years, in 1994:

> In a real sense, the drunks, the derelicts, the winos and panhandlers have lost their homeland and been scattered all over the city, sharing their wine and tall stories and, as much as they can, looking out for one another. The Bowery may no longer be what it was, but it is still a state of mind.

The Bowery may indeed be a state of mind, but throughout its long history it never really was what people looking through the lens of memory and nostalgia imagined it to have been. Despite its remarkable continuity from one generation to the next, change has always been taking place along the Bowery. Yet each different version of the Bowery had its roots in the version that came before it. The Tea Water Spring gave rise to the Indian trail, the trail became the Post Road, the Post Road brought the taverns and the horse races, the taverns and horse races gave way to the pleasure gardens. The pleasure gardens in turn gave way to the beer halls and the theaters, the beer halls and theaters gave rise to the concert halls, and the concert halls gave rise to the dime museums, saloons, and burlesque houses. The saloon culture helped create Prohibition, which at last broke the Bowery and left it derelict, living in the shadows of its past fame, until at last the city's continued growth, which had once left the Bowery behind, turned back and started to recolonize the Bowery. The Bowery, living in the memory of its long history, may yet become a promenade where affluent urbanites listen for what strange tales its remaining old buildings might tell them.

At twilight on a clear winter's evening you can walk up from Grand Street by the windows of the "lighting district," where hundreds of lamps and chandeliers jam the shop windows and bathe the sidewalks in a warm yellow glow. You can feel the shadows of the Bowery's past. And perhaps in your imagination you can see them too.

The taxis and delivery vans vanish into the fog of history. Instead, you spy Peg-Leg Peter Stuyvesant riding his carriage up the Bowery, happy to turn his back on New Amsterdam and looking forward to the evening on his country estate. Henry Astor gallops past in search of cattle herds while Washington Irving nips in to the Bull's Head to hear tales of Knickerbocker New York. That girl with the kid must be poor Charlotte Temple distract-edly wandering in search of shelter. There's the Mighty Mose running to the fire bell or manning the brakes on Lady Washington of Company 40. Henry Chanfrau is looking at him kind of squinty-eyed, confident that he'll dethrone him someday soon. There're some tough-looking kids on the corner—Bowery B'hoys no doubt—and one of them is sitting on the fireplug. You'd cross the street to avoid them, but over there the Prophet Matthias is ranting and raging about the end of the world.

That guy with the sword must be Ned Buntline, heading up the Bow-ery to Astor Place to shut down that foreign opera house. P. T. Barnum is tipping his hat to a fashionable lady in crinolines over on the corner of Bond Street. Max Malini plays card tricks on the sidewalk while Harry Houdini and his brother Theo look on, planning even more amazing feats. A ragged Stephen Foster is over there knocking on the door of a minstrel house, hoping to sell another song or two, while Colonel Corco-ran leads the Fighting 69th down the street and off to the war in Virginia. Owney Geoghegan's two widows jostle each other's carriages as they drive up the Bowery. The earth shakes as the great Jacob Adler passes by.

If you listen now you can hear the rattle of the Third Avenue El pull-ing out of the Chatham Square station. The fellow ahead is John McGurk, yes, *that* John McGurk, chatting with Eat-Em-Up McManus. Carrie Joy

Lovett is ringing the bell at the Salvation Army place, and Carry Nation heads up the street looking fierce. Zip the Pinhead is ringing the doorbell at Charles Eisenmann's studio, planning to get his picture taken. Mr. Worth is stepping into his museum—is that a boa constrictor he's got there? Ludwig the Bloodsucker ambles by, looking hungry.

No, ignore these characters. Head down to Steve Brodie's place and he'll take you to his room in the back and tell you the story of how he jumped off the Brooklyn Bridge. Stephen Crane is standing in the soup line around the corner. Chuck Connors in his bowler hat and pea jacket is talking to Big Tim Sullivan about his next racket up at Tammany. And there goes Teddy Roosevelt charging down the street with Jake Riis in tow.

White-haired Professor Peck is talking with Professor Seagull, while Mazie Gordon hands out her dimes, and the satin blonde smiles at the rumpled Weegee. You're just in time for the last call at Sammy's, and Jeanne Jordan stands on the bar and takes a bow.

Acknowledgments

I would like to take this opportunity to thank the many individuals and organizations who have generously and graciously contributed to the creation of this book.

I extend particular thanks to my mom, Patricia Edwards Clyne, who has given me much professional insight into the craft of research and writing, and whose personal library of New York State history has been an invaluable resource. It is to her that this book is respectfully dedicated. I thank my grandparents Neta and Ray Augustus Edwards, who even in its worst years never grew tired of New York City and the curiosities it contained. Thanks also to my dad Francis Clyne, for his immigrant's perspective and entrée to New York's Irish community.

I also extend my gratitude to the unseen librarians down in the stacks of the New York Public Library, who somehow retrieve the most obscure items with astonishing dispatch. Thanks also to New York University's Bobst Library, the New-York Historical Society, the Museum of the City of New York, and the Bronx County Historical Society, as well as the members of the East Bronx History Forum, who have been more than generous in sharing their knowledge, insights, and research discoveries.

I likewise extend my gratitude to a number of additional individuals who have helped advance this project:

Evan T. Pritchard shared his insights and knowledge of the Native Americans of the New York area, and led wonderful walking tours that explored the native trails and sacred sites of lower Manhattan.

Kevin Walsh, whose book, *Forgotten New York*, is an indispensable guide to the little-known aspects of the city, and whose website www.forgotten-ny.com is a browser's delight.

Greg Young and Tom Meyers, whose podcast, "The Bowery Boys: New York City History" has been a continuing revelation of new details of the past of a city I thought I knew.

My friend Jane Williams has shared a number of urban adventures with me, and lent an artist's perspective to our discoveries.

Special thanks to the Celtic League American Branch, for hosting my series of "Macabre New York" walking tours, which helped focus my researches and storytelling skills.

Source Notes

1. The Great Bouwerie

John S. Abbott, *Peter Stuyvesant: The Last Dutch Governor of New Amsterdam*.
Charles J. Addams III, *New York City Ghost Stories*.
Reginald Pelham Bolton, *Indian Paths in the Great Metropolis*.
———, *New York City in Indian Possession*.
Lindsay Denison and Max Fischel, *Villages and Hamlets within New York City*.
Alan F. Harlow, *Old Bowery Days: The Chronicles of a Famous Street*.
Frederica W. Hertel, *A Guide to Historic St. Mark's Church In-the-Bouwerie*.
M. A. Jagendorf, *The Ghost of Peg-leg Peter*.
Thomas A. Janvier, *In Old New York*.
Henry H. Kessler and Eugene Rachlis, *Peter Stuyvesant and His New York*.
A. A. Rikeman, *The Evolution of Stuyvesant Village*.

2. Taverns and Tea Water

Michael and Ariane Batterbury, *On the Town in New York*.
The City History Club of New York, *Historical Guide to the City of New York*.
Thomas J. Davis, *A Rumor of Revolt: The "Great Negro Plot" in Colonial New York*.
Alan F. Harlow, *Old Bowery Days: The Chronicles of a Famous Street*.
Stewart H. Holbrook, *The Old Post Road*.
Kenneth Holcomb Dunshee, *As You Pass By*.
Charles Hemstreet, *Nooks and Carnnies of Old New York*.
Thomas A. Janvier, *In Old New York*.
Stephen Jenkins, *The Old Boston Post Road*.
Gregg Smith, *Beer: A History of Suds and Civilization from Mesopotamia to Microbreweries*.

3. Bowery Bunker Hill

Bruce Bliven Jr., *Under the Guns: New York, 1775–1776*.
Patricia Edwards Clyne, "The Legend of Charlotte Temple."
Alan F. Harlow, *Old Bowery Days: The Chronicles of a Famous Street*.
William A. Polf, *Garrison Town: New York in the Revolution*.

4. Pleasure Gardens

Michael and Ariane Batterbury, *On the Town in New York*.
Richard Albert Edward Brooks, ed., *The Diary of Michael Floy, Jr., Bowery Village 1833–1837*.
Carl Carmer, *The Years of Grace 1808–1858*.
Patricia Edwards Clyne, "Room at the Inn."
Howard Crosby, *Sketch of the Fourth Avenue Presbyterian Church*.
Kenneth Holcomb Dunshee, *As You Pass By*.
Thomas M. Garrett, *A History of Pleasure Gardens in New York City 1700–1865*.
Alan F. Harlow, *Old Bowery Days: The Chronicles of a Famous Street*.
Charles Hemstreet, *Nooks and Carnnies of Old New York*.
Frederica W. Hertel, *A Guide to Historic St. Mark's Church In-the-Bouwerie*.
Thomas A. Janvier, *In Old New York*.
Paul C. Johnson and Sean Wilentz, *The Kingdom of Matthias*.
St. Clair McKelway, "The Marble Cemeteries."
Frank Monaghan and Marvin Lowenthal, *This Was New York: The Nation's Capital in 1789*.
Stanley Nadel, *Little Germany: Ethnicity, Religion and Class in New York City, 1845–1880*.
Oscar Schisgall, *The Bowery Savings Bank of New York: A Social and Financial History*.
Derek Wilson, *The Astors, 1763–1992: Landscape with Millionaires*.

5. Humbug

William T. Anderson, ed., *Mermaids, Mummies and Mastodons: The Emergence of the American Museum*.
Charles A. Huguenin, "Joice Heth Hoax."

6. The Mighty Mose

Herbert Asbury, *Ye Olde Fire Laddies*.
Walter Blair, *Tall Tale America: A Legendary History of Our Humorous Heroes*.
Benjamin Albert Botkin, *New York City Folklore*.
Richard K. Dorson, *American Folklore*.
Kenneth Holcomb Dunshee, *As You Pass By*.
David S. Reynolds, *Walt Whitman's America*.

7. Dead Rabbits and Plug Uglies

Herbert Asbury, *The Gangs of New York*.

Ned Buntline, *Mysteries and Miseries of New York*.

———, *Three Years After*.

J. T. Headley, *The Great Riots of New York 1712–1873*.

Jay Monaghan, *The Great Rascal: The Life and Adventures of Ned Buntline*.

8. Dear Friends and Gentle Hearts

Ernest A. McKay, *The Civil War and New York City*.

9. Women in Tights

Robert C. Allen, *Horrible Prettiness: Burlesque and American Culture*.

Maxwell F. Marcuse, *This Was New York!*

James D. McCabe Jr., *Lights and Shadows of New York Life*.

Luc Sante, *Low Life: Lures and Snares of Old New York*.

Christine Stansell, *City of Women: Sex and Class in New York, 1789–1860*.

10. Suicide Hall

Herbert Asbury, *The Gangs of New York*.

Benson Bobrick, *Labyrinths of Iron: Subways in History, Myth, Art, Technology and War*.

Clifton Hood, *722 Miles: The Building of the Subways and How They Transformed New York*.

James D. McCabe Jr., *Lights and Shadows of New York Life*.

Luc Sante, *Low Life: Lures and Snares of Old New York*.

Isabelle K. Savell, *Politics in the Gilded Age in New York State and Rockland County: A Biography of Senator Clarence Lexow*.

11. Living Curiosities

Robert Bogdan, *Freak Show: Presenting Human Oddities for Amusement and Profit*.

James J. Flynn and Charles Huguenin, "Abbott Parker's Picture of the Crucifixion, August 1904."

Michael Mitchell, *Monsters of the Gilded Age: The Photographs of Charles Eisenmann*.

Luc Sante, *Low Life: Lures and Snares of Old New York*.

Samuel M. Steward, *Bad Boys and Tough Tattoos: A Social History of the Tattoo with Gangs, Sailors, and Street-corner Punks, 1950–1965*.

12. The Mayor of the Bowery
Herbert Asbury, *Carry Nation.*
Carleton Beals, *Cyclone Carry: The Story of Carry Nation.*
Chuck Connors, *Bowery Life.*
Stewart P. Evans and Paul Gainey, *The Lodger: The Arrest and Escape of Jack the Ripper.*
C. Desmond Greaves, *The Life and Times of James Connolly.*
Ernest Jarrold, *Tales of the Bowery.*
Gwen Kinkead, *Chinatown: Portrait of a Closed Society.*
William Brown Meloney, "Slumming in New York's Chinatown."
Dave Ramney, *Thirty Years on the Bowery.*

13. Nickel Kickers
Robert C. Allen, *Horrible Prettiness: Burlesque and American Culture.*
Herbert Asbury, *All Around the Town.*
Michael and Ariane Batterbury, *On the Town in New York.*
Arnold and L. Marc Fields, *From the Bowery to Broadway: Lew Fields and the Roots of American Popular Theater.*
Ricky Jay, *Learned Pigs and Fireproof Women.*
Kathy Peiss, *Cheap Amusements: Working Women and Leisure in Turn of the Century New York.*

14. I'll Never Go There Anymore
Herbert Asbury, *The Gangs of New York.*
Christopher Benfrey, *The Double Life of Stephen Crane.*
George Chauncey, *Gay New York: Gender, Culture and the Making of the Gay Male World 1890–1940.*
The Committee of Fifteen, *The Social Evil.*
Stephen Crane, *Sketches and Reports.*
John Hopkins Denison, *Beside the Bowery.*
Timothy J. Gilfoyle, *City of Eros: New York City, Prostitution and the Commercialization of Sex 1790–1920.*
Ernest Jarrold, *Tales of the Bowery.*
Marilyn Wood Hill, *Their Sisters' Keepers: Prostitution in New York City, 1830–1870.*
H. Paul Jeffers, *Commissioner Roosevelt: The Story of Theodore Roosevelt and the New York City Police 1895–1897.*
Joseph Mitchell, *McSorley's Wonderful Saloon.*
Lulla Rosenfeld, *Bright Star of Exile: Jacob Adler and the Yiddish Theatre.*
Stanley Wertheim and Paul Sorrentino, *The Crane Log: A Documentary History of Stephen Crane 1871–1900.*

15. Boulevard of the Forgotten
Call I. Cohen, *Old Men of the Bowery*.
Louis Stettner, ed., *Weegee*.
Works Projects Administration, *The WPA Guide to New York City*.

16. Sneaky Pete
Harry Baronian, "The Bowery Social Register." *The Bowery News*.
Call I. Cohen, *Old Men of the Bowery*.
Michael D. Zettler, *The Bowery*.

17. Operation Bowery
Elmer Bendiner, "Immovable Obstacle' In the Way of a New Bowery."
Colonel S. H. Bingham, *Report to the New York City Transit Authority: Demolition of Third Avenue Elevated Line South of 149th Street*.

18. A New Bowery?
Jack Henry Abbott, "On the Bowery."
Michael D. Zettler, *The Bowery*.

Bibliography

Books and Manuscripts

Abbott, John S. *Peter Stuyvesant: The Last Dutch Governor of New Amsterdam.* New York: Dodd & Mead, 1873.

Addams III, Charles J. *New York City Ghost Stories.* Reading, Pennsylvania: Exeter House Books, 1996.

Allen, Irving Lewis. *The City in Slang: New York Life and Popular Speech.* New York: Oxford University Press, 1993.

Allen, Robert C. *Horrible Prettiness: Burlesque and American Culture.* Chapel Hill, North Carolina: University of North Carolina Press, 1991.

Anderson, William T. ed. *Mermaids, Mummies and Mastodons: The Emergence of the American Museum.* Philadelphia, Pennsylvania: American Association of Museums, 1992.

Asbury, Herbert. *All Around the Town.* New York: A. A. Knopf, 1934.

———. *Carry Nation.* New York: A. A. Knopf, 1929.

———. *The Gangs of New York.* New York: A. A. Knopf, 1927.

———. *Ye Olde Fire Laddies.* New York: A. A. Knopf, 1930.

Batterbury, Michael and Ariane Batterbury. *On the Town in New York.* New York: Scribner's, 1973.

Beals, Carleton. *Cyclone Carry: The Story of Carry Nation.* Philadelphia, Pennsylvania: Chilton Co., 1962.

Benfrey, Christopher. *The Double Life of Stephen Crane.* New York: A. A. Knopf, 1992.

Bingham, Colonel S. H. *Report to the New York City Transit Authority: Demolition of Third Avenue Elevated Line South of 149th Street.* Typescript, 4 May 1954, New York Public Library.

Blair, Walter. *Tall Tale America: A Legendary History of Our Humorous Heroes.* New York: Coward-McCann, 1944.

Bliven, Bruce Jr. *Under the Guns: New York, 1775–1776.* New York: Harper & Row, 1972.

Bobrick, Benson. *Labyrinths of Iron: Subways in History, Myth, Art, Technology and War.* New York: Newsweek Books, 1981.

Bogdan, Robert. *Freak Show: Presenting Human Oddities for Amusement and Profit.* Chicago, Illinois: University of Chicago Press, 1988.

Bolton, Reginald Pelham. *Indian Paths in the Great Metropolis.* New York: Museum of the American Indian, Heye Foundation, 1922.

———. *New York City in Indian Possession.* New York: Museum of the American Indian, Heye Foundation, 1975.

Botkin, Benjamin Albert. *New York City Folklore.* New York: Random House, 1956.

———. *Sidewalks of America.* Indianapolis, Indiana: Bobbs-Merrill, 1954.

Brooks, Richard Albert Edward, ed. *The Diary of Michael Floy, Jr., Bowery Village 1833–1837.* New Haven, Connecticut: Yale University Press, 1941.

Buntline, Ned. *Mysteries and Miseries of New York.* New York; H. Long & Brother, 1848.

———. *Three Years After.* New York: Edward Z. C. Judson, 1872.

Carmer, Carl. *The Years of Grace 1808–1858.* New York: Grace Church, 1958.

Chauncey, George. *Gay New York: Gender, Culture and the Making of the Gay Male World 1890–1940.* New York: Basic Books, 1994.

City History Club of New York (The). *Historical Guide to the City of New York.* New York: F. A. Stokes Company, 1909.

Cohen, Call I. *Old Men of the Bowery.* New York: Guilford Press, 1989.

Committee of 15 (The). *The Social Evil.* New York: G. P. Putnam's Sons, 1902.

Connors, Chuck. *Bowery Life.* New York: R. K. Fox, 1904.

Crane, Stephen. *Sketches and Reports.* Charlottesville, Virginia: University of Virginia Press, 1973.

Crosby, Howard. *Sketch of the Fourth Avenue Presbyterian Church.* New York: E. French, 1864.

Davis, Thomas J. *A Rumor of Revolt: The "Great Negro Plot" in Colonial New York.* New York: Free Press, 1985.

Denison, John Hopkins. *Beside the Bowery.* New York: Dodd, Mead and Company, 1914.

Denison, Lindsay and Max Fischel, *Villages and Hamlets Within New York City.* New York: Press Publishing Company, 1925.

Dorson, Richard K. *American Folklore.* Chicago, Illinois: University of Chicago Press, 1959.

Dunshee, Kenneth Holcomb. *As You Pass By.* New York: Hastings House, 1952.

Evans, Stewart P. and Paul Gainey, *The Lodger: The Arrest and Escape of Jack the Ripper.* London: Century Publishing, 1995.

Fields, Arnold and L. Marc Fields, *From the Bowery to Broadway: Lew Fields and the Roots of American Popular Theater.* New York: Oxford University Press, 1993.

Garrett, Thomas M. *A History of Pleasure Gardens in New York City 1700–1865.* Ph.D. dissertation, New York University, 1978.

Gilfoyle, Timothy J. *City of Eros: New York City, Prostitution and the Commercialization of Sex 1790–1920.* New York: W. W. Norton, 1992.

Gilmartin, Gregory F. *Shaping the City: New York and the Municipal Arts Society.* New York: Clarkson Potter, 1995.

Goldstone, Harmon H. and Martha Dalrymple, *History Preserved: A Guide to New York City Landmarks and Historic Districts.* New York: Simon & Schuster, 1976.

Greaves, C. Desmond *The Life and Times of James Connolly.* London: Lawrence & Wishart, 1961.

Harlow, Alan F. *Old Bowery Days: The Chronicles of a Famous Street.* New York: D. Appleton & Company, 1931.

Headley, J. T. *The Great Riots of New York 1712–1873.* New York: E. B. Treat, 1873.

Hemstreet, Charles. *Nooks and Crannies of Old New York.* New York: C. Scribner's Sons, 1899.

Henderson, Helen W. *A Loiterer in New York.* New York: C. Scribner's Sons, 1917.

Hertel, Frederica W. *A Guide to Historic St. Mark's Church In-the-Bouwerie.* New York, 1949.

Hill, Marilyn Wood. *Their Sisters' Keepers: Prostitution in New York City, 1830–1870.* Berkeley, California: University of California Press, 1993.

Holbrook, Stewart H. *The Old Post Road.* New York: McGraw-Hill, 1962.

Hood, Clifton. *722 Miles: The Building of the Subways and How They Transformed New York.* New York: Simon & Schuster, 1993.

Howe, Irving and Kenneth Libo, *How We Lived: A Documentary History of Immigrant Jews in America.* New York: R. Marek Publishers, 1979.

Israelowitz, Oscar. *Lower East Side Tourbook.* New York: Israelowitz Publishing, 1996.

Jagendorf, M. A. *The Ghost of Peg-leg Peter.* New York: Vanguard Press, 1965.

Janvier, Thomas A. *In Old New York.* New York: Harper & Brothers, 1903.

Jarrold, Ernest. *Tales of the Bowery.* New York: J. S. Ogilvie Publishing Co., 1905.

Jay, Ricky. *Learned Pigs and Fireproof Women.* New York: Villard Books, 1990.

Jeffers, H. Paul. *Commissioner Roosevelt: The Story of Theodore Roosevelt and the New York City Police 1895–1897.* New York: J. Wiley & Sons, 1994.

Jenkins, Stephen. *The Old Boston Post Road*. New York: G. P. Putnam's Sons, 1913.

Johnson, Paul C. and Sean Wilentz, *The Kingdom of Matthias*. New York: Oxford University Press, 1994.

Kessler, Henry H. and Eugene Rachlis. *Peter Stuyvesant and His New York*. New York: Random House, 1959.

Kinkead, Gwen. *Chinatown: Portrait of a Closed Society*. New York: Harper Collins,1992.

Kouwenhoven, John A. *The Columbia Historical Portrait of New York*. New York: Harper & Row, 1953.

Marcuse, Maxwell F. *This Was New York!* New York: Carlton Press, 1965.

McCabe Jr., James D. *Lights and Shadows of New York Life*. New Illinois: National Publishing Company, 1872.

McKay, Ernest A. *The Civil War and New York City*. Syracuse, New York: Syracuse University Press, 1990.

Mitchell, Joseph. *McSorley's Wonderful Saloon*. New York: Duell, Sloan, & Pierce, 1938.

Mitchell, Michael. *Monsters of the Gilded Age: The Photographs of Charles Eisenmann*. Toronto, Canada: Gage Publishing Co., 1979.

Monaghan, Frank and Marvin Lowenthal. *This Was New York: The Nation's Capital in 1789*. New York: Doubleday, Doran & Co., 1943.

Monaghan, Jay. *The Great Rascal: The Life and Adventures of Ned Buntline*. Boston, Massachusetts: Little, Brown, 1952.

Nadel, Stanley. *Little Germany: Ethnicity, Religion and Class in New York City, 1845–1880*. Urbana, Illinois: University of Illinois Press, 1990.

Peiss, Kathy. *Cheap Amusements: Working Women and Leisure in Turn of the Century New York*. Philadelphia, Pennsylvania: Temple University Press, 1986.

Polf, William A. *Garrison Town: New York in the Revolution*. New York: New York State American Revolution Bicentennial Commission, 1976.

Ramney, Dave. *Thirty Years on the Bowery*. New York: American Tract Society, 1910.

Reynolds, David S. *Walt Whitman's America*. New York: Knopf, 1995.

Rikeman, A. A. *The Evolution of Stuyvesant Village*. Mamaroneck, New York: C. G. Peck, 1899.

Rosenfeld, Lulla. *Bright Star of Exile: Jacob Adler and the Yiddish Theatre*. New York: Crowell, 1977.

Rovere, Richard H. *Howe and Hummel: Their True and Scandalous History*. New York: Farrar, Strauss, & Giroux, 1947.

Sante, Luc. *Low Life: Lures and Snares of Old New York*. New York: Farrar, Strauss, & Giroux, 1993.

Savell, Isabelle K. *Politics in the Gilded Age in New York State and Rockland County: A Biography of Senator Clarence Lexow.* Historical Society of Rockland County, New York: American Management Association, 1984.

Schisgall, Oscar. *The Bowery Savings Bank of New York: A Social and Financial History.* New York: American Management Association, 1984

Schwartzman, Paul and Rob Polner. *New York Notorious.* New York: Crown Publishers, 1992.

Seitz, Sharon and Stuart Miller. *The Other Islands of New York City.* Woodstock, Vermont: Countryman Press, 1996.

Smith, Gregg. *Beer: A History of Suds and Civilization from Mesopotamia to Microbreweries.* New York: Avon Books, 1995.

Stansell, Christine. *City of Women: Sex and Class in New York, 1789–1860.* New York: Knopf, 1986.

Stelzle, Charles. *A Son of the Bowery: The Life Story of an East Side American.* New York: George H. Doran Company, 1926.

Stettner, Louis, ed. *Weegee.* New York: Knopf, 1977.

Steward, Samuel M. *Bad Boys and Tough Tattoos: A Social History of the Tattoo with Gangs, Sailors, and Street-corner Punks, 1950–1965.* New York: Haworth Press, 1990.

Ulmann, Albert. *A Landmark History of New York.* New York: D. Appleton & Co., 1939.

Van Every, Edward. *Sins of New York.* New York: B. Blom, 1972.

Werner, M. R. *It Happened in New York.* New York: Coward-McCann, 1957.

———. *Tammany Hall.* New York: Greenwood Press, 1928.

Wertheim, Stanley and Paul Sorrentino. *The Crane Log: A Documentary History of Stephen Crane 1871–1900.* New York: G. K. Hall, 1994.

Willard, Eugene Bartram. *The Bowery.* New York: *American Psychologist,* 1936.

Wilson, Derek. *The Astors, 1763–1992: Landscape with Millionaires.* London: Weidenfeld and Nicholson, 1993.

Wolfe, Gerard R. *New York: A Guide to the Metropolis.* New York: McGraw-Hill, 1994.

Works Projects Administration. *The WPA Guide to New York City.* New York, 1939.

Zettler, Michael D. *The Bowery.* New York: Drake Publishers, 1975.

Articles

Abbott, Jack Henry. "On the Bowery," in Kirk Hollander, ed. *Low Rent: A Decade of Prose and Photographs from The Portable Lower East Side.* New York, 1994.

Baronian, Harry. "The Bowery Social Register." *The Bowery News,* 1960.

Bendiner. "Immovable Obstacle' In the Way of a New Bowery." *New York Times Magazine,* 21 January 1962.

Clyne, Patricia Edwards. "The Legend of Charlotte Temple," *Hudson Valley*, v.10, n.4, August 1981.

———. "Room at the Inn." *Hudson Valley*, v.25, n.8, December 1996.

Flynn, James J. and Charles Huguenin. "Abbott Parker's Picture of the Crucifixion, August 1904." *New York Folklore Quarterly*, v. XVII, n. 2, Summer 1961.

Hewitt, Edward Ringwood and Mary Ashley Hewitt. "The Bowery," in Maud Wilder Goodwin etal, eds., *Historic New York*. New York, 1899.

Huguenin, Charles A. "Joice Heth Hoax." *New York Folklore Quarterly*, v. 12, n.4, Winter 1956.

McKelway, St. Clair. "The Marble Cemeteries." *The New Yorker*, 4 August 1934.

Meloney, William Brown. "Slumming in New York's Chinatown." *Munsey's Magazine*, August, 1909.

Newspapers

The New York Times
The Daily News
The New York Herald
New York Newsday
The New York Clipper

Index